OTHER BOOKS BY KATHY GUNST

Lundy's (coauthored with Robert Cornfield)

The Parenting Cookbook

Roasting

Leftovers

The Great New England Food Guide
(coauthored with John Rudolph)

Condiments

Relax, Company's Coming!

150 Recipes for Stress-Free Entertaining

Kathy Gunst

SIMON & SCHUSTER

New York   London   Toronto   Sydney   Singapore

To my father, Lee Gunst,
for his never-ending support and love.

SIMON & SCHUSTER
Rockefeller Center
1230 Avenue of the Americas
New York, NY 10020

SIMON & SCHUSTER and colophon are
registered trademarks of Simon & Schuster, Inc.

For information about special discounts for bulk purchases,
please contact Simon & Schuster Special Sales:
1-800-456-6798 or business@simonandschuster.com

Designed by Katy Riegel

Manufactured in the United States of America

10   9   8   7   6   5   4   3   2   1

Library of Congress Cataloging-in-Publication Data is available.

ISBN 0-7432-0258-9

Acknowledgments

Many thanks to my agent, Deborah Krasner, who simultaneously became my agent, friend, and traveling buddy all in one year. To Janice Easton, my editor, who gave me guidance, advice, and a clear vision. Thank you to Sydney Miner, who took over the book and saw it to publication.

Thanks to Valerie Jorgensen, longtime and always-there friend who helped me so much with the "Setting the Table" section of this book. To Karen Frillmann, my soul mate and friend, who supports me in ways too numerable to record here. Thanks to Elisa Newman, whose California kitchen was the scene of some great meals and warm times.

Thanks to friends and family who shared recipes: Sue Schardt, Isabel Achoa, Kathleen O'Neill, Ronnie Maddelena, Andrea Gunst, Glenn Smith, Nancy Rudolph, and Eve Edelstein-Williams. Many thanks to Mary O'Connor, who helped create the kitchen of my dreams—a place to cook, create, and entertain. And to Steve Lomprey for his help with the cover.

Thank you to my editors at the following publications where some of these recipes have previously appeared: *Parenting* magazine, *Bon Appétit*, the *Los Angeles Times, Diversion, Kitchen Garden,* and *Cooking Light.* Many thanks to my producers at WBUR in Boston, Graham Smith and Jon Marston.

Thank you to my friend Cat Lee who, on one of our many walks through the Maine woods, helped me come up with the title for this book. You are a source of huge inspiration to me.

To Nancy Rudolph, my mother-in-law, who provides encouragement, love, and an always-willing palate.

To John, my constant. Thank you for going over this (and through this) with such patience and care and for devouring everything I put on our table with such honesty and enthusiasm. Thanks to my girls, Emma and Maya, for their spirit and discerning taste buds, and their ability to put up with their mother's "weirdness" in the kitchen.

Contents

A Guide to the Recipes

When you're getting ready to entertain, you want to know as much as possible about the recipes you're using before you begin cooking. *Always take the time to read a recipe through completely so there are no surprises once you start.* Make a list of ingredients and create a shopping list of *everything* you need.

Each recipe in this book is followed by a graphic symbol, letting you know just how simple or complex the recipe is. If you're just starting out and inviting friends over for dinner isn't something you do regularly, choose recipes with only one . If you want to be more adventurous and you have some extra time, look for recipes that are rated and .

    Recipe requires little or no effort to put together.

    Recipe needs some planning ahead and organization.

    Recipe is more elaborate and requires several steps.

Zen and the Art of the Party

It's a Saturday night, and my mother has just tried on her sixth outfit. "How does this one look?" she asks, turning from side to side in a kind of mock model swirl. She's dressed in the latest '60s suburban chic fashion—cocoa brown pants with a matching cowl-neck cashmere sweater. "Good," I say, trying to put this excruciating part of the evening to rest. "Really good," I emphasize. My mother seems pleased and begins to clip on oversized gold hoop earrings and a  necklace. She brushes out her gorgeous thick hair. And then, showing my teenage naïveté, I make a crucial mistake. "But how will you cook in that sweater?" I ask. "What?" she snaps back at me, panic sweeping over her face. "What did you say? Cook? I forgot all about that."

The guests are expected in an hour. The good thing is that the chicken casserole, which she made two days ago, is already warming in the oven and the dining room table has been set. The dining room is one of those showplace rooms that our family doesn't actually use. Like a secret vault, it's unsealed only a few times a year—on major holidays and when my parents throw a dinner party. Sometimes, between these events, I sneak into the room to run my hands over the smooth wooden table, marvel at the silver all tucked away in individual velvet bags, and finger the delicate lace napkins that are used only on the rarest occasions.

While my mother changes again (this time she opts for a more casual man-tailored shirt that doesn't look nearly as good), she shouts for me to put the stuffed potatoes into the oven. "Oh my God, the dessert!" she shrieks, stuffing her feet into high-heeled sandals, and rubbing a quick smear of rouge along her high cheekbones.

She runs to the kitchen and begins to whip the cream for her signature chocolate mousse. This is the dessert she makes for every dinner party. When the cream splatters all over her shirt, I retreat to my room to avoid the hysterics I know will soon follow. Like clockwork, the doorbell rings and my father ushers in the first guest. He pours the Scotch, and takes the deviled eggs and a wedge of Brie out of the refrigerator. In the bedroom, my mother changes her shirt, cursing under her breath.

Soon the house is filled with friends and neighbors, and my brothers and I are sent off to the den with our T.V. dinners to watch our favorite shows. Before bed we come downstairs in our clean pajamas, teeth brushed, and say a brief, polite hello to the assembled guests. This ritual always reminds me of the Von Trapp children as they are marched in front of the crowd at their father's gala dinner for the rousing chorus of "So Long, Farewell, Auf Wiedersehen, Goodnight."

Despite this hysteria, I was still able to hold on to the storybook idea little girls have about what fun it is to throw a party. I began hosting birthday parties for my parents, setting an immaculate table with matching paper plates, napkins, tablecloth, party favors, and streamers from the nearby Hallmark Party Store. I stuffed cream cheese into fat ribs of celery and spooned Boursin cheese onto Ritz crackers in swirly patterns. I made meat loaf and begged my mother to teach me her recipe for baked stuffed potatoes. I may have borrowed recipes from my mother, but I did not seem to adopt her attitude. Making dinner for my family gave me a deep sense of calm and girlhood accomplishment.

Unfortunately, the feeling didn't last. As I got older, got my first apartment, and began giving real dinner parties, the family propensity for tensing up to the point of breakdown took hold of me. The more I wanted to impress my guests by cooking show-off dishes, the higher the stress level became. Once the lessons I learned from observing my mother kicked in, it took years for me to really let go and enjoy the parties I hosted.

I entered adulthood wondering why people bothered to give dinner parties. To me, they were tortuous exercises that always ended with a sinkful of dishes and extreme exhaustion by the host. What exactly was the appeal? Even today, the titles of recent books and articles on entertaining teach that one must strive for perfection to impress one's guests. "Entertaining Like a Millionaire," "The Beach House Party Book," "Entertaining Tips from the Stars," "Entertaining with the Leading Fashion Designers," "Perfect Wine for Perfect Food," and so on.

In a leading food magazine there is an "entertaining" column written by a New York society woman. She tells tales of playing hostess to the rich and famous. As far as I can see, she doesn't actually cook, but she knows how to buy take-out food and hire New York's hottest chefs to cater her soirees. Since when did millionaires become our advisors on how to cook for friends? Since when did good food and money become synonymous?

Think about the best parties you've ever been to. What do you remember about these evenings? Was it the perfectly matched napkins and impeccable wines? Was it the floral arrangements or the candles? Chances are it wasn't any of those details. If you're anything like me, the best parties were ones where the food was simple, homemade, and served with a generous spirit; the ones where you laughed the hardest or met some great new people. Some of these parties may have been in exotic, wonderful places—on a gorgeous beach or by the fire in someone's elegant home. But some of them probably also happened in a studio apartment at a cramped little table, or in a house full of laughing children. The point is that it's not the location of the party that matters most, but the spirit of the event.

Entertaining is about giving. It may be as simple as sharing a summer salad grown in a friend's garden, enjoying a chicken roasted the way your grandmother taught you, savoring a cake made from an old family recipe, or sharing an outstanding bottle of wine simply because you are getting together with old friends. It's about the stories that are told and the feeling of being included—a feeling that makes you want to sit and eat and drink and linger around a table for a long time.

The good host isn't necessarily someone who spends a lot of money or dedicates three days to cooking the perfect meal. The good host is the person who makes you feel welcome, relaxed, and a part of his or her life.

I was recently invited to a friend's house for dinner. It was a cool summer night and she had set a table under a huge shade tree. A small group of us arrived and she was nowhere in sight. We went looking for her and discovered she was in the kitchen, cooking furiously next to a sink piled high with dishes, with a look of sheer panic on her face. She welcomed us, gave us each a glass of wine, and sent us back outside. We sat out there, under the tree, for close to forty-five minutes. We wandered back into the kitchen and asked to help, begged her to come outside and sit with us, but she insisted she wanted to finish up in the kitchen—alone.

We managed to laugh and drink and get exceedingly hungry, but mostly we felt bad. We felt like a burden. When we finally ate, over an hour and a half after arriving, rain began to sprinkle and none of us felt particularly hungry, although the food was superb. The hostess had outdone herself—baked bread, made a beautiful soup and a delicious salad of roasted vegetables—but there was no joy in that food, no sense of being a welcomed guest in her home. Instead of politely saying thanks, I wanted to tell my friend, "We are the reason you had this party, not so you could lock yourself in your kitchen and try to control the food. No one came for perfect food. We came to see you." That party stands out for me because it was such a good example of how hard people work to make party food taste and look good, while forgetting what the party was really about.

If you find yourself obsessing about making a good impression, you need to stop and sit down. There were many times while I was writing this book I would review the recipes and think, "This isn't party food. These dishes aren't fancy enough. I'd better make a complex bouillabaisse or a four-layer cake with homemade ice cream." But then I would remind myself that the whole point of this book is to show that good, creative, simple food is the very best thing you can serve to people you care about. If you want complex, show-off, trend-of-the-moment food you can go out to a restaurant. Entertaining at home should be about something different.

The ritual of sharing food is undoubtedly one of our earliest social conventions, yet the basic act of eating and drinking with others is disappearing in everyday life. We eat alone in our cars or in front of the television or computer. In a world where solitary eating has become the norm, it's no wonder that the art of sharing food with others—entertaining—is being lost.

My first hope is that you will use this book to find recipes, ideas, and mostly inspiration to invite people to share food with you. I have offered recipes and ideas that I hope are approachable, that just might change your definition of "party food." My second hope is that this book helps you to relax and take it slow. Begin with a very simple menu and take your time as you cook, set the table, and open the wine. Look into the faces of your guests and realize that it's not perfection they're looking for, it's your presence. So, Relax, Company's Coming!

—Kathy Gunst
South Berwick, Maine
June 2001

2

Getting Organized

An Entertaining Primer

During the year and a half I spent writing this book, friends and acquaintances would constantly ask, "What are you working on these days?" When I told them I was developing a new cookbook called *Relax, Company's Coming,* many people just laughed. *Relax, Company's Coming?* Oh, you mean you're going to publish a list of the best caterers in the country?" asked one friend. "Isn't that title a bit of an oxymoron?" said another. My oldest daughter said, "Why don't you just call it *Get a Grip on Yourself and Order a Pizza?*" After the laughter died down

 and I had a chance to explain my ideas, many people followed with, "Yes! I get it. But tell me, how do you do it?"

The truth is there are choices you can make that will allow you to feel more in control when you give a party: choosing recipes that match your level of skill in the kitchen, simplifying the way you clean your house and set your table, shopping strategically, and taking stock of your strengths and weaknesses as a host and playing to your strengths. Let this book be your guide.

To get to know yourself and your habits better you need to pinpoint exactly what makes you most nervous about entertaining. I have talked with dozens of people about this subject. Listed below is a compilation of the most common responses I received, followed by some very specific suggestions that may put some, or perhaps all, of your fears to rest.

I'm going to get in over my head and nothing will come out right.

- *Choose a menu and recipes that you are comfortable with.* There is no shame in this— a well-made, simple meal served by a relaxed host is far preferable to an elaborate meal served by a stressed-out host. Most people are grateful to simply be invited to your home for a meal.
- *Pick recipes by the level of preparation they require.* As you look through the recipes in this book you'll see ☕'s listed after each. The ☕'s let you know how easy or complex the dish is. See page 11 for a guide.
- *Plan your preparation time realistically.* As you read through the book, you'll notice that every recipe tells you how much of the dish can be made ahead of time. If you are the type of host that gets really anxious, you'll want to choose recipes that can be done completely ahead of time. You'll want to either avoid dishes that require preparation at the last minute, or leave only one dish that requires last-minute preparation.

    If you're comfortable with finishing the cooking when guests are already there, you should take a look at recipes that can be done partially ahead of time and those that need to be put together at the last minute.

No matter how thoroughly I follow a recipe, something always seems to go wrong. The food is overcooked and tasteless, or there is some other sort of culinary disaster.

- *Try out the recipe ahead of time.* Make the recipe for yourself or your family and see if it works. Make sure you're comfortable with it. Did you have trouble? Did it take too much time? Was it too salty or spicy? Adjust the recipe to your liking and then, when you serve it to your guests, you'll feel comfortable with it, like an old friend.

I'm scared people will judge me, and the food won't be good. My sister is an amazing cook. My mother fed eight people every night and made it look so easy. I can't stop wishing I were Martha Stewart.

- *Don't try to be someone you're not:* Be glad that your sister is a great cook and that your mother can cook for a crowd. If that's not what you're good at, don't fake it. Choose a menu that feels doable and reflects what you're good at. Don't overshoot for the sake of trying to impress someone.
- *Make food you love, and everyone will love what you make.* If you want the meal to feel like something really special without spending all day cooking, choose one or two simple dishes and make them with real loving care. When I'm having someone to dinner on a weeknight and don't want to make a big deal of it, I'll simply cook a regular family meal and add an extra side dish, a special salad, or a dessert. Don't think you always have to go out of your way to create an elaborate meal. And don't be too proud to ask a friend to bring a dessert, soup, or bread to help complete the meal and make the event more relaxed for you.

  I had an experience that illustrates this point well. Eight people were coming to dinner. I didn't know any of them well, but I really wanted to wow them. I was in a foul mood as I prepared a rather elaborate four-course meal that I thought would impress a king. The guests arrived on time and we had drinks and a few appetizers. They seemed far more interested in drinking than in eating the homemade chicken liver pâté I had painstakingly prepared. We sat down and I served the soup. They drank the wine and stirred their soup. The chicken stuffed with wild rice and hazelnuts, baked stuffed tomatoes, and garlic bread were met with equal indifference. At one point during the meal, I pulled my husband into the kitchen and, with a look of desperation on my face, whined, "They hate it. They hate me. Why did I bother cooking all day?" He shrugged and said, "I think they like to drink. They have no appreciation of this good food. Forget it. I love it." Conversation was strained, I was a miserable wreck, and half the dinner sat untouched in the kitchen. When I brought out a chocolate soufflé (at this point I felt like telling them I hadn't made dessert and that it was time for them to leave) they all perked up considerably. "Ooh, chocolate," one woman cooed. "I just love chocolate. Is there any more wine?" They ate every last bite of the soufflé, polished off all the wine, and eventually left. "Cook to please yourself," some wise soul told me years later. I try to recall that advice every time I feel compelled to try to impress someone at my table. It's usually the simplest, home-cooked meals that are remembered, and appreciated the most.

I never feel organized. So many of the foods I enjoy have to be made at the last minute. What can I do ahead of time that will make the party easier for me, and help me not to panic when the doorbell rings?

- *Proper preparation is key.* No matter what type of recipes you choose you can make things easier by having all your ingredients ready ahead of time: Select the correct pans and skillets you'll need for cooking, preheat the oven, prechop your ingredients (anything with milk, cream, butter, cheese, or any raw meat obviously needs to be covered and refrigerated until you're ready to cook).
- *Before you begin to cook, read each recipe thoroughly.* You don't want any surprises when you're halfway through a recipe and up to your elbows in flour. Review all the steps that can, and can't, be done ahead of time and plan accordingly.
- *Set the table.* The morning of, or the evening before, your event, choose plates, silverware, platters, serving spoons and forks, carving knives, glasses, candles, and flowers. There's nothing worse than frantically looking for a spoon or knife when the food is ready and getting cold. (For more tips about creating a great table, see page 272.

I never seem to find the right ingredients. The food in my supermarket looks awful and doesn't provide much inspiration.

- *Shopping is key!* Being a good shopper can make the difference between a good meal and a great meal. Always read through recipes thoroughly and make a complete shopping list. However, don't be a slave to your list. If you plan to make an eggplant gratin, and you get to the store only to find that the eggplants are soft with large brown spots all over them, forget it. Look at the zucchini. They look fabulous. Why not make a zucchini gratin instead? Many recipes offer suggestions for ingredient substitutions. Look at the end of the recipe under the heading "You Can Also Add . . ."
- *There's plenty to be said for the picky shopper.* Be persistent about finding the freshest, best-looking ingredients. The truth is that beautiful food inspires us to cook. Old, sad-looking food makes us feel like a failure before we even start.

- *New foods can provide new inspiration.* Each time you shop pick up a new item for your pantry. Read through "The Party Pantry" (page 25) to get some ideas for new ingredients to keep around that will help you create quick hors d'oeuvres, sauces, salad dressings, or desserts. One new ingredient (like lemongrass, coconut milk, or olive tapenade) can give your everyday cooking a whole new twist.

   I don't live in an urban area, so I have to drive a minimum of fifteen to twenty minutes to buy food. However, I manage to find fresh-baked baguettes, beautiful fruit and vegetables year-round, Asian ingredients, and much more. My freezer and pantry are stocked with foods that I've bought on trips from even further away. I also try to find ingredients on the Internet through the dozens of new companies that have sprouted up in the last few years offering mail-order foods from all over the world; (see page 39 for a list).

   Even when I shop in my local area I try to branch out. Instead of constantly doing my shopping in one store, buying the same ingredients week after week, I try to visit different shops. It takes more time, but varying my shopping patterns keeps me so much more interested in cooking and entertaining. When you have some extra time, try visiting a new food shop that you don't usually go to. Why not finally check out that Asian vegetable market, the health food store, or that little bakery or cheese shop in the next town or neighborhood?

There won't be enough food!

- *Buy in quantity.* Deciding how much to buy can be tricky. Read the recipe thoroughly and figure out how many people you'll be serving, then shop accordingly. My philosophy is that *it's always better to have more than less.* Some would disagree (talk to my husband). But I am a big fan of leftovers, and as far as I'm concerned, running out of food during a dinner party is not fun, and certainly not the way to stay relaxed.

   One winter we were having a big party and I thought, OK, I'll let my husband do the shopping. I told him how many people were coming and what we needed, pumping up the figures ever so slightly so that there would be enough. He came home with much less than I would have and said, with complete conviction, "There will be enough food. Just relax!" The party was going well and everyone wanted seconds. We dished out the food, leaving behind empty serving plates and dishes, a sight I have dreaded for years. I looked at my husband and held up an empty platter as if to say, "Last time I let *you* go shopping." He smiled a grin of deep satisfaction. After everyone had gone home, he looked at me and said, "I know that was hard for you, but an empty dish is the sign of a successful party. It means everyone loved everything and that's why there's nothing left. No one went home hungry." I was too mad to answer. But somewhere in the deep recesses of my overbuying brain, I knew he was right. But did that change my buying or cooking habits? Not a bit.

I don't know a thing about wine. I'm scared I'll serve the wrong kind and be embarrassed.

- *Find a reputable wine shop.* It may not be as easy as it sounds, but it is the best thing you can do. It's not always the shop with the largest selection that has the best advice. If you have more than one shop in your neighborhood, go in, look around, and talk to the salespeople. Ask questions. Talk about your menu and get advice on which wines will complement the food you're serving. You don't need to splurge to discover a really good wine. Do you want to serve white and red wine and let your guests choose? Do you want a different wine for each course? Talk to someone you trust or go online and find a reputable wine site like wine.com or wineshopper.com for ordering, or winetoday.com for detailed tasting reviews. Also provide beverage alternatives. You could serve beer, sparkling cider or water, or your own favorite beverage. Think about whether or not you want to offer liquor and stock up accordingly.

People will think I'm cheating if I don't cook the whole meal, but I don't really have time to make a complete meal from scratch.

- *Takeout is your friend.* It's Thursday night and an old friend is in town. Rather than meet in some bar or mediocre restaurant, you'd like to invite her to dinner at your house. However, you have to work late or there's a meeting at your daughter's school. There's hardly any food in the refrigerator, you haven't planned a thing, and, quite frankly, it's been a tough week. Despite these obstacles, eating at home *can* be the most relaxing solution. The trick is not to feel that you have to cook a full dinner.

  All around the country, from rural country stores to the most sophisticated urban gourmet food shops, excellent take-out food is available. Why not pick up a deli-roasted chicken and simply bake some potatoes, sauté a green vegetable, buy premixed, prewashed salad greens, and make a simple dessert (see "Desserts," page 219). Or you may want to make a simple main course such as Salmon Cakes, (page 116), or Rigatoni in Creamy Walnut-Pea Sauce, (page 108), and supplement the meal with store-bought bread, deli salads, sorbet, and cookies from the bakery. You can put on sweatpants and have a really relaxed time talking with your friend *at home.* Throughout this book you'll find recipes for evenings exactly like this.

I work long days and I don't have time to put together a weekday dinner party, and I'm too exhausted at the end of the week to think about entertaining.

- *Weekend preparation is your answer.* Think about spending a Saturday or Sunday afternoon cooking a few dishes that can be served later in the week or frozen for a later date. Soups, stews, casseroles, stocks, pies, piecrust, pesto, and sauces are all ideal make-ahead (or cook-to-freeze) foods. Check each recipe to see if it can be frozen or made in advance.

People will judge my house. Some of my friends have really great apartments and houses.

- *This is where you live.* Good food and fun times don't come from grand houses. They come from friends who are relaxed and happy to see you. They come from friends who have had a good time cooking. Some of the best meals I've ever enjoyed were served at a cramped table in a dark studio apartment. Work with what you have!

I don't want to spend hours cleaning my house just so some friends can come over and eat dinner.

- *You don't need to clean your entire house in order to serve dinner to your friends.* Clean up your kitchen and whatever room you will be eating and sitting in. Straighten up the bathroom, but don't go nuts. A friend of mine does what she calls "diverting cleanup." She places a table runner on the island in her kitchen and puts flowers out where the food will be served. She shoves dirty laundry into closets and forces her guests' eyes to go to the food table and not to the pile of kids' toys lying on the floor in the next room.
- *Start clean: Don't start your evening with a sink full of dirty dishes.* Leave time to clean up before the party begins. Always clean the dishes you've used to cook with, and put them away. You'll feel so much more organized if your sink and dishwasher

are empty when you begin the party! And it will make cleanup after the event so much easier.

- *Set the mood.* What else can you do ahead of time to feel better about your environment and help create a relaxed mood? Do you want music? Candlelight? Do you want to eat in the kitchen, or do you have a dining room/living room where the mood might be more relaxed? You can set the mood by thinking about these kinds of details ahead of time.

I won't have fun at my own party. I get so worried about everything being right and everyone else having a good time that I generally feel miserable at my own events.

- *Imagine the worst thing that can possibly happen.* Go ahead and visualize the most disastrous party. Sometimes imagining the worst helps put things in perspective. This is about sharing, not perfection. Entertaining is about laughing and telling stories and getting to know people on a new level. If something goes wrong, the best thing you can do is laugh and enjoy yourself anyhow.

  I once spent an entire day cooking a soup—chopping vegetables, making a homemade broth, and adjusting the spices. I baked bread and made a pie while the soup simmered. I was really looking forward to seeing some old friends. At the last minute I decided the soup wasn't flavorful enough and I added a dash of hot pepper sauce. Somehow the little white plastic thing that controls the amount of sauce that comes out fell off and, within a split second, about half a cup of hot pepper sauce ended up in my soup—along with the little piece of plastic. Disaster! The soup was inedible—a pot of fire that would hurt the most macho eater. Everyone was due to arrive in ten minutes. I felt like crying. Not only did I not have dinner to serve, but I had wasted an entire day making a soup that was inedible. When the first guest arrived, I told her what had happened and she started to laugh. Then I started laughing uncontrollably, with tears pouring down my face. She helped me dump the soup and we boiled water for pasta (that wonderful old standby). We had a great time that night and the pasta was delicious. No one missed the ruined soup.

3
The Party Pantry

When it comes to entertaining, a well-stocked pantry is your best friend. Whether you're planning a cocktail party or a dinner party, or friends drop by unexpectedly, having a well-stocked pantry can make cooking and planning a lot easier. Grab a jar of anchovies and a jar of olives and whip up a tapenade to serve with breadsticks. Open a box of linguine and sauté a few cloves of garlic with olive oil and roasted red peppers and you can put dinner on the table in about twenty minutes. Open cans of coconut milk and chicken broth, toss in a few spices, and you've got a Thai-flavored soup in no time.

The following chapter is meant to provide ideas and inspiration, so when you open your pantry dozens of ideas will jump out. I'll introduce you to some foods you may not have tried before, as well as others that you may already be familiar with. If you pick up one new item each time you go shopping, you'll find that your pantry, and your cooking, will stay full of new possibilities.

ANCHOVIES

These fish fillets, packed in salt or oil, are an invaluable ingredient for making food festive and flavorful. I find that anchovies sold in small glass jars are superior to the ones in tins. When using anchovies packed in salt, always rinse the fillet under cold running water, separate the fillets, and remove the spines before serving.

I mash anchovies into vinaigrettes, or drape them over crunchy romaine lettuce with croutons and thin shavings of Parmesan cheese to make a quick Caesar salad. You can make a quick appetizer by serving them on thin pieces of grilled bread or crackers. One of my favorite instant pasta sauces is made with anchovies: In a small saucepan sauté 2 cloves of chopped garlic in 1 teaspoon olive oil. Open a can of anchovies and add to the heated pan. Let the fillets "melt down," then add a few capers and chopped tomatoes or sun-dried tomatoes, and toss with hot linguine or spaghetti. Add anchovies to bottled tomato sauce for a rich, salty flavor. A classic Italian dip, *bagna cauda,* is a warm mixture of olive oil, garlic, and anchovies melted down to a paste and then served with raw vegetables.

ARTICHOKES (Marinated Artichoke Hearts, Artichoke Puree)

Marinated artichoke hearts in oil and herbs are great for adding to antipasti platters, pasta sauces, or served as a quick hors d'oeuvre. Artichoke puree, available in specialty food shops, is a blend of artichoke hearts, olive oil, vinegar, and salt. It's excellent spread on crackers or as a pizza topping. You can use the puree as the basis of an artichoke-flavored pasta sauce, or for adding flavor to stuffing or rice dishes.

ASIAN INGREDIENTS

Chinese chile oil is fiery hot, with an orange hue, and the flavor of chile peppers. It's frequently used to season stir-fries, marinades, sauces, and vegetable dishes and can be stored in the refrigerator for several months.

Chinese chile sauce is a thick, spicy paste used to flavor sauces and stir-fries. You can use Chinese chile paste or Chinese black bean paste to add spice to glazes, marinades, and stir-fries, or to rub a rich, spicy flavor under the skin of chicken or duck.

Chinese fermented black beans are small soybeans that have been fermented and preserved with salt and ginger. Because they are so salty, the beans should always be rinsed under cold running water before using. They are usually chopped before being added to noodle and tofu dishes, stir-fries, or sauces.

Hoisin sauce is a thick, mahogany-colored sauce made from mashed and fermented soybeans, garlic, chiles, spices, and flour. Hoisin has a sweet, almost smoky flavor that is excellent added to marinades, barbecue sauces, stir-fries, soups, and stews. For a quick Asian-flavored glaze for fish, poultry, or meat, try mixing hoisin with a touch of soy sauce and sesame oil.

Rice wine is made from fermented rice. It is colorless and adds good flavor to soups, stews, marinades, and sauces. It's a great choice for deglazing pans when sautéing poultry, fish, or meat, particularly with dishes that have other Asian flavors.

Soy sauce can be used in marinades, sauces, glazes, and for dipping sauces. It's also used as a table condiment that can take the place of salt. Look for soy sauce that indicates "naturally fermented" on the label and is made only from the following ingredients: soybeans, wheat or flour, salt, and water. Chinese soy sauce tends to be stronger than the Japanese variety, with a more pronounced flavor. You can choose between light (also called pure), dark, and heavy. You can also choose between regular soy sauce and low-sodium soy sauce, which is brewed in the traditional manner but contains up to 43 percent less sodium. Tamari and soy sauce have an almost identical look and flavor, but tamari contains little, if any, wheat. Store in a cool, dark spot.

BROTH (Chicken, Beef, Vegetable)

I always keep a few cans of low-sodium chicken, beef, and vegetable broth on hand for making quick soups and sauces, or for adding to stews or casseroles. The low-sodium varieties have more flavor than the standard broth. I also look for vegetable and mushroom bouillon cubes that can be easily reconstituted into a liquid base with hot water. Vegetable broth is great to have around when making vegetarian dishes or when the flavor of chicken or beef isn't needed. I especially like vegetable and mushroom broth in pasta sauce and risotto, and for making mushroom-flavored polenta.

CANNED BEANS, CHICKPEAS, AND DRIED BEANS

Canned beans go a long way to create interesting meals. In my pantry, I always have several cans of white cannellini beans, kidney beans, black beans, pinto beans, and chickpeas. Always drain canned beans thoroughly and rinse off under cold running water to remove any "canned" flavor. Use beans to create an instant dip (see page 61) or to make a quick antipasto plate combining beans with canned tuna (tossed with olive oil and lemon juice), olives, capers, and roasted peppers. I also add beans to soups and stews for texture, flavor, and fiber. I add beans to tacos and burritos, mash them with onions, garlic, and cumin for instant refried beans, and make a quick stew with sausage, white beans, and tomatoes (see page 138).

When you have the time, dried beans are even better than the canned variety. Dried beans need to be soaked in a large bowl of cold water for several hours, or overnight, and then cooked until tender with the seasonings of your choice.

CAPERS AND CAPERBERRIES

Capers are the flower bud of a bush that grows throughout the Mediterranean. The small buds are picked, sun-dried, and then pickled in a brine solution or preserved in salt. The very tiny nonpareil variety are considered the finest, though many people prefer the fatter, plumper capers.

Caperberries are the size of a medium-small green olive, with the stem still attached. An oval berry forms if the flower buds of the caper bush are allowed to open and set fruit, creating the caperberry. Serve them with antipasti, add to sauces and salads, or use as a topping for sautéed or grilled fish, poultry, or meat. To make a quick tartar sauce for fish or fried foods, add a few teaspoons of capers or chopped caperberries to a cup of mayonnaise and season with salt, pepper, a dash of hot pepper sauce, and the juice of a fresh lemon.

CHILES (Green Chiles and Chipotle Chiles)

Canned vegetables are not high on my list of good food, but canned green chiles can be great to have on hand for putting together a quick salsa or adding a fresh "bite" to soups, stews, dips, guacamole, quesadillas, tacos, or burritos. Try whirling up a small can of green chiles or a tablespoon of chipotle chiles into a quick, spicy dip with $1\frac{1}{2}$ cups sour cream (or plain yogurt), a generous touch of cumin, and the juice of a lime.

Chipotle chiles, or smoked jalapeño peppers, are available dried or canned in adobo sauce. They add a smoky intensity to sauces, guacamole, salsa, vinaigrette, stews, and soups. Remember that a little bit goes a long way, so start with a small amount and then keep adding the peppers to taste.

CHOCOLATE

Having a variety of chocolate on hand can help you put together instant desserts. **Baking or unsweetened chocolate** contains chocolate liquor, 50 percent to 58 percent cocoa butter, and no sugar, and is ideal for melting into sauces and using for cakes, tarts, soufflés, and so on. **Semisweet or bittersweet chocolate** must be at least 35 percent chocolate liquor and is ideal for baking. **Sweet or dark chocolate** has at least 15 percent chocolate liquor and varying amounts of sugar, cocoa butter, and flavorings. Often used in baking, it is delicious served with ripe fruit. **Milk chocolate** has at least 10 percent chocolate liquor and is better for eating than for baking. And **white chocolate**, which is not really chocolate at all, is a mixture of cocoa butter, sugar, and milk.

Use a vegetable peeler to shave thin slices of chocolate to sprinkle over fruit salads or onto slices of pound cake or angel's food cake, or use the shavings as a quick topping for ice cream or fruit-flavored sorbet. When melting chocolate be sure to use the lowest heat possible, or it will clump up and become difficult to work with.

COCONUT

Look for cans of **unsweetened coconut milk** in Asian and specialty food shops. Unsweetened coconut milk adds an instant exotic flavor to soups, stews, and sauces. Try tossing steamed fresh green beans with coconut milk and finely chopped fresh ginger. Make a quick Thai soup by adding coconut milk to chicken, vegetable, or fish broth and garnish with chopped scallions, cilantro, and sliced mushrooms (see page 80). It adds a rich, sweet flavor to sauces, noodle dishes, and curries (see page 120).

Grated coconut can be kept in the freezer for sprinkling over cakes, cupcakes, and sweet breads, or to add a crunchy sweetness to curries, stews, chutney, and salads. Coconut is particularly good sprinkled over fresh fruit salad. Lightly toasted coconut brings out a nutty sweetness: Heat the grated coconut in an ungreased skillet over moderate heat for about 4 minutes, shaking occasionally to prevent the coconut from burning.

COFFEE

Keep a jar of good-quality instant coffee or espresso around to add a mocha flavor to whipped cream and icings, and to give pudding, sweet sauces, or cake and bread batters a mocha essence.

COOKIES

I love butter cookies, chocolate cookies, chocolate wafers, biscotti—all kinds of cookies. Serve cookies with fresh fruit and you have an instant dessert. Serve with ice cream, frozen yogurt, or sorbet for a cool treat. To make plain cookies more festive, ice them with a simple chocolate sauce (melt 1 bar good chocolate over very low heat and add a small amount of cream, orange juice, or liqueur to thin it out). Biscotti can be served with coffee, hot chocolate, cappuccino, or espresso. Top butter cookies or biscotti with lemon curd (see page 32) and chocolate shavings for a quick dessert. Make an instant ice cream cookie sandwich using store-bought cookies (see page 258).

CRACKERS

Keep a variety of crackers around the pantry for quick hors d'oeuvres, or to serve with cheeses, dips, or seasoned cream cheese or goat cheese topped with savory pepper or herbal jellies.

FISH BROTH AND CLAM JUICE

Look for homemade fish broth or clam broth in the freezer section of a fish market or specialty food shop. Bottled clam juice tends to be extremely salty, but can be useful for making seafood stew, soup, or a seafood-flavored risotto.

FROZEN PASTRY (Puff, Phyllo, Pastry Shells)

Keeping frozen pastry on hand can be a great help in putting together appetizers, pies, quiches, and tarts—without a lot of fuss. You can fill a frozen pie shell (either a commercially made one or a homemade crust) to make a quick quiche or tart by sautéing onions and other vegetables. Add 2 beaten eggs, 1 cup of grated cheese, and a pint of sour cream and bake for about 50 minutes at 400 degrees, or until set and golden brown.

GARLIC

Always keep several heads of fresh garlic in the kitchen. A good friend from California sends me a braid of local garlic for the holidays every year, and I cook from it year-round. There is no substitute for fresh garlic (I never use bottled garlic). I use garlic in virtually everything and find that it has an uncanny ability to highlight other flavors. One of my favorite comfort foods is as simple as can be: Heat 4 tablespoons olive oil in a small skillet. Chop 4 to 5 garlic cloves and sauté in the oil for about 2 minutes, until just beginning to turn golden brown. Don't let the garlic burn. Toss with 1/2 pound cooked pasta, sprinkle with freshly ground black pepper, chopped fresh parsley or herbs, and freshly grated Parmesan cheese.

GINGERROOT

Fresh gingerroot is called for quite a bit in these recipes. Although dried powdered ginger can be substituted in some dishes, there is nothing like the fresh, bracing, pungent flavor of fresh gingerroot. It is simultaneously hot and sweet and is considered by many to be a digestive aid. Look for firm, fresh gingerroot with light brown skin in a gnarled root. To prepare fresh ginger, simply peel off the skin using a small, sharp knife or vegetable peeler and chop the root finely. Use the back of a large knife to smash the peeled ginger before chopping; it releases fresh juices that can be added to any dish that calls for fresh gingerroot.

HERBS AND SPICES

I use quite a lot of fresh herbs in my cooking. I have a south-facing windowsill where I grow cilantro, basil, tarragon, chives, and rosemary year-round. Fresh herbs wake up the flavors in other foods and add a depth and mystery to food that dried herbs often don't provide. Use fresh herbs whenever possible. Dried herbs work best when they have a chance to simmer and release their flavor. They will stay fresh for nearly a year if they are kept away from heat or direct sunlight.

Spices—ground cinnamon, cloves, nutmeg, curry powder, cumin, turmeric, red cayenne, hot and sweet paprika—should also be stored in a cool, dark spot.

HONEY

Keep good-quality honey on hand for baking, to sweeten sauces, glaze a duck or chicken, add sweetness to a marinade or barbecue sauce, or to drizzle into tea and spoon on top of ice cream, pound cake, or cookies.

HOT PEPPER SAUCE

I use hot pepper sauce to flavor all kinds of dishes—everything from scrambled eggs and omelettes to soups, stews, and casseroles. Keep hot pepper sauce in a cool spot, out of direct sunlight.

JAMS, JELLIES, AND PRESERVES

Heat the preserves or jam over low heat and spoon over ice cream, cookies, angel food cake, or pound cake for a quick dessert. To make a quick fruit tart, pierce a frozen pie crust with a fork and bake until golden brown. Brush with warm jam or jelly and layer with fresh fruit, then brush the top of the fruit with more of the warm preserves. Tea sandwiches can be as simple as butter and preserves on bread, crusts removed, and cut into triangles. Serve with hot tea with mint and lemon. You can also brush a chicken, duck, or Cornish hen with sweet preserves to create a fruity, sweet glaze; simply brush the meat during the last 10 minutes of cooking.

LEMON CURD

Look for lemon curd in specialty food shops. This sweet-and-sour spread is fabulous for putting together last-minute desserts. Serve lemon curd with homemade or store-bought cookies (butter cookies and shortbread are a particularly good match), pound cake, angel food cake, scones, and muffins, or spoon over ice cream or sorbet with a shaving of chocolate or a sprinkling of chopped chocolate chips.

NUTS

Almonds, cashews, walnuts, pecans, brazil nuts, hazelnuts, and pine nuts are handy for sprinkling over salads, into sauces and stews, or for creating a topping for fish or chicken fillets. Make a quick pesto by blending (but not pureeing) 2 cups fresh herbs (use traditional basil or experiment with parsley, cilantro, or mint), with $1/2$ cup extra-virgin olive oil, salt, pepper, and $1/2$ cup of your favorite nuts. Stir in $1/3$ cup grated Parmesan cheese. Nuts also add great flavor and texture to stuffing and rice dishes. Keep nuts in the freezer and use as needed.

OILS (Olive, Herb-Flavored, Sesame, and Vegetable)

Olive oil is my oil of choice, particularly for sauces, vinaigrettes, salad dressings, marinades, or moistening and adding flavor to foods while roasting. I try to keep a gallon of relatively inexpensive extra-virgin oil around for everyday cooking, and have a few bottles of really special olive oils—with their delicate olive essence—on hand for drizzling over foods where its flavor can really shine. A few of my current favorites come from Spain, Morocco, Tuscany, and Turkey. Many specialty food shops offer olive oil tastings, which is a great way to discover oils you really enjoy. When you're spending $15 to $40 for a bottle of olive oil you want to make sure you really like its flavor!

I also like to keep a bottle of herb-infused oil (basil, garlic, cilantro, or rosemary) for adding fresh herb flavor to sautéed fish, beef, and chicken. Herb-flavored oils are a delicious base for a salad dressing, pesto, or an herb sauce.

If you're frying over very high heat you may want to think about using a more neutral, and less expensive, vegetable oil, such as canola oil. Vegetable oil won't add flavor to foods, but it doesn't burn when exposed to high heat.

Nut oils (walnut, almond, and hazelnut) are particularly rich and are delicious sprinkled over steamed vegetables, salads, or pizza. Store them in the refrigerator as they tend to go rancid more quickly than other oils.

Sesame oil, which is used in many Asian dishes and stir-fries, has the rich, intense scent and flavor of toasted sesame seeds. It's delicious in barbecue sauces, marinades, and glazes, and can add an interesting twist to salads and sauces. Try sautéing vegetables with a touch of sesame oil added to other oils or butter.

OLIVES AND OLIVE PUREE

Keep a good variety of black and green olives in the refrigerator. They will keep for several weeks and can be served as a quick snack or added to many dishes—pasta sauce, salads, sandwiches, stews, rice, and couscous. They can be marinated with a wide variety of flavors (see page 43). The pitted, canned variety, despite what my children say, are virtually tasteless and have the texture of a stick of gum.

Olive puree, available at specialty food shops, is a blend of black or green olives, olive oil, and salt. It's extremely flavorful and can be useful in whipping up last-minute appetizers. In fact, it's so enticing you can simply eat it straight from the jar. When olive puree is mixed with anchovies it is called tapenade. Mix several tablespoons of olive puree or tapenade with sour cream or yogurt for a quick dip. Spread it on grilled bread, or add a teaspoon or two to soups, stews, and salad dressings for an olive essence. Make an olive-flavored deviled egg by mashing the yolk of a hard-boiled egg with a teaspoon of olive puree, and stuff the mixture back into the whites. Toss a few tablespoons of olive puree with pasta, or top a baked potato. Brush a teaspoon on top of grilled or panfried chicken breasts or fish fillets, or heat a tablespoon in a small saucepan with an anchovy or two to make a dipping sauce for steamed vegetables.

ONIONS AND POTATOES

Keep these staples in a cool, dark aerated bin to use with virtually everything—stews, soups, sauces, dips, tarts, and quiches. Potatoes can be baked at the last minute and filled with a variety of toppings, or cut into wedges and roasted at high temperatures and served as a quick snack with sour cream and salsa.

PASTA AND NOODLES

We play a game at our house called "What If You Were Stranded on a Desert Island and Could Only Eat One Food for the Rest of Your Life?" I know I should choose something with vitamin C and lots of water—fresh fruit or some other equally healthful choice. But every time we play, I answer "pasta." There are few foods in the world that provide such comfort and satisfaction. I can eat it three or four times a week and never get bored. Keep a good variety of pasta shapes on hand—spaghetti, linguine, fettuccine, angel hair, rotelle (or wagon wheels), orecchiette, orzo, egg noodles, Chinese rice noodles, cellophane noodles, and more. Pasta should be stored in a cool, dark spot.

RICE

Try to keep a variety of rice on hand for making pilaf, risotto, stuffing, and salads, and serving with stir-fries. Arborio rice is an Italian variety of short-grain rice that is highly prized for its high starch, which creates a very creamy texture. This is the classic ingredient for risotto, as it is shorter than other short-grain rice. Basmati rice, a long-grained rice with an excellent texture, is grown in the foothills of the Himalayas and is renowned for its perfumed, nutlike flavor. Regular long- and short-grain white rice is invaluable for side dishes, stuffings, and salads. Wild rice is prized for its nutty texture and flavor and is excellent to serve with rich foods, as a special stuffing, or mixed with regular white rice for a pilaf.

ROASTED RED BELL PEPPERS

Although nothing beats homemade roasted peppers (see page 46), I have been able to find jars of good-quality Italian roasted red bell peppers in specialty food shops and even some supermarkets (packed in water and salt, and sometimes in high-quality olive oil). I keep a few jars on hand at all times for making an instant antipasto: Arrange peppers on a platter with tuna, olives, small pickles, and thin slices of crusty bread or breadsticks. Chop red bell pepper into salads and sauces, and use them to top sandwiches, pizza, pasta, grilled fish, or chicken, or to add a sweet flavor to stews and casseroles. You can also puree roasted red bell peppers with garlic and olive oil for a quick dip, or add to mayonnaise for a sandwich spread or topping for grilled bread. For a quick appetizer, serve a plate of roasted pepper strips crisscrossed with anchovy fillets, sprinkled with basil or parsley and a drizzle of high-quality olive oil and balsamic vinegar.

SALSA

I always keep a few jars of salsa around for a quick appetizer. Serve with taco chips, raw vegetables, sour cream, and chopped fresh cilantro. Use salsa to accompany tacos, burritos, grilled fish, poultry, or meat. Once opened, salsa will stay fresh in the refrigerator for about a week.

SALT AND PEPPER

Good sea salt is not a marketing gimmick. Unlike regular table salt, which can be bitter, sea salt adds a fresh, briny taste to foods without overwhelming other flavors. Kosher salt can be used as a substitute for sea salt. It is highly flavorful and can be used for pickling foods and seasoning meats and vegetables.

The "right" amount of salt is a personal decision. Many of us are convinced that salt is bad. Food shouldn't taste salty, but it should be full of flavor. Salt can help achieve this fullness. Always undersalt to begin with; taste and adjust as needed.

If you don't already have one, invest in a pepper mill. Freshly ground black pepper (or a combination of pink, green, and black peppercorns) adds excellent flavor to most foods. The peppercorns' fragrant scent and volatile oil is released as you grind it.

SARDINES

Sardines strike me as the cliché of what cooks pull out of their pantry when guests stop by unexpectedly and there's no other food in the house. But don't just think of these tiny fish as a food of last resort. Sardines are delicious drizzled with lemon juice on top of crackers, thinly sliced grilled bread, or focaccia. You can also use sardines to make a quick dip (whirl in a food processor with olive oil, lemon juice, and pepper) and call it a fish pâté.

SUGAR

I keep a jar of plain sugar around for baking, adding sweetness to marinades and sauces. I have a jar of vanilla-flavored sugar for sweetening cake batters, French toast, muffins, sauces, and chocolate dishes. Vanilla sugar is ideal in any dish that would benefit from sweetness and the musty flavor of vanilla. To make vanilla sugar, simply cut a whole vanilla bean down the middle lengthwise. Bury the two halves of the vanilla bean in about 4 cups sugar and seal tightly. The sugar will be flavored within a few days and will keep for months.

TAHINI

Also called sesame paste, tahini is made by grinding roasted, hulled sesame seeds into a thick paste similar to unhomogenized peanut butter. Most tahini is light golden brown in color, with a rich flavor and smooth texture. It adds a nutty sesame flavor and creamy thickness to sauces, noodle dishes, vinaigrettes, and dips. Tahini will stay fresh, refrigerated, for several months.

TARAMASALATA

This Greek-style caviar dip or spread is made from carp roe. It can be difficult to find if you don't live in an area with a Greek population or near a well-stocked specialty food shop. I love having a jar of this salty, pink fish spread on hand for making a quick dip (mix it with sour cream, a touch of olive oil, and a squeeze of fresh lemon juice and pepper). Serve with warm triangles of pita bread or sesame crackers. It also makes a wonderful sandwich spread, layered with cucumbers, thinly sliced radishes, and a variety of other fresh vegetables. Try a spoonful on top of a piping hot baked white potato or sweet potato.

THAI CURRY PASTE

There are several Thai curry pastes now available at Asian and specialty food shops. I've even found red Thai curry paste in the Asian section of my supermarket. These spicy, full-flavored pastes are made from a combination of spices (which often include lemongrass, coriander, chiles, lime zest, and ginger); they make a great foundation for a number of Thai-style noodle dishes and curries. They can be kept in the pantry (a dark, cool spot) for up to a year.

TOMATO SAUCE

I always prefer homemade tomato sauce over canned, but there are many instances when there's no time to make my own and canned or bottled sauce must suffice. Prepared tomato sauce has improved dramatically in recent years, with companies competing for the best homemade taste. Look for a variety with herbs, garlic, and no additives. Good, canned whole, peeled Italian tomatoes are another good choice.

Tomato sauce and canned whole tomatoes are essential for pasta sauces, pizza toppings, or as a sauce for sautéed or grilled chicken or fish. To make a store-bought tomato sauce taste homemade, try this simple recipe: Heat 1 tablespoon olive oil in a medium saucepan. Add 2 cloves minced garlic and a handful of chopped fresh herbs (or a pinch of dried), such as rosemary, basil, thyme, and oregano. Add 1/4 cup dry red wine and let simmer. Add a bottle of tomato sauce and freshly ground pepper, and simmer about 10 minutes. You could also add capers, chopped caperberries, or sun-dried tomatoes; chopped olives or olive puree, a few anchovies, and a bay leaf.

TORTILLAS AND TACOS

Corn and wheat tortillas are now available in grocery stores all over the country. Look for a brand that doesn't contain additives. Heat tortillas (corn or wheat) or taco shells in a low oven, or on an ungreased skillet over low heat. Fill them with cooked, thinly sliced meats, poultry, fish, vegetables, herbs, beans, salsa, salads, grated cheese—virtually anything. Tortillas are great wrappers for leftovers from any party. You can make taco chips by cutting tacos into small triangles and baking them in a hot, 400 degree oven until crisp; flip over and brown the other side. Sprinkle with sea salt and serve with guacamole, salsa, and sour cream.

TUNA AND CANNED SALMON

Both of these canned fish can be used in antipasti platters, to make a quick fish cake (see page 116), or mixed with capers, lemon juice, pepper, chopped scallions, and very finely chopped red onion for a salad or sandwich filling.

VINEGAR (Wine, Cider, and Balsamic)

Balsamic vinegar, or *aceto balsamic,* is a dark, richly flavored vinegar imported from Italy. It is made by fermenting grape juice in wooden casks, often for years. Balsamic vinegar can vary widely in price and quality; better products usually indicate "aged in wood" and "made in Italy" on the label. Its tangy flavor and natural sweetness adds great flavor and aroma to salad dressings, marinades, sauces, and poultry and meat dishes. I sometimes add a tiny splash of high-quality balsamic vinegar to a hearty soup to cut the richness.

I go through lots of wine vinegar; it's the most versatile vinegar. A well-made wine vinegar can transform an ordinary salad into something extraordinary. I keep a bottle of good French red and white vinegar around for sprinkling on salads and coleslaw; for making vinaigrettes, marinades, and sauces; for sprinkling over fresh garden vegetables (with a drizzle of good olive oil), and to add tartness to soups and stews.

Cider vinegar adds a tart, fruity flavor to salad dressings and is the traditional vinegar used for making pickles. Look for cider vinegar with at least 5 percent to $5^1/_2$ percent acidity. All vinegar should be stored in a cool, dark spot.

WINE, VERMOUTH, AND SHERRY

Keep a bottle of high-quality dry red or white table wine on hand for deglazing pans and adding to marinades, soups, stocks, and sauces. Dry vermouth is useful for adding to marinades, splashing over roasts, and deglazing pans (particularly with fish and seafood). Dry sherry is also handy for marinades and deglazing pans; it can also be used as a substitute for Chinese rice wine.

WONTON AND EGG ROLL WRAPPERS

My supermarket now carries fresh wonton and egg roll wrappers on a regular basis. These wheat-based wrappers are terrific for making dumplings, ravioli, egg rolls or spring rolls, crepes, or small lasagna rolls (see page 56 for directions for making your own dumplings). If you live near a Chinese grocer, check to see if they sell homemade wrappers. Keep wonton and egg roll wrappers in the freezer unless you'll be using them right away.

Finding Specialty Ingredients

If you have trouble finding some of the ingredients called for in the recipes, you might want to look at one of the following food Web sites where you can order specialty ingredients.

- *www.EthnicGrocer.com:* Wide variety of ethnic ingredients.
- *www.DeanDeluca.com:* Cookware, household items, great cheeses, and specialty foods from around the world.
- *www.tienda.com:* An excellent collection of Spanish olive oils, rice, saffron, and more.
- *www.Epicurious.com:* Equipment and foods from all over the globe.
- *www.esperya.com:* Italian specialty foods.
- *www.allthingsdutch.com:* Dutch cheeses, Indonesian spices, and more.
- *www.shamra.com:* Mediterranean foods.
- *www.ThaiGrocer.com:* Everything you need for cooking Thai specialties.
- *www.orientalpantry.com:* A wide assortment of Asian foods.
- *www.fromages.com:* Cheese from around the world.
- *www.rogersintl.com:* An excellent selection of international olive oils and specialty foods.

4
Appetizers

Nibbles, Dips, Sauces, and Salads

Spiced Nuts

Orange-Marinated Olives

Endive Spears Stuffed with Herbed Goat Cheese

Sautéed Fresh Figs with Pancetta

Roasted Red Bell Peppers

Spinach, Prosciutto, and Red Bell Pepper Crostini

Clams in Green Sauce (*Almejas en Salsa Verde*)

Beef Satay with Coconut-Ginger Dipping Sauce

Cheese and Pepper Twists

Vietnamese-Style Spring Rolls with Shrimp

Shrimp and Pork Dumplings with Soy-Sesame Dipping Sauce

Turkish-Style Stuffed Grape Leaves (*Zeytinyagli Asma Yaprak
   Sarma*)

Gingered Crab Cakes

White Bean Dip

Red Caviar Dip

Spiced Nuts

Offer these sweet and savory nuts with cocktails before dinner, or sprinkle them over salads. They can be made three days ahead of time. A great gift idea: a Mason jar filled with nuts and decorated with bright ribbon or raffia.

Vegetable oil for greasing the baking sheet
2 tablespoons olive oil
½ teaspoon ground ginger
½ teaspoon curry powder
¼ teaspoon cayenne
2 tablespoons sugar
1 tablespoon honey
¾ cup walnut halves
¾ cup pecan halves
Salt

Line a baking sheet with foil. Spread vegetable oil lightly over the foil. Heat the olive oil in a large skillet over medium heat. Add the ginger, curry, and cayenne; sauté until fragrant, about 30 seconds. Stir in the sugar and honey. Add the nuts and stir until honey mixture is amber in color and nuts are well coated, about 6 minutes.

Transfer the nut mixture to the prepared baking sheet. Working quickly, separate the nuts with a spoon. Sprinkle with salt. Cool. Store in an airtight container at room temperature.

Makes 1½ cups

You Can Also Add . . .

- Almonds, pistachios, cashews, or hazelnuts instead of, or in addition to, the walnuts and pecans.
- ¼ to ½ teaspoon cumin.
- Maple syrup instead of honey.

Orange-Marinated Olives

Use any good-quality olive for this spicy dish. An assortment of black and green olives looks particularly nice.

1 cup brine-cured olives
¼ cup fresh orange juice
¼ cup olive oil
About 8 strips orange peel, cut into very thin julienne strips
2 cloves garlic, very thinly sliced
About ½ teaspoon crushed red pepper
Salt

In a medium bowl, mix the olives, orange juice, oil, orange peel, and garlic. Season to taste with the pepper and salt. Cover and refrigerate overnight. Can be prepared 4 days ahead of time. Keep refrigerated.

Makes 1 cup

You Can Also Add . . .

- Lemon juice and lemon peel instead of orange.
- 1 teaspoon fennel or cumin seeds.
- 1 tablespoon chopped fresh rosemary, thyme, or oregano, or 1 teaspoon dried herbs.

Endive Spears Stuffed with Herbed Goat Cheese

A quick, simple hors d'oeuvre that can be served with cocktails or alongside a first-course salad with French bread or toast points. You can make the herbed goat cheese a day ahead of time, or assemble the endive spears up to four hours before serving.

4 ounces soft goat cheese
About 2 tablespoons heavy cream
1½ tablespoons fresh rosemary, finely chopped, or 1½ teaspoons dried, crushed
1½ tablespoons fresh thyme, finely chopped, or 1½ teaspoons dried
1½ tablespoons fresh parsley, finely chopped
1 tablespoon fresh chives, minced
Freshly ground pepper
1 large head endive, or 2 small heads
Sweet paprika, optional

In a medium bowl, cream the goat cheese with the back of a kitchen spoon. Add the cream, rosemary, thyme, parsley, chives, and pepper and mix until smooth and creamy. Add more cream if the cheese is particularly thick. Cover and refrigerate until ready to use. Bring to room temperature before assembling.

Core the endive and separate into spears. Spoon the filling into 20 endive spears, filling each spear about halfway. Assemble on a plate and sprinkle with the paprika, if using. Cover and refrigerate.

Makes 20 endive spears

You Can Also Add . . .

- Finely chopped vine-ripened tomatoes scattered over the cheese.
- Toasted and finely chopped hazelnuts, pine nuts, almonds, walnuts, or cashews.
- A tiny bit of red salmon caviar on top of the cheese.

Sautéed Fresh Figs with Pancetta

The season for figs is fairly short, midsummer through early fall, but fresh figs are such a treat. A friend of mine who lives in Northern California has a gorgeous fig tree that literally drips with fruit for more than a week. Figs are delicious eaten raw in fruit salads, served cold with paper-thin slices of prosciutto, or simmered into a fruit compote. This very simple appetizer can be put together in minutes and has a very sophisticated flavor. Serve at a cocktail party, as a first course, or place on top of mixed greens for an interesting salad.

⅛ pound pancetta or prosciutto, thinly sliced
1 teaspoon olive oil
8 fresh figs, stemmed and cut in half lengthwise
Freshly ground pepper

In a large skillet cook the pancetta about 4 minutes on each side, until crisp and cooked (like bacon). Remove from the skillet and drain on paper towels. (If using prosciutto cook in ½ teaspoon olive oil for 1 minute on each side.) Cut the pancetta into thin strips or chop.

Add the olive oil to the skillet and place over moderate heat. Add the figs, flesh side down, and cook 1 minute. Gently flip the figs over and cook 1 minute on the other side. Sprinkle with pepper. Place on a serving plate and scatter the figs equally with the pancetta. If serving the figs at a cocktail party, use toothpicks. Serve hot.

Makes 4 servings

Roasted Red Bell Peppers

Sweet, tender, and exceedingly adaptable, these red bell pepper strips can be used for a quick appetizer, or to top more complex dishes. Keep a few red bell pepper strips on hand, or roast the peppers a few days before your party and let them marinate in olive oil. If the peppers are placed in a glass jar and completely covered with olive oil, they will keep for up to two weeks in the refrigerator.

3 large, firm red bell peppers
   (works with green, yellow, and orange bell peppers as well)
Good-quality olive oil

There are two methods for roasting peppers. The first is to cook them under the broiler: Preheat the broiler. Place the peppers directly under the broiler and broil on each side about 4 minutes, or until blackened. (There's a fine line between blackened pepper skin, which just blisters and begins to peel off, and peppers that are over-cooked and drying out, so watch it!)

Alternatively, you can place the pepper directly over the flame of a gas stove and, using a pair of tongs, flip it from side to side, or until just blackened on all sides.

When the peppers are blackened and still hot, place them in a brown paper bag,

folding the edges to seal the bag tightly. Let the peppers sit in the bag for about 2 minutes. The steam in the bag will loosen the skin from the pepper flesh. Remove from the bag and, when cool enough to handle, remove the skin, core, and inner ribs. Cut into thin or thick wedges and cover with olive oil. Any or all of the possible additions listed below can be served on top, or on the side, of the peppers.

Makes 4 to 6 servings

You Can Also Add . . .

- Shredded fresh basil.
- Chopped fresh or dried thyme, rosemary, or oregano.

- 2 cloves minced or very thinly sliced garlic.
- Roasted garlic: Place 1 head garlic drizzled with 1 tablespoon olive oil in a small ovenproof skillet. Roast in a 400 degree oven until soft, about 20 minutes. Pop the garlic cloves out of their skin and scatter on top of the peppers with the oil from the skillet.
- Capers or caperberries.
- Anchovy fillets.
- Black and green olives.
- Crumbled goat cheese or blue cheese.

Spinach, Prosciutto, and Red Bell Pepper Crostini ☕ ☕

Crostini and bruschetta are popular Italian appetizers where any variety of fresh or cooked foods are used to top grilled Italian or French bread. The crostini can be assembled two hours ahead of time. Cover and refrigerate until ready to broil and serve.

2 tablespoons plus 2 teaspoons olive oil
½ red bell pepper, cut into thin strips
10 ounces fresh spinach, stemmed
1 teaspoon minced garlic
¼ cup chopped prosciutto
Salt and freshly ground pepper
1 tablespoon heavy cream
Twelve ½-inch-thick slices cut from French baguette
6 tablespoons freshly grated Parmesan cheese

Heat 1 teaspoon of the oil in a heavy skillet over medium heat. Add the pepper and sauté until almost tender, about 8 minutes. Transfer to a small bowl.

Heat the same skillet over moderately high heat. Add 1 teaspoon of the oil and then the spinach and sauté about 4 minutes, or until tender, stirring constantly. Transfer the spinach to a work surface and let cool slightly. Chop and set aside.

Heat 1 tablespoon of the oil in the same skillet. Add the garlic and cook about 30 seconds. Add the prosciutto and sauté 30 seconds. Add the chopped spinach, salt and pepper to taste, and cook 2 minutes. Remove from heat and add the cream, then set aside.

Preheat the broiler. Arrange the bread slices on a large baking sheet. Broil until lightly toasted. Turn bread slices over, and brush the top of the bread slices with the remaining 1 tablespoon of oil. Broil until lightly toasted. Cool. Cover spinach mixture and pepper strips separately and refrigerate. Store toasts in an airtight container at room temperature.

To serve: Spoon a generous tablespoon of the spinach mixture on top of each toast slice. Arrange a pepper strip on top. Sprinkle with the cheese and broil until the cheese bubbles and the spinach mixture is hot, about 2 minutes. Transfer to a serving plate.

Makes 12 crostini

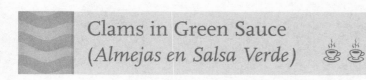

Clams in Green Sauce
(*Almejas en Salsa Verde*)

Isabel Achoa, a friend living in Granada, Spain, taught me to make this simple classic. Baby littleneck clams are simmered in a garlic and parsley sauce until they just open and release their salty essence. Serve hot, with chunks of crusty bread to soak up the delicious green sauce.

2 pounds littleneck clams, or mahogany clams (the smaller and fresher the better)
Coarse sea salt
1½ tablespoons olive oil, preferably Spanish
5 cloves garlic, finely chopped
1 tablespoon flour
½ cup dry white wine, or dry Spanish sherry
½ cup water
2 cups fresh parsley, minced
Crusty bread, cut into thick slices

Scrub the clams well and place in a bowl covered with cold water. Sprinkle in 1 teaspoon coarse sea salt and let sit for at least 15 minutes, and up to 1 hour.

Drain the clams, rinse, and drain again.

In a medium saucepan, heat the oil over moderate heat. Add the garlic and cook about 2 minutes, stirring. Sprinkle in the flour, stirring to create a paste, and let cook 1 minute. Add the clams, stirring well to thoroughly coat them. Add the wine, water, and parsley and stir well. Let cook 7 to 10 minutes, depending on the size of the clams, or until they just open. Do not let them overcook or they will be tough. Stir the clams well. If the sauce tastes too winey, remove the clams with a slotted spoon and simmer the sauce another 2 to 3 minutes, over moderately high heat. Serve hot with the bread.

Makes 4 servings

You Can Also Add . . .

- Mussels, scrubbed and debearded, instead of, or in addition to, the clams. Cook about 8 minutes, or until the mussel shells are completely open.
- 1 pound linguine or spaghetti and pour the clams and sauce on top.
- Medium shrimp instead of the clams. Cook until the shrimp are pink and cooked through, about 5 minutes.

Beef Satay with Coconut-Ginger Dipping Sauce ☕ ☕

Thin strips of flank steak are marinated in coconut milk, ginger, and soy sauce and then threaded onto bamboo skewers and grilled. The grilled beef strips are served with a spicy coconut-ginger dipping sauce. The beef can be marinated an hour, several hours, or a day ahead of time and the dipping sauce can be prepared a day ahead of time. Both should be covered and refrigerated until ready to serve.

THE BEEF:
1½ pounds flank steak
½ cup unsweetened coconut milk*
2 tablespoons soy sauce
1 tablespoon gingerroot, minced
1 tablespoon fresh lemongrass, chopped, optional *
Freshly ground pepper

THE DIPPING SAUCE:
1 tablespoon peanut oil or vegetable oil
1½ tablespoons gingerroot, minced
2 cloves garlic, minced
1 teaspoon Chinese chile paste, or chopped fresh chiles, or a few dashes
    hot pepper sauce*
½ cup smooth or chunky natural peanut butter
2 tablespoons soy sauce
¾ cup unsweetened coconut milk*
⅓ cup water
2 tablespoons cilantro, finely chopped, optional

Cut the beef into very thin (about ½-inch thick), long strips and place in a medium bowl; you should have about 25 thin strips. (Alternatively, you can cut the beef into small 1-inch cubes.) Cover with the coconut milk, soy sauce, ginger, lemongrass, and pepper.

Soak about 25 wooden bamboo skewers in a bowl of cold water for at least 1 hour. Soaking prevents the wooden sticks from burning.

*Available at Asian and specialty food shops.

Make the dipping sauce by heating the oil in a medium saucepan over moderately low heat. Add the ginger and garlic and cook about 2 minutes, stirring frequently. Add the chile paste and cook 10 seconds, stirring. Stir in the peanut butter, mashing it to create a smooth paste. Add the soy sauce, coconut milk, and water and whisk to create a smooth sauce. Let simmer over low heat for 5 minutes, stirring. Remove from the heat and stir in the cilantro, if using. Transfer the sauce to a serving bowl, cover, and refrigerate until ready to use. The sauce should be served at room temperature; remove it from the refrigerator about 15 minutes before serving, stirring to smooth out the sauce.

Thread the beef onto the soaked bamboo skewers, by placing the thinnest end of the beef strip onto the skewer first and then weaving the beef onto the stick, piercing it in three or four spots. (Alternatively, place about four or five chunks of beef onto each skewer.) If broiling the beef, place the skewers on a baking sheet lined with aluminum foil.

Preheat the broiler with the rack about 4 inches from the heat. Alternatively, light a charcoal, wood, or gas fire until red hot. Broil or grill the beef about 3 minutes on each side, being careful not to let the skewers burn. (Have some water on hand in case the wood catches fire.) Test the thickest piece of beef to make sure it's medium-rare. Serve the satay hot with the dipping sauce at room temperature.

Makes about 25 skewers

You Can Also Add . . .

- Skinless boneless chicken breasts instead of beef, cooking for 2 to 3 minutes on each side, or until cooked through.
- 1 cup shredded, unsweetened coconut as a topping. Heat the coconut in a dry skillet over low heat for about 4 minutes, shaking the pan occasionally to prevent the coconut from burning. It should just begin to turn a very light golden-brown. Place the coconut in a small bowl and invite guests to dip the beef into the sauce and then into the bowl of coconut. You could also sprinkle the coconut on one side of the beef skewers just as they come off the fire.
- 1 cup chopped unsalted peanuts as a topping. Place peanuts in a bowl and let guests dip the beef into the sauce and then coat them in the peanuts. You could also sprinkle the beef skewers with peanuts just as they come off the fire.
- A collection of hot pepper sauces for guests who desire a spicier dish.

Cheese and Pepper Twists

These breadsticks, twisted with coarsely ground pepper and grated Parmesan cheese, are ideal to serve with cocktails. Although they require a yeast rising, they can be made from start to finish in less than two hours. Experiment with different herbs and cheeses; see ideas on page 53. You can adjust the setting on your pepper grinder for a coarser grind. The twists can be made up to four days ahead of time; store in an airtight container at room temperature.

2 teaspoons active dry yeast

1½ cups lukewarm water

2 tablespoons olive oil, plus additional for coating the bowl and the baking sheets

1 teaspoon salt

Generous amounts of coarsely ground pepper

About 3 cups flour, plus additional for kneading

About 1 cup freshly grated Parmesan cheese

1 egg white

Dissolve the yeast and water in a large bowl and set aside in a warm spot. Let stand for 10 minutes, or until the yeast begins to bubble.

Add the 2 tablespoons of oil, the salt, and a generous grinding of pepper. Sprinkle on the flour and stir until the dough comes together.

Flour a clean work surface and knead the dough, working in ¾ cup of the cheese. Knead about 10 minutes, or until smooth and the pepper and cheese are well incorporated. Lightly oil a large bowl. Add the dough and flip so it's coated in oil on both sides. Cover with a clean tea towel and set in a warm, draft-free spot for 1 hour, or until the dough doubles in size.

Lightly oil two baking sheets. Preheat the oven to 400 degrees.

Place the egg white in a bowl and lightly whisk.

Cut the dough into three equal parts. Roll out one third of the dough on a floured work surface into a rectangle about 8 by 8 inches. Brush the dough with some of the beaten egg white and sprinkle with 2 tablespoons of the remaining cheese and a light grinding of pepper. Cut the dough, using a kitchen knife or a serrated pizza cutter, into 8 long strips. Take a strip and twist it from both ends, creating a swirl. Place the twist on the oiled baking sheet. Repeat with the remaining dough. Repeat with the remaining two rounds of dough, brushing with egg white and then sprinkling with cheese and pepper before twisting.

Bake the twists on the middle and top third shelf of the oven for 20 to 25 minutes, making sure they don't burn. Switch the baking sheets after about 10 minutes, so they cook evenly. Remove from the oven and let cool on a cooling rack. Bake the remaining twists.

Makes 24 twists

You Can Also Add . . .

- $1\frac{1}{2}$ tablespoons chopped fresh rosemary, thyme, oregano, basil, or a combination of fresh herbs, or $1\frac{1}{2}$ teaspoons dried herbs.
- A combination of grated cheeses.
- A dash of cayenne to the dough to give the cheese twists a spicier flavor.

Vietnamese-Style Spring Rolls with Shrimp ☕ ☕ ☕

Making your own spring rolls may sound like a major commitment, but you'll be surprised to find that this procedure is quite easy and fun. The lime juice, gingerroot, cilantro, cucumber, and mint are typical Southeast Asian flavors. Serve these spring rolls as appetizers, as an hors d'oeuvre with cocktails, or as part of a buffet. They go particularly well with Thai beer. The spring rolls can be made several hours ahead of time; cover and refrigerate until ready to serve.

THE DIPPING SAUCE:
¼ cup fish sauce (nam pla),* or soy sauce
2 tablespoons scallions, thinly sliced
1½ tablespoons fresh lime juice
Pinch crushed red pepper

THE ROLLS:
2 teaspoons olive oil
2 teaspoons minced gingerroot, minced
16 uncooked medium shrimp, peeled, deveined, and halved lengthwise
¼ cup cilantro, chopped
Salt and freshly ground pepper
4 cups hot water
Eight 6-inch-diameter Vietnamese spring rolls sheets†
4 small bibb lettuce leaves, halved
½ cup scallions, cut into thin strips
½ cup cucumber, peeled, seeded, and cut into thin strips
4 teaspoons fresh mint leaves, minced

To make the dipping sauce: Mix the fish sauce, the 2 tablespoons of scallions, lime juice, and crushed red pepper in a small bowl and set aside.

To make the rolls: Heat the oil in a medium skillet over medium-high heat. Add the ginger and sauté about 10 seconds, stirring frequently. Add the shrimp and cilantro

*Available at Asian markets and in the Asian food section of many supermarkets.
†Thin Vietnamese wrappers made from wheat flour, also called *Banh Trang*, are also found at Asian food markets.

and sauté until the shrimp are just cooked through, about 1 minute. Remove from the heat and season with salt and pepper to taste.

Pour the hot water into a large bowl. Using tongs, dip 1 spring roll sheet into the water for 5 seconds. Remove from the water and place on a wet towel. Let stand for 30 seconds (spring roll sheets should be soft and pliable; if still stiff sprinkle with more water).

Place half a lettuce leaf across the top third of the spring roll sheet. Arrange 4 shrimp halves on the lettuce. Top with 1 tablespoon each of the scallions and cucumber. Sprinkle ½ teaspoon mint over each filing. Fold sides of spring roll sheet over ends of filling. Starting at the filled side, roll into a cylinder. Place on a plate. Repeat with the remaining spring roll sheets, lettuce, shrimp, scallions, cucumber, and mint. Serve with the dipping sauce.

Makes 4 to 8 servings

Shrimp and Pork Dumplings with Soy-Sesame Dipling Sauce

Living in an area without a really good Chinese restaurant isn't easy. I find myself fantasizing about the great restaurants of Hong Kong, New York, and San Francisco. I learned to make these dumplings at home as a matter of survival and, if I do say so, they are almost as good as any you'll find in your favorite Chinese restaurant. The dumplings can be made a day ahead of time; cover and refrigerate until ready to cook. You can also very carefully wrap in plastic or a plastic container and freeze the dumplings for up to two months.

You'll need a Chinese steamer basket to make these dumplings. Look for a two-leveled bamboo Chinese steamer basket and wonton wrappers in Asian food markets or specialty food shops.

THE DUMPLINGS:
½ pound medium shrimp (26/30 count), peeled, deveined, and coarsely chopped
1 pound ground pork
2 tablespoons scallions, very finely chopped
1 tablespoon minced gingerroot
¼ teaspoon soy sauce
¼ teaspoon sesame oil
1 tablespoon chopped cilantro, optional
About 30 wonton wrappers
Lettuce leaves, preferably iceberg

THE DIPPING SAUCE:
1 tablespoon minced gingerroot
1½ tablespoons chopped cilantro
½ cup chopped scallions
6 tablespoons soy sauce
2 teaspoons sesame oil

To make the dumpling filling, use your hands or a spoon to gently but thoroughly mix the shrimp, pork, scallions, ginger, soy sauce, sesame oil, and cilantro. The filling can be made several hours ahead of time; cover and refrigerate until ready to use.

To make the dipping sauce: Mix the ginger, cilantro, and scallions in a small serving bowl. Add the soy sauce and sesame oil. The sauce can be made several hours ahead of time; cover and refrigerate until ready to serve.

To make the dumplings: Fill a small bowl with water. Place a dumpling wrapper on a clean work surface and place about 1 heaping teaspoon of the filling in the center. Wet your fingertips and lightly dab the edges of the wrapper with some water and fold two opposite corners into the middle and press together to seal. Lift the other 2 sides in to meet in the middle and press together, using the water to help the dough stick together if necessary. Pinch all the edges so a sealed pocket is formed. Repeat with the remaining wrappers and filling, making about 30 dumplings.

To cook the dumplings, line a two-leveled Chinese steamer basket with lettuce leaves (this will keep the dumplings from sticking to the bottom of the basket and provide extra moisture as the lettuce steams). Place 10 dumplings in each basket on top of the lettuce leaves.

Fill the bottom of a wok or a large skillet with 1 to 2 inches of water. Bring to a boil. Place the steamer baskets on top of the boiling water, making sure the water isn't touching the bottom tray and steam for 6 to 8 minutes. Test one dumpling from the bottom steamer tray by cutting in half and making sure the pork is thoroughly cooked. Serve hot with the dipping sauce.

Makes about 30 dumplings

Turkish-Style Stuffed Grape Leaves
(*Zeytinyagli Asma Yaprak Sarma*)

There is no denying that this is a time-consuming recipe. You should plan on spending at least two hours in the kitchen. Despite the long preparation time, this is not a difficult recipe.

This is my adaptation of a recipe from Kathleen O'Neill, a Californian who lives in Bodrum, Turkey, and runs culinary tours of southeastern Turkey and market tours of Istanbul.

In this recipe, grape leaves are stuffed with rice, currants, nuts, spices, and onions cooked in olive oil. Fresh dill is used to flavor the stuffing, and the leaves are then simmered in lemon juice and water until tender. A tip I learned from O'Neill: If you soak the grape leaves in hot water it removes the strong brine flavor found in so many bottled grape leaves.

These morsels will be a hit at any party—ideal to bring to a potluck or to serve at a cocktail party, as a first course, or as part of any buffet. They can be made up to a day ahead of time.

1 bottle grape leaves, 35 to 45 leaves*
½ cup good-quality olive oil
3 medium onions, finely chopped
¼ cup pine nuts or chopped walnuts or almonds
1 cup short-grain white rice
¼ cup currants or raisins
½ teaspoon cinnamon
½ teaspoon allspice
1 teaspoon salt
1½ teaspoons sugar
Generous grinding of pepper
¼ cup fresh dill, finely chopped
Juice of 1 large lemon
1 lemon, very thinly sliced, for garnish
Large fresh dill head or few sprigs of fresh dill, for garnish

*Available in specialty food shops and supermarkets.

Drain the brine solution off the grape leaves and place the leaves in a colander. Gently rinse in hot water. Place the leaves in a large bowl and cover with warm water; let soak for 30 minutes to an hour. Drain and set aside.

Bring 2 cups of water to a boil in a saucepan.

Meanwhile, heat the olive oil in a large saucepan over medium heat. Add the onions and sauté for 15 minutes, stirring frequently, being careful not to let them brown. Add the nuts and cook for another minute. Add the rice and sauté for 3 minutes. Stir in the currants, cinnamon, allspice, salt, sugar, and pepper. Stir in 1 cup of the boiling water. Cover, reduce the heat to low, and simmer for about 10 minutes, or until the water has been absorbed. At this point, *the rice will only be partially cooked.* Remove from the heat and place the rice filling into a bowl and allow to cool. When cool, stir in the fresh dill and add salt and pepper to taste.

Line the bottom of a large skillet with a lid with 10 of the drained (unstuffed) vine leaves. From the stack of leaves, take one leaf and pinch off the stem with your fingers. Place the leaf in front of you and, with the vein side up and the stem end pointing toward you, place about a tablespoon of the filling in the center lower half of the leaf, near the stem end. Fold in both sides over the filling and roll up from the stem end. Place the stuffed leaves in the prepared pan, seam side down. Continue to stuff the leaves and fill the pan, placing them side by side tightly in the pan. When the bottom of the pan has a complete layer, begin a second layer placing them directly on top of the first.

Sprinkle the stuffed leaves with a pinch of salt. Pour the lemon juice on top of all the leaves and slowly add the remaining cup of boiling water. Cover with a piece of wax paper, pushing the paper down snugly over the grape leaves. Cover the pan with the lid. Place the pan over medium-low heat and simmer for 30 minutes. Remove from the heat and set aside until the leaves have cooled. Place on a platter and refrigerate until serving time.

Garnish the plate with the lemon slices and dill and serve cold.

Makes about 35 stuffed grape leaves

Gingered Crab Cakes

Make tiny versions of these gingery crab cakes (one-inch) and serve them as hors d'oeuvres, or make them larger and serve as a first course with lemon and lime wedges and a simple tartar sauce. Fresh gingerroot gives the crab a delicious, fresh zing!

2 tablespoons olive oil
1 small onion, finely chopped
¼ cup green or red bell pepper, finely chopped
1 scallion, finely chopped
Salt and freshly ground pepper
1 tablespoon gingerroot, finely chopped
6 ounces fresh crabmeat
1 egg, whisked
1½ tablespoons heavy cream
1 teaspoon fresh lemon or lime juice
About ½ cup bread crumbs, fresh or dry
1 lemon or lime, cut into wedges
Tartar Sauce (see page 67), optional

In a medium-large skillet, heat 1 tablespoon of the oil over moderate heat. Add the onion and cook 3 minutes. Add the bell pepper, scallion, salt, pepper, and ginger and cook another 5 minutes, stirring frequently.

In a large bowl, separate the crabmeat with a fork. Add the egg and mix well. Add the cream, salt, pepper, and lemon juice. Add the cooked onion and pepper mixture and enough bread crumbs to hold the mixture together; it will still appear moist. You can make the mixture about 6 hours ahead of time up to this point. Cover and refrigerate until ready to cook.

Heat a large, heavy skillet with the remaining tablespoon of oil. Form the mixture into 1-inch- or 3-inch-diameter cakes and cook about 4 minutes. Gently flip the cakes, and cook another 3 to 5 minutes, or until golden brown and cooked through. You can cook the cakes and keep in a warm, 250 degree oven for about 1 hour before serving. Serve hot with lemon or lime wedges and tartar sauce, if desired.

Makes 6 three-inch cakes, or about 12 one-inch cakes

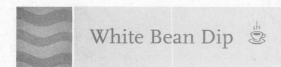

White Bean Dip ☕

With a can of beans, a blender or food processor, a drizzle of olive oil, and a few dry herbs you'll have an instant, unbelievably satisfying dip in no time. Serve with crackers, pita toasts (page 63), chips or taco chips, or raw vegetables.

1 can white cannellini beans (15.5 ounces), drained
1½ tablespoons olive oil
1 clove garlic, chopped
Salt and freshly ground pepper
½ teaspoon dried rosemary
½ teaspoon dried thyme

In the container of a food processor or blender, puree the beans, oil, garlic, salt, pepper, rosemary, and thyme. Serve within 1 to 2 hours.

Makes about 1½ cups

You Can Also Add . . .

- 1 ripe tomato, chopped and placed around the finished dip.
- ½ cup pitted black or green olives, placed around the finished dip.
- 1 tablespoon chopped fresh herbs instead of dried.
- A dash of hot pepper sauce to taste.
- Basil oil or other herb-flavored oil for the olive oil.
- Black or kidney beans or chickpeas for the white beans.
- 2 tablespoons chopped fresh basil or parsley sprinkled on top of the dip.

Red Caviar Dip

Red caviar, which comes from salmon, is relatively inexpensive (compared to black stur-geon caviar) and makes a delicious dip. Serve with toast triangles, crackers, or assorted raw vegetables like steamed asparagus spears, thinly sliced fennel, radish halves, celery, or endive spears. The dip can be made up to eight hours ahead of time.

1 cup sour cream
2 scallions, very thinly sliced
1 tablespoon fresh lemon juice
1 tablespoon plus 1 teaspoon chopped fresh chives
¼ cup plus 3 tablespoons fresh salmon caviar

Mix the sour cream, scallions, lemon juice, and the 1 tablespoon chives in a medium serving bowl. Gently fold in the ¼ cup caviar. Sprinkle the dip with the remaining chives and caviar and serve cold.

Makes about 1 cup

Spinach Dip with Pita Triangles and Vegetables ☕ ☕

Fresh spinach is sautéed with garlic and then pureed with sour cream and scallions to create this simple, delicious dip. You can use more garlic depending on how pronounced you want the garlic flavor to be. Serve with raw or cooked vegetables, pita triangles, and cooked shrimp. The dish can be made up to a day before.

1½ teaspoons plus 2 tablespoons olive oil
1 to 2 cloves garlic, chopped
8 cups (about 5 ounces) fresh spinach leaves, stemmed
1 to 2 scallions, chopped (about ½ cup), white and green parts
1 cup sour cream
1 teaspoon fresh lemon juice
Salt and freshly ground pepper
Two 6-inch-diameter pita breads
Assorted raw or cooked vegetables

Heat the 1½ teaspoons oil in a large skillet over moderate heat. Add the garlic and sauté about 10 seconds. Add the spinach and sauté, stirring frequently, until wilted and tender, about 2 minutes. Cool.

Place the spinach and scallions in a food processor and puree. Transfer to a bowl and mix in the sour cream, lemon juice, salt, and pepper. Cover and chill.

Preheat the broiler. Slice each pita bread horizontally in half, forming 2 circles. Cut each circle into 4 triangles. Place the triangles on a baking sheet and brush lightly with the remaining 2 tablespoons oil. Sprinkle with pepper. Broil until golden, watching closely to avoid burning, about 2 minutes. Cool.

Keep the dip covered and chilled. Store pita in airtight container. Serve spinach dip with pita triangles and assorted raw vegetables.

Makes 6 servings

Yogurt "Cheese" with Mint, Scallions, and Cucumber ☕ ☕

When yogurt is drained in a colander or strainer it thickens and transforms into a delicious, thick "cheese." Yogurt cheese is popular in Middle Eastern cooking, where it's used for making dips and sauces, and for thickening soups and stews. With this dip, the yogurt needs to drain for at least two hours, or overnight. The longer it drains, the thicker the yogurt cheese will be. Once you've drained the yogurt, this pungent sauce can be put together in about five minutes.

Serve as a dip or sauce with raw or steamed vegetables, with cooked or grilled shrimp, crackers, chips, or skewers of grilled chicken, beef, or lamb.

4 cups plain, low-fat yogurt
1 medium cucumber, peeled, seeded, and grated
2 scallions, thinly sliced, white and green parts
⅓ cup fresh mint, chopped
1 clove garlic, minced, optional
Salt and freshly ground pepper
Dash hot pepper sauce

Place a large, fine sieve over a medium bowl. Pour the yogurt into the sieve and let it drain for 2 hours, or up to 24 hours. If you want the sauce to be very thick and cheesy, you should let it drain for close to 24 hours. If you prefer a thinner sauce, let it drain for just a few hours. Remove the drained yogurt from the sieve and throw away the juices gathered in the bowl.

Mix the yogurt cheese with the cucumber, scallions, mint, garlic, salt, pepper and hot pepper sauce to taste. Cover and refrigerate. Serve within 2 to 3 hours.

Makes 8 servings

You Can Also Add . . .

- ½ cup finely chopped walnuts or almonds.
- ½ teaspoon ground cumin.
- A touch of crumbled dried red chile pepper or chile paste for a spicier dip.
- 1 tablespoon chopped cilantro.
- The dip to a scooped-out round peasant bread and use the bread as the serving bowl.

Mango Salsa

I doubt you'll find a fresher-tasting, more appealing salsa than this one made with juicy, ripe mangoes tossed with green chiles, red bell pepper, red onion, cilantro, and lime juice. The recipe comes from my friend Glenn Smith, a massage therapist and "recovering chef" who spends summers on Martha's Vineyard and winters in Aspen, Colorado.

For appetizers, I'd serve the salsa with chips, guacamole, and margaritas, or try it as a dipping sauce for cooked (steamed or grilled) shrimp, raw vegetables, or quesadillas. It's also fabulous as a side dish for tacos, burritos, enchiladas, or just about any grilled or roasted food. The canned green chiles are not particularly hot; if you want your salsa to have bite, add a dash or two of your favorite hot pepper sauce. If using a fresh chile, add the seeds. The salsa should be served within one to three hours; cover and refrigerate until ready to eat.

2 large, ripe mangoes, pitted and peeled into ½-inch cubes, about 2 cups*
1 red bell pepper, cut into small dice, about 1½ cups
1 medium red onion, cut into small dice, about ½ cup
One 4.5-ounce can chopped green chiles, or 1 fresh green chile, seeded and finely
    chopped
⅓ cup cilantro, chopped
2 tablespoons olive oil
Juice of 2 large limes
Salt and freshly ground pepper
Dash hot pepper sauce

Mix all the ingredients in a medium bowl and let sit for 1 to 3 hours before serving. Cover and refrigerate.

Makes about 4 cups

*Be sure to cut the mangoes over a bowl to catch all the juices.

Ultimate Guacamole

This guacamole is fresh and chunky, with the vibrant flavors of Mexico—not a mush of indistinguishable flavors like that found in so many mediocre Mexican restaurants. Avocados are considered by some to be aphrodisiacs, making this an ideal dish to serve to people you love.

4 ripe avocados, preferably Hass variety (Californian or Mexican)
½ fresh jalapeño pepper
⅓ cup cilantro, chopped
Juice of 1 lime
1 large ripe tomato, chopped
2 scallions, finely chopped, white and green parts
¼ cup red or white onion, finely chopped
Dash hot pepper sauce, optional
Salt to taste
Garnishes: 2 cups salsa (hot, medium, or mild, homemade or bottled)
    1 cup sour cream
    ½ cup finely chopped cilantro
    1 to 2 tablespoons pureed chipotle peppers
    1 large bag tortilla chips

Cut the avocados lengthwise and remove the pit. Using a teaspoon, gently scoop out the flesh and place in a medium bowl. Using the back of a fork, break the avocados up into chunks, being careful not to overwork it into a mush. Cut the jalapeño in half lengthwise. Remove the seeds if you don't want a spicy dish; leave them in if you like a "bite." Chop the pepper and seeds, if using, and add to the avocados. Gently fold in the cilantro, lime juice, tomato, scallions, onion, hot pepper sauce, and salt to taste. Serve within 1 hour, accompanied by bowls of salsa, sour cream, cilantro, peppers, and chips.

Makes 6 servings

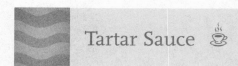

Tartar Sauce

Serve this sauce with crab cakes, salmon cakes, cooked shrimp, or other deep-fried, panfried, or grilled seafood.

1 cup mayonnaise
⅛ cup onion, diced
⅛ cup fresh lemon juice
⅛ cup capers, or caperberries, chopped
⅛ cup parsley, finely chopped
⅛ cup gherkins, very finely chopped
Salt and freshly ground pepper
Hot pepper sauce

In a bowl, mix all the ingredients and taste for seasoning; the sauce should have a slight peppery taste. The sauce can be made several hours before serving. Cover and refrigerate until ready to serve.

Makes about 1 cup

Nana's Quick Ideas for Appetizers and Hors d'Oeuvres

My grandmother, Leona Levy, was not a cook, but she knew how to give a party—including choosing the right menu. As a little girl, I remember being awed by the selection of finger foods served at holidays and family gatherings in her big Manhattan apartment. When I was about six or seven, I asked her how she made a certain dish. She rolled her head back and gave a huge, deep laugh. "Kathy, I can't even boil an egg," she admitted, without a trace of remorse in her voice. That's when I realized that the women in the kitchen were the ones who ran my grandparents' household.

I lost my beloved grandparents several years ago. When we cleared out their apartment I found an old, battered index file stuffed with handwritten cards in my grandmother's elegant script. Inside was a collection of recipes—gathered from old friends, magazines, and now-faded clippings from *The New York Times*—that were like a treasure from a lost time. The following ideas all come from my grandmother's file; these are the recipes, gathered from old friends, that she served at cocktail and dinner parties she and my grandfather hosted from around 1940 through the 1980s. Some of them may strike you as old-fashioned, but they are all quick and easy, and full of flavors that remain very popular today.

- Mix 2 cups softened cream cheese with ½ cup grated or very thinly sliced radishes. Mix in 2 to 3 tablespoons milk to thin and 3 tablespoons chopped chives. Spread on thin brown rye bread or those cute little party pumpernickels.

- Mix crabmeat with mayonnaise to taste and sprinkle in a dash of cayenne. Spread into endive spears.
- Mash Roquefort or blue cheese with a fork. Add sour cream to thin the cheese and a touch of mustard and stuff into celery ribs.
- Spread cream cheese on thin slices of toast or small party bread. Add paper-thin slices of smoked salmon, a sprinkling of fresh chives, and a paper-thin slice of lemon. Cut the toast in two triangles and serve with a sprig of fresh dill.
- Mash 4 anchovy fillets into a paste. Mix with 1 cup softened cream cheese and add 1 to 2 tablespoons of milk to thin the mixture. Add freshly ground pepper and a tablespoon or two of finely chopped red onion and serve as a dip with crackers or raw vegetables.

Caribbean Roasted Banana Chutney

In the dead of a New England winter I always start to crave color. After months of soups, stews, and a limited choice of fresh vegetables and fruit, this vibrant Caribbean-style chutney wakes up my senses, but you may serve it any time of year with chips, curries, seafood, cold roast beef, lamb, or pork.

3 bananas, cut into 1-inch pieces
2 tablespoons finely chopped onion
1 teaspoon plus 2 tablespoons olive oil
2 tablespoons light brown sugar
1 tablespoon butter, cut into small pieces
½ red bell pepper, chopped
½ green bell pepper, chopped
3 scallions, trimmed and chopped
About 1 tablespoon jalapeño pepper, seeded and chopped, or several dashes hot
    pepper sauce
1½ tablespoons chopped fresh mint
Juice of 2 limes
Juice of 1 lemon
About 1 tablespoon rum, preferably dark, optional

Preheat the oven to 400 degrees. Place the bananas and chopped onion in a small roasting dish or ovenproof skillet and sprinkle with the 1 teaspoon oil. Roast for 8 minutes. Remove from the oven and sprinkle the bananas and onions with the sugar and butter and roast another 5 minutes.

Meanwhile mix the red and green pepper, scallions, jalapeño, mint, lime and lemon juices, and remaining 2 tablespoons olive oil together in serving bowl.

Remove the bananas from the hot oven and deglaze the pan with the rum, if using. Stir the hot bananas and juices into the bowl with the peppers, making sure to get all the juices up from the bottom of the skillet. Taste for seasoning, adding more salt, pepper, or hot sauce if needed. Serve cold or at room temperature. Serve within 24 hours.

Makes about 1½ cups

Spanish Chopped Salad

A colorful chopped salad that goes well with egg dishes, roasted meats, chips, or as a topping for toasted crusty bread or tortilla chips. Serve as an appetizer with taco chips, quesadillas, or cooked shrimp.

¼ cup fresh parsley, minced
¼ cup green or red bell pepper, chopped
1 scallion, finely chopped
¼ cup good quality black or green olives, pitted and chopped
2½ tablespoons good-quality olive oil, preferably Spanish
1 tablespoon Spanish sherry vinegar, or wine vinegar
Salt and freshly ground pepper

Mix all the ingredients and serve within 1 hour.

Makes about 1 cup

A Few Quick Ideas for
Throw-It-All-Together Appetizers

- Take a wedge or wheel of Brie or Camembert and surround it with sun-dried cranberries, cherries, and golden raisins scattered over the cheese. The intense flavors and chewy texture of the dried fruit provide a great contrast to the rich cheese.

- Quick dips: Mix bottled taramasalata (Greek fish roe) with sour cream, lemon juice, and touch of olive oil for an instant dip. Serve with raw fennel wedges and warm pita bread.

- Mix 2 cups sour cream with ½ cup olive puree or tapenade, a squirt of lemon, and a drizzle of olive oil for an instant dip. Serve with a variety of raw vegetables, toast points, crackers, or cooked shrimp.

- Surround a log of soft goat cheese with chopped ripe tomatoes, chopped olives, scallions, and chopped fresh basil or rosemary. Drizzle with olive oil and bake at 350 degrees for about 15 minutes, or until the cheese just begins to ooze and melt and the tomatoes soften. Serve hot with French bread toasts or crackers.

- Serve an assortment of smoked fish cut into small, bite-sized pieces with a horseradish cream. Whip 1 cup heavy cream until just stiff and gently fold in 1 to 2 tablespoons horseradish (beet horseradish gives the cream a gorgeous pink color and sweet flavor), and salt and pepper to taste. Serve with small triangles of party rye (or dark rye) bread or crackers.

- Cut the end off a fresh fennel bulb and cut the bulb into quarters. Serve with a small bowl of coarse sea salt and a bowl of extra-virgin olive oil and dip the raw, anise-flavored vegetable into both.

- Mix a can of drained tuna fish or canned salmon with 1 table-spoon olive oil, juice from half a lemon or lime, and a table-spoon of capers and serve on warm toast points.
- Boil a few eggs. Cut in half and scoop out the yolks. Mix the yolks with a tablespoon or two of tapenade or olive puree. Stuff the filling back into the egg whites and sprinkle with paprika or cayenne for a quick, olive-flavored deviled egg.
- Serve thinly sliced smoked salmon or trout on black bread (or any thin toast) and top with capers, chopped onion, and a dollop of horseradish.
- Filet mignon on horseradish toast: Light a charcoal, gas, or wood fire, or preheat the broiler, and grill 2 pounds filet mignon, sprinkled with coarsely ground pepper, for 6 to 10 minutes, or until medium rare. Remove from the heat and let sit 2 minutes. Cut into thin slices and then cut each slice into 2-inch pieces. Place the warm steak on croûtes, grilled French bread, or toast triangles that have been spread with horseradish cream. To make the horseradish cream, see smoked fish idea on page 72.
- Buy half a pound of lump crabmeat (if frozen, thaw completely) and mix with the juice of 1 lime, ¼ cup toasted, slivered almonds, and serve with tortilla chips, crackers, or pita toasts (see page 63).
- Cut fresh figs or fresh melon into thin wedges and wrap with paper-thin slices of prosciutto and a grinding of pepper.
- Mix 1 cup soft cream cheese with pepper, 1 tablespoon lemon juice, and 1 tablespoon minced scallions and/or chives. Spread 1 to 2 tablespoons onto a slice of smoked salmon and roll up tightly. Cut into bite-sized pieces and serve with lemon wedges.

Turkish Shepherd's Salad

Found throughout Turkey and the Middle East, this fresh vegetable salad is served along with other salads and dips as part of the meze, or appetizer course. Serve with warm pita triangles (see page 63). To make a Middle Eastern platter, serve the shepherd's salad accompanied by pita bread, assorted olives, and hummus, and tabbouleh sprinkled with fresh mint. The salad is also a delicious accompaniment to grilled or roasted lamb, beef, chicken, or fish.

1½ cups chopped ripe tomato
1 cup diced green bell pepper
1 cup diced cucumber, peeled and seeded
½ cup fresh parsley, chopped
⅓ cup chopped scallions
¼ cup fresh lemon juice
1 tablespoon olive oil
Salt and freshly ground pepper

Combine all the ingredients in a medium bowl and let sit for 1 hour at room temperature or in refrigerator.

Makes 8 servings

5
Casual Parties

Soups, Breads, Salads, Sandwiches,
Comforting Meals, and Sides

Grilled Shrimp, Mango, and Spinach Salad

Asian Chicken Salad with Mandarin Oranges and Soy-Glazed
Pecans

Grilled Chicken Baguettes with Mango, Tomato, and Garlic
Mayonnaise

Steak Sandwiches on Garlic Baguettes with Arugula and
Tomatoes

Summer Vegetable Hero with Green Yogurt Dressing

Spanish Potato and Pepper Tortilla

Potato and Cheese Pancakes

Leek, Mushroom, and Asparagus Risotto

Rigatoni in Creamy Walnut-Pea Sauce

Summer Tomato and Basil Linguine

Tan Tan Noodles

Spicy Noodles with Ginger and Fresh Vegetables

Grilled Salmon with Dill and Lemon

Salmon Cakes

Roast Haddock with Roasted Garlic, Tomato,
and Capers

Green Curry Chicken with Peas and Basil

African Chicken, Spinach, and Peanut Stew

Chinese-Flavored Fried Chicken with Ginger
  Dipping Sauce

Grilled Chicken Done Two Ways

Grilled Flank Steak with Fresh Corn-Tomato-Basil Sauté

Braised Oriental-Style Short Ribs

Ma Po Dofu (Spicy Szechuan-Style Tofu Stew)

Turkish Lamb Kabobs

Grilled Steak with Provençal Herbs

Greek Lamb Burgers

Quick Sausage and White Bean Stew

Pork Chops with Caramelized Apples and Onions

Maple-Glazed Ham Steaks

Roasted Garlic

White Beans Provençal

Pickled Red Onions

Grilled Zucchini with Lemon

Panfried Summer Tomatoes

Sautéed Baby Spinach with Garlic

Roasted Summer Beans with Sesame-Soy Glaze

Roasted Winter Root Vegetables

Roasted Potato Wedges

Spring Pea Soup

There are few things that make me happier than the arrival of the first peas in our garden each spring. This soup is as simple as can be—a true celebration of the vibrant taste, texture, and color of spring peas. Serve hot or cold, or with a garnish of chopped fresh mint and a dollop of crème fraîche or heavy cream.

1 tablespoon olive oil
2 leeks, cleaned and cut into 1-inch pieces
3 tablespoons minced fresh chives
2½ cups fresh shell peas, shelled*
4 cups homemade chicken broth or low-sodium canned, or vegetable broth or pea stock†
Salt and freshly ground pepper
Chopped fresh mint and crème fraîche, for garnish, optional

In a large pot heat the oil over a moderately low heat. Add the leeks and sauté about 10 minutes, stirring frequently until soft and lightly golden brown. Add the chives and the peas and cook 1 minute, stirring to coat the peas. Add the broth, salt, and pepper, and bring to a boil. Let simmer about 15 minutes, or until the peas are soft (but not falling apart) and the broth is flavorful.

Working in batches, place the soup in the container of a food processor or blender and puree. Transfer the soup back to the pot. The soup can be made a day ahead of time up to this point. Cover and refrigerate until ready to serve. Reheat the soup over low heat until simmering hot, or serve cold. Taste for seasoning and adjust as needed. Top the soup with the mint and crème fraîche, if using.

Makes 4 servings

*Shell peas are available in the late spring. They are mature peas that are eaten after the pod has been discarded.
†To make a pea stock: Place the pea shells in a large pot. Chop 1 carrot, 1 rib of celery, and 1 large onion and add to the pot along with a dash of salt and 4 peppercorns. Cover with 4 cups water. Simmer, covered, over moderately low heat for 20 minutes. Reduce the heat to low, uncover, and simmer another 20 minutes. Strain.

Quick Thai-Style Coconut Soup

A friend called at the last minute and needed to talk. I invited her to lunch and decided to try something a bit different. My goal was to transform some leftover chicken soup into a Thai-style coconut soup. In just about twenty minutes, I simmered the broth with a can of unsweetened coconut milk, a chunk of gingerroot, a lime, and a piece of fresh lemongrass. The resulting soup was full of the fresh flavors of Thailand.

3 cups chicken broth, homemade or canned
One 2-inch piece gingerroot, cut into thin strips
One 2-inch piece fresh or dry lemongrass, optional*
Two 1-inch strips lime peel
1½ cups cooked chicken meat, skinless and cut into thin strips
1 cup unsweetened coconut milk*
Salt and freshly ground pepper
Dash hot pepper sauce
1 scallion, chopped
3 tablespoons finely chopped cilantro or parsley, optional

In a medium saucepan heat the chicken broth over moderate heat. Add the ginger, lemongrass, if using, and lime peel and simmer 3 minutes. Add the chicken, coconut milk, salt, pepper, hot pepper sauce, and scallion and let simmer for 15 minutes. Taste for seasoning and adjust as needed. Sprinkle with half the cilantro, if using, and cook another 5 minutes, until slightly thickened and the flavors come together. Using a slotted spoon, remove the ginger, lemongrass, and lime peel. Serve hot with a sprinkling of the remaining cilantro, if using.

Makes 4 servings

*Available in Asian and specialty food shops.

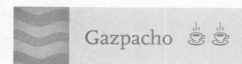

Gazpacho

My Spanish friend, Isabel Achoa, taught me how to prepare this authentic gazpacho in her kitchen in Granada, Spain. "I grew up drinking gazpacho out of tall, icy cold glasses all summer as a child. It was like a milkshake," Achoa reminisced. This is a great way to use up the freshest summer ingredients. Serve in tall glasses (chilled well in the freezer) or in large bowls. Serve the toppings in small bowls and pass at the table.

2 pounds ripe tomatoes
2-inch chunk French or Italian bread, preferably day old
2 cucumbers, peeled and chopped
1 small green bell pepper, chopped
2 to 3 cloves garlic, peeled and chopped, optional
1 small onion, chopped
2 tablespoons olive oil
About ¼ cup water
1 to 2 tablespoons sherry vinegar, or red wine vinegar
Salt

THE GARNISHES:
1 cucumber, peeled and cut into small cubes
1 green and/or red bell pepper, cut into small cubes
1 scallion, thinly sliced

Bring a pot of water to a boil over high heat. Place the tomatoes in the boiling water for 10 seconds; remove immediately and place in a bowl of ice cold water for just a minute. Remove and peel the tomatoes. If seeds bother you, remove the seeds by slicing the tomatoes in half and squeezing them over a bowl. Core and cut the tomatoes into quarters.

Soak the bread in water for 2 minutes. Soak and squeeze out the excess moisture.

Place the tomatoes, cucumbers, pepper, garlic, if using, onion, oil, water, 1 tablespoon of the vinegar, a pinch of salt, and the moistened bread into a large bowl and mix well. Transfer in batches to a food processor or blender and blend until almost smooth. You don't want to completely puree the gazpacho. Taste for seasoning and add the additional vinegar and salt if necessary. Serve within 1 to 2 hours, with the raw vegetable garnishes in small bowls.

Makes 4 to 6 servings

Double Corn Muffins with Chives and Cheddar ☕

Fresh corn kernels, cornmeal, and fresh chives are mixed into this muffin mixture and then topped with grated cheddar cheese and baked until golden. Serve anytime—as part of a brunch or breakfast, for lunch with a salad, or to accompany chili, grilled foods, or roast chicken or meat. Although these muffins can be made several hours ahead of time, they are particularly good hot from the oven with sweet butter and accompanied by strong coffee.

Butter for greasing the muffin tin
5 tablespoons butter
1 egg
1 cup milk
¾ cup fresh corn kernels, cut off the cob, or frozen corn
½ cup grated cheddar cheese
1 cup flour
¾ cup cornmeal, preferably yellow
1 tablespoon baking powder
1 teaspoon salt
Freshly ground pepper
1½ teaspoons sugar
2 tablespoons minced fresh chives

Preheat the oven to 400 degrees. Grease eight ⅓-cup muffin cups and set aside.

Melt the butter in a small saucepan.

In a large bowl, whisk the egg. Add the milk, corn, half the cheese, and the melted butter and whisk well. Sift the flour, cornmeal, baking powder, and salt over the egg mixture. Add a good grinding of pepper, the sugar, and chives. *The batter can be made several hours ahead of time; cover and refrigerate the batter until ready to bake. Whisk the batter well before placing in the muffin tin.*

Divide the batter among the muffin cups and sprinkle with the remaining cheese. Bake on the middle shelf of the oven for 18 to 20 minutes, or until golden brown and a toothpick inserted in the center comes out clean.

Makes 8 muffins

You Can Also Add . . .

- Dash cayenne or chopped chile peppers for spicy corn muffins.
- 1 tablespoon chopped fresh thyme or rosemary, or 1 teaspoon dried, to the batter for a corn-herb muffin.
- 2 tablespoons chopped sun-dried tomatoes or sun-dried cranberries or cherries to the batter.

Garlic Bread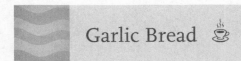

Sometimes all it takes to make a meal feel really special is a loaf of garlic bread. Serve this bread with virtually any soup, salad, stew, roast, savory dish, or grilled food, or use for making sandwiches. The garlic bread can be prepared, but not baked, up to twenty-four hours ahead of time.

About 2 tablespoons olive oil
About 2 tablespoons butter
4 cloves garlic, very finely chopped
Freshly ground pepper
1 baguette, or loaf of Italian bread, about 18 inches long

In a small saucepan, heat the oil and butter over moderately low heat. Add the garlic and cook about 4 minutes, making sure the garlic doesn't burn. Add a generous grinding of pepper and set aside. (If your baguette is particularly large, you may need to add another tablespoon of oil and butter.)

Tear off a long piece of aluminum foil. Cut the baguette into thin slices. Reassemble the loaf of bread by brushing the garlic butter onto one side and placing it on the foil. Add the next slice of bread until the bread slices are all coated with the garlic butter. Drizzle any remaining garlic butter over the whole loaf. Wrap the foil tightly around the bread. Refrigerate until ready to bake.

Preheat the oven to 350 degrees. Bake the garlic bread for 15 to 20 minutes, or until the bread is hot.

Makes 4 to 6 servings

You Can Also Add . . .

- 1$^1/_2$ tablespoons chopped fresh herbs (like basil, rosemary, oregano, tarragon, thyme, or sage), or 1$^1/_2$ teaspoons dried, for a Garlic-Herb Bread.
- 2 tablespoons fresh lemon juice for a Lemon-Garlic Bread.
- $^1/_4$ cup grated cheese (Parmesan, cheddar, or any hard cheese) over the bread before wrapping in foil and baking for a Garlic-Cheese Bread.

Green Salad with Sun-Dried Tomato Croûtes

You can add any assortment of lettuce, watercress, greens, or raw or cooked vegetables to this salad.

8 thin slices crusty bread, preferably 1 or 2 days old
1 tablespoon olive oil
2 tablespoons finely chopped sun-dried tomatoes
4 cups assorted lettuce greens or baby spinach
Basic Vinaigrette (see page 86) or Green Yogurt Dressing (page 100)

Place the bread slices in a toaster oven or the oven and bake at 200 degrees for 3 minutes. Flip the toast over and spread each piece lightly with the oil and the sun-dried tomatoes. Bake another 3 to 4 minutes or until golden brown. The croûtes can be made several hours ahead of time. Cover and keep at room temperature.

Toss the greens in a large bowl with about ⅓ cup vinaigrette. Top with the croûtes.

Makes 4 servings

You Can Also Add . . .

- 3 tablespoons grated Parmesan cheese or crumbled goat cheese on top of the tomatoes on the croûtes and place under the broiler until melted, golden, and bubbling.
- 2 tablespoons tapenade instead of sun-dried tomatoes.
- 2 tablespoons chopped fresh herbs, or 2 teaspoons dried herbs, on top of the sun-dried tomatoes.
- 2 tablespoons chopped pimientos or roasted red bell pepper strips instead of the sun-dried tomatoes.

Roasted Pear and Mixed Green Salad

The pear's natural sweetness mellows and takes on an almost savory flavor when roasted. Toss these pear slices into a mixture of your favorite greens.

1 tablespoon butter
1 Bosc pear, almost ripe, cored and cut into 8 wedges, peeled or unpeeled
Freshly ground pepper
1 teaspoon Dijon mustard
Salt
1 tablespoon fresh tarragon, chopped, or ½ teaspoon dried
2 tablespoons balsamic, red, or white wine vinegar, or fresh lemon juice
4½ tablespoons olive oil
3 cups mixed greens or mesclun mix
¼ cup Parmesan cheese, thinly shaved, optional*

Preheat the oven to 350 degrees. Melt the butter in a small, ovenproof skillet. Add the pear wedges and a grinding of pepper and place in the oven to roast for about 15 minutes, or until tender but not falling apart. Remove and let cool slightly. Although the pears taste best served hot, they can be roasted several hours ahead of time. Cover and refrigerate. Bring to room temperature before adding to the salad.

In the bottom of a salad bowl, mix the mustard, salt, pepper, and tarragon. Whisk in the vinegar, and then the oil, and taste for seasoning. Place the greens in the salad bowl and top with the pear wedges and the Parmesan cheese shavings. Toss just before serving.

Makes 2 to 4 servings

You Can Also Add . . .

- Sliced roasted beets.
- Crumbled blue cheese instead of the Parmesan.
- 1 leek cut into 1-inch pieces; roast along with the pear and toss with the greens.
- Peeled wedges of roast apples instead of pear.

*Use a vegetable peeler to shave thin slices off a chunk of Parmesan cheese.

Grated Carrot and Sun-Dried Cranberry Salad

This colorful winter salad combines beautiful colors, flavors, and textures that wake up a winter palate. Serve with sandwiches, soups, roasted meat or poultry, and crusty bread.

3 cups grated carrots, about 2 large carrots
¼ cup finely chopped fresh parsley
3 tablespoons chopped sun-dried cranberries, cherries, or raisins
Salt and freshly ground pepper
3 tablespoons wine vinegar
6 tablespoons olive oil

In a bowl, mix the carrots, parsley, and cranberries. Add salt and pepper. Mix in the vinegar and oil, and stir well. Taste for seasoning. The salad can be made about 2 hours ahead of time. Cover and refrigerate until ready to serve.

Makes 6 servings

You Can Also Add . . .

- ½ cup thinly sliced fresh, peeled water chestnuts, or rinsed and drained canned water chestnuts.
- 2 tablespoons finely chopped scallions or chives.
- ½ cup finely chopped toasted walnuts, pecans, or almonds.
- Thin slivers roasted duck or chicken to make a main course salad.

Tomato, Avocado, and Red Onion Salad with Roquefort Dressing ☕

This salad combines the buttery texture of avocado, juicy, ripe tomatoes, the bite of red onion, and the creamy tang of blue cheese. Serve as a first course or as a side salad with grilled steak, chicken, or fish.

3 tablespoons red wine vinegar
¼ cup plus 1½ teaspoons olive oil
1 tablespoon fresh chives, minced
Salt and freshly ground pepper
2 medium ripe tomatoes, cut into ¼-inch-thick slices
1 small red onion, thinly sliced
1 large avocado, cut crosswise into ⅓-inch-thick slices
4 ounces Roquefort cheese, crumbled

Place vinegar in a small bowl. Gradually whisk in the oil in a thin stream. Stir in the chives, salt, and pepper.

Arrange the tomatoes, onion, and avocado in an overlapping pattern on serving plate. Sprinkle with the cheese. Pour the dressing on top.

Makes 4 servings

Italian-Style Bread and Tomato Salad with Toasted Pine Nuts ☕

Use a good crusty bread that is preferably one or two days old to make this Italian-style salad. You can assemble the ingredients and toss the salad with the dressing an hour or less before serving. Roast chicken or any grilled food makes a great accompaniment.

¼ cup pine nuts
2½ cups crusty bread, cut into cubes with the crust
1½ cups chopped fresh parsley
1½ cups chopped ripe tomatoes, or halved cherry tomatoes
1 red bell pepper, cubed
2 tablespoons red or white wine vinegar
4 to 5 tablespoons good-quality olive oil
Salt and freshly ground pepper

Place the pine nuts in a small skillet and warm over moderately low heat for about 5 minutes, or until they are fragrant and just beginning to brown; be careful not to  let them burn. You can toast the nuts several hours ahead of time. Cover and keep at room temperature until ready to use.

Place the bread, parsley, tomatoes, and bell pepper in a salad bowl and mix well.

Sprinkle the nuts over the salad and add the vinegar, 4 tablespoons of the oil, the salt and pepper, and toss well. Taste for seasoning and add the remaining oil if needed.

Makes 4 servings

Warm Potato Salad with Lovage

Lovage is a beautiful, tall herb with celery-like leaves and a bracing, fresh, celery-like fla-vor. Its bright green leaves and hollow stems can be chopped and used as a celery substi-tute—although lovage has much more flavor and dimension than celery. It's an ideal match for potatoes, with their buttery texture and ability to take on other flavors. In this potato salad, the just-cooked potatoes are tossed with a light vinaigrette and lovage (or celery and celery leaves).

Serving this potato salad warm really takes advantage of the flavor of the lovage. The salad can also be made ahead of time and served at room temperature or chilled.

1½ pounds new potatoes, red and white, unpeeled
1 tablespoon Dijon mustard
Salt and freshly ground pepper
⅓ cup chopped fresh lovage, chopped, or chopped celery with the attached celery
   leaves
3 to 4 tablespoons white wine vinegar
About ¼ cup good-quality olive oil

Bring a large pot of lightly salted water to a boil. Add the potatoes and cook, over mod-erate heat, for 15 to 20 minutes, or until tender (they should feel tender throughout when pierced with a small, sharp knife). Drain and let cool slightly.

In a serving or salad bowl, mix the mustard, salt, pepper, and lovage. Cut the warm potatoes into chunks and place in the serving bowl. Add the vinegar and oil while the potatoes are still hot, and toss well. Taste for seasoning, adding more vinegar, oil, salt, or pepper as needed.

Makes 4 to 6 servings

You Can Also Add . . .

- 1 to 2 tablespoons capers.
- 1 tablespoon fresh chopped thyme, or 1 teaspoon dried.
- ⅓ to ½ cup heavy cream, plain low-fat yogurt, or mayonnaise for a creamier salad.

Asian Slaw with Peanuts

This slaw is colorful, fresh tasting, and considerably lighter than traditional cole slaw. The dish can be made three hours ahead of time. Cover and chill until ready to serve.

½ cup vegetable oil
¼ cup rice vinegar
2 tablespoons sesame oil
1½ tablespoons minced gingerroot
2 teaspoons soy sauce
Salt and freshly ground pepper
6 cups thinly sliced napa cabbage
6 scallions, very thinly sliced
6 ounces snow peas, stringed, thinly sliced lengthwise
1 large red bell pepper, thinly sliced
½ cup roasted peanuts

Whisk the vegetable oil, vinegar, sesame oil, ginger, and soy sauce together to blend. Season with salt and pepper. (You don't want to add much salt because of the soy sauce.)

In a large salad or serving bowl, mix the cabbage, scallions, snow peas, bell pepper, and peanuts. Toss with enough dressing to coat. Taste for seasoning.

Makes 4 to 6 servings

Grilled Shrimp, Mango, and Spinach Salad

Shrimp are briefly marinated in an Asian-flavored marinade—lime juice, cilantro, and a dash of chile paste—and then sautéed quickly in a hot pan and placed on top of fresh spinach with cubes of ripe mango. Serve as a light main course for lunch or dinner, or as a first course to any meal.

If you clean the spinach, chop the mango, and marinate the shrimp ahead of time the salad can be put together in about ten minutes. Serve immediately because the hot pan juices are delicious as they soften the raw spinach.

THE SHRIMP:
½ pound medium shrimp in the shell (12 shrimp), slit lengthwise down the middle
    and deveined
Juice of 1 lime
3½ teaspoons olive oil
2 tablespoons cilantro, chopped
Dash Chinese chile paste or hot pepper sauce, to taste*
1 large clove garlic, cut into thin slivers

THE SALAD:
½ pound fresh baby spinach, or regular spinach, well-washed and stemmed
1 large ripe mango, peeled and cut into medium cubes (about 1 to 1½ inches)
1 tablespoon olive oil
1½ tablespoons fresh lime juice
2 tablespoons chopped cilantro
½ lime cut into small wedges

Place the shrimp in a bowl and cover with the lime juice, 1 teaspoon of the olive oil, the cilantro, chile paste, and garlic. Stir well to thoroughly coat and let marinate for 10 minutes and up to several hours; if marinating for more than a few minutes, cover and refrigerate.

To prepare the salad: Place the spinach in the middle of a serving plate or on 4 salad plates. Surround the spinach with the mango cubes. The recipe can be made ahead of time up to this point. Cover and refrigerate for up to 4 hours.

*Available in Asian and specialty food shops.

To cook the shrimp: Place a heavy, medium skillet over high heat. Add the remaining 2½ teaspoons olive oil and let heat 1 minute until almost smoking. Drain the shrimp from the marinade and add to the hot oil. Cook 1 minute; flip the shrimp over and cook another minute. Add the marinade from the shrimp and let simmer about 1 minute, rapidly boiling. Remove the shrimp from the pan and arrange on the spinach; pour the hot marinade on top. Drizzle with the 1 tablespoon olive oil and the 1½ tablespoons lime juice. Sprinkle the top of the salad with the 2 tablespoons chopped cilantro, and arrange the lime wedges along the outside near the mango cubes.

Makes 2 to 4 servings

You Can Also Add . . .

- Scallops instead of, or in addition to, the shrimp.
- ⅓ cup slivered, toasted almonds on top of the salad.
- Peach, nectarine, or papaya instead of mango.

Asian Chicken Salad with Mandarin Oranges and Soy-Glazed Pecans ☕ ☕

This is a wonderful winter chicken salad with the flavors of the Orient. If you buy a rotisserie or preroasted chicken at your supermarket or deli (or use leftover cooked chicken), this salad can be put together in very little time. You can make the vinaigrette and the pecans a day ahead of time and toss it all together at the last minute.

THE PECANS:

1½ teaspoons olive or vegetable oil

½ teaspoon sesame oil

½ cup pecan halves

1 tablespoon soy sauce

THE CHICKEN AND SALAD:

2 cups cooked chicken, skinned and cut into thin slices or cubes

½ cup chopped scallions

2 seedless Mandarin oranges, Clementines, or tangerines, peeled and separated into sections

2 cups tender lettuce greens, or raw spinach, stemmed

THE ORANGE VINAIGRETTE:

1 tablespoon grated or chopped gingerroot

Freshly ground pepper

1 tablespoon wine vinegar

Juice of 1 large orange, or 3 tablespoons orange juice

¼ cup olive oil

1½ teaspoons soy sauce

To prepare the pecans: Heat the olive oil and sesame oil in a small skillet over moderate heat. Add the pecans and cook, stirring frequently, for 2 minutes. Add the soy sauce and cook another 2 minutes, stirring until all the nuts are coated. Remove from the heat and set aside. Place in an airtight container and refrigerate if making ahead of time.

Gently mix the chicken, scallions, and oranges together in a bowl.

Finally, make the vinaigrette in a small bowl by mixing the ginger, pepper, vinegar, orange juice, and olive oil. Add the soy sauce and taste for seasoning. Place in airtight container and refrigerate if making ahead of time.

Gently mix the vinaigrette with the chicken and oranges. Mix in half the pecans. Place the chicken salad on a bed of greens or spinach and top with the remaining nuts.

Makes 2 to 4 servings

You Can Also Add . . .

- Ripe summer peach or nectarine slices for the Mandarin oranges.
- Grapes for the Mandarin oranges.
- 1 teaspoon grated orange zest to the vinaigrette.
- $1/4$ teaspoon ground cumin to the vinaigrette.
- 1 tablespoon honey to the pecans when you add the soy sauce.
- $1/8$ teaspoon curry powder to the pecans when you add the soy sauce.
- Whole cloves of roasted garlic: Roast 10 cloves of unpeeled garlic at 350 degrees for 15 minutes, or until soft. Squeeze out of the peel and toss with the Mandarin oranges.

Grilled Chicken Baguettes with Mango, Tomato, and Garlic Mayonnaise

Light, satisfying, and full of fresh flavors, these sandwiches are ideal on a hot summer night. Marinate the chicken the day before serving, grill it a day ahead if time allows, and you can put these sandwiches together in a flash.

THE CHICKEN:
2 whole skinless boneless chicken breasts
1 tablespoon soy sauce or tamari
2 cloves garlic, chopped
1 tablespoon fresh lime juice
Dash hot pepper sauce or Chinese chile paste

GARLIC MAYONNAISE:
8 cloves garlic, unpeeled
Salt and freshly ground pepper
1 tablespoon olive oil
1 cup mayonnaise

THE SANDWICHES:
1 large baguette, cut into quarters
1 ripe mango, cut into thin slices
2 ripe tomatoes, red or yellow, thinly sliced
Several tender lettuce leaves

Place the chicken in a bowl and cover with the soy sauce, garlic, lime juice, and hot pepper sauce. Cover and let marinate for at least 1 hour and up to 24 hours ahead of time.

To make the mayonnaise: preheat the oven to 350 degrees. Place the garlic in a small, ovenproof skillet and sprinkle with the salt and pepper and drizzle the olive oil on top. Roast for 15 to 20 minutes, or until the cloves feel tender. Let cool and squeeze the garlic out of the skin; chop coarsely and place in a small bowl. Add the mayonnaise and season to taste. The mayonnaise can be made up to 2 days ahead of time; cover and refrigerate until ready to serve.

Preheat the broiler or light a barbecue with charcoal or wood. Remove the chicken from the marinade, and grill for 6 minutes, flip the breasts, brush with the marinade, and grill another 6 to 8 minutes, or until cooked through. Let cool slightly and cut into thin slices on the diagonal.

To serve: Place the baguette slices in a basket. Serve the chicken on a plate and surround with plates or bowls of the mango, tomatoes, lettuce, and garlic mayonnaise. Let guests assemble their own sandwiches.

Makes 4 servings

You Can Also Add . . .

- 1 pound steak instead of the chicken breasts. Broil or grill until medium-rare, about 5 minutes on each side, depending on the thickness of the steak.
- Pickled Red Onions (see page 146.)

Steak Sandwiches on Garlic Baguettes with Arugula and Tomatoes ☕ ☕

Grilled steak is thinly sliced and sandwiched between crusty chunks of French bread flavored with garlic. The sandwich is then layered with tangy arugula and ripe summer tomatoes. The steak can be cooked a day ahead of time, but the sandwiches should be assembled at the last minute to prevent them from getting soggy. This is ideal picnic food.

THE STEAK:

1 pound Delmonico, Porterhouse, or sirloin steak

1 teaspoon olive oil

1 teaspoon herbes de Provence,* or ½ teaspoon thyme mixed with ½ teaspoon rosemary

THE SANDWICHES:

2 crusty baguettes

About 2 to 3 tablespoons olive oil or herb-flavored olive oil

1 large clove garlic

1 large bunch arugula, trimmed

2 large, ripe tomatoes, sliced

Salt and freshly ground pepper

Rub the steaks on both sides with the oil and herbs and set aside.

Preheat a large skillet over moderately high heat. Add the steak and cook, covered, for 6 to 8 minutes on each side for medium-rare. Alternatively, preheat the grill until red-hot and grill the meat for 6 to 8 minutes on each side. Let the meat cool. If prepar-

*Available in gourmet and specialty food shops

ing the meat ahead of time, wrap tightly and refrigerate. Thinly slice the meat just before assembling the sandwiches.

Preheat the broiler. Cut each baguette in half horizontally then cut each half into four pieces and place on a baking sheet. Lightly brush the bread with the olive oil and broil for about 1½ minutes, or until a light golden brown. Remove from the oven and immediately rub each piece of bread with the garlic clove; the idea is to just get the essence of the garlic absorbed into each piece of bread.

Assemble the sandwiches in the following fashion: Line each piece of bread with some of the arugula. Top half of the bread with the steak and the other half with a slice of tomato. Season with a touch of salt and a grinding of pepper. Place a tomato slice on top of a steak half and cut the sandwich in half.

Makes 4 servings

Summer Vegetable Hero with Green Yogurt Dressing ☕ ☕

Use the freshest vegetables from your own garden or a farmer's market. Layer the vegetables on crusty French or Italian bread. The simple dressing that tops the sandwich—a beautiful fresh, green puree of yogurt, chives, parsley, and scallions—brings out the vegetables' fresh flavor.

THE DRESSING:

3 tablespoons fresh parsley, chopped
1 scallion, chopped
2 tablespoons minced fresh chives
Salt and freshly ground pepper
½ cup plain, low-fat yogurt
2 tablespoons olive oil
1 tablespoon wine vinegar

THE SANDWICH:

1 good-quality loaf French bread (baguette), about 12 inches long
1 cup grated carrots, about 1 large
1 cup thinly sliced cucumbers, peeled and seeded
1 cup thinly sliced radishes
½ cup shredded lettuce
1 ripe tomato, thinly sliced
1 cup cheese, grated (I recommend Parmesan or another sharp hard cheese)

To make the dressing: Place all the dressing ingredients in a blender or food processor and puree. Taste for seasoning. The dressing can be made several hours ahead of time; cover and refrigerate until ready to serve. The dressing will keep for 2 to 3 days, covered and refrigerated.

Cut the bread in half lengthwise. Layer the carrots, cucumbers, radishes, lettuce, tomatoes, and cheese and any other optional ingredients you like on half the bread. Spoon the dressing on the other half of the bread. Place the two halves together and cut into 4 sandwiches.

Makes 2 to 4 servings

You Can Also Add . . .

- Pitted black and/or green olives.
- Bean sprouts.
- ½ cup red or green bell pepper, chopped.
- ½ cup young zucchini, grated.
- Sliced raw mushrooms or roasted or grilled mushrooms.
- Fresh shelled peas.
- Raw baby spinach, or sautéed spinach.
- Chopped fresh herbs.
- Roasted red bell pepper slices (see page 46).
- Roasted garlic cloves (see page 143).
- Pickled Red Onions (see page 146).
- Slices of roasted or grilled zucchini or eggplant.

Spanish Potato and Pepper Tortilla

In tapas bars throughout Spain, tortillas (omelettes) are filled with potatoes, peppers, olives, shrimp and fish, cheese, and various other fillings and served at room temperature with crusty bread and glasses of local sherry or fruity red wine. This Spanish-style tortilla features tender slices of potato and strips of red and green bell pepper. It can be served hot or at room temperature. Unlike the French and American omelette, this egg dish is served flat, not folded over. Accompany it with crusty bread and Spanish Chopped Salad (page 71). This tortilla is excellent served at brunch or lunch, or as a light dinner.

About 1½ tablespoons olive oil, preferably Spanish
2 small potatoes or 1 large potato, peeled and cut in half lengthwise and then cut
    crosswise into thin slices
1 small green bell pepper, very thinly sliced
1 small red bell pepper, very thinly sliced
1½ tablespoons fresh thyme, chopped, or 1 teaspoon dried
Salt and freshly ground pepper
5 eggs
2 tablespoons fresh parsley, finely chopped
Spanish Chopped Salad (see page 71)

In a 10-inch, heavy-bottomed skillet, heat the oil on low. Add the potatoes, making sure they don't stick and clump together, and cook 8 minutes, stirring frequently. The potatoes shouldn't turn brown, but don't worry if a few of them do. Add the pepper strips, thyme, and salt and pepper and cook another 8 minutes, stirring frequently.

Meanwhile, in a large bowl whisk the eggs with salt and pepper. Remove the potatoes and peppers from the skillet with a slotted spoon, allowing the excess oil to remain in the skillet. Add the potato mixture to the whisked eggs. Let sit about 3 minutes.

Preheat the broiler. Heat the remaining oil in the skillet over moderate heat. There should be enough to coat the bottom of the pan; if needed, add another ½ tablespoon oil. Add the eggs and vegetables, spreading the mixture evenly on the skillet. Cook about 3 minutes, until the bottom of the omelette is set and golden brown. (The top will still be wet.) Remove from the stovetop and place under the preheated broiler for 1 to 2 minutes or until *almost set*. The tortilla should still be slightly moist, but not wet.

Remove from the broiler and use a spatula to loosen the tortilla from the skillet. Place a plate on top of the skillet and flip the tortilla over onto the plate. Sprinkle with the parsley and serve hot or at room temperature, cut in wedges.

Makes 2 to 4 servings

You Can Also Add . . .

- Crumbled goat cheese over the tortilla just before you place it under the broiler.
- 1 cup chopped ripe tomato.
- Chopped fresh rosemary, mint, cilantro, and other herbs.
- ½ cup pitted chopped olives.
- Cooked shrimp or fish cut into bite-sized pieces.
- Leftover cooked sausage or cured ham, cut into bite-sized pieces.

Potato and Cheese Pancakes

A cross between a grease-free latke (potato pancake) and a delicious grilled cheese sandwich, these pancakes are delicious plain, or can be topped with melted herb butter, sour cream, or plain, low-fat yogurt. Serve for brunch, or as a side dish with roasted chicken, grilled fish, or meat, or as a main course accompanied by crusty bread and a green salad. The recipe can easily be doubled.

THE PANCAKES:
1 medium potato
2 tablespoons butter
1 egg
¼ cup low-fat milk
Salt and freshly ground pepper
½ cup flour
½ teaspoon baking powder
¼ cup freshly grated Parmesan cheese
¼ cup grated cheddar cheese, or your favorite hard cheese
2 tablespoons minced chives
1 tablespoon fresh thyme or sage, chopped, or ½ teaspoon dried
Butter or vegetable oil for greasing the pan

THE TOPPINGS:
2 tablespoons butter melted with 1 tablespoon chopped chives and 1 teaspoon
     chopped thyme or sage
1 cup plain, low-fat yogurt or sour cream or 1 cup applesauce

Peel the potato and grate on the large hole opening of a grater. Melt the butter in a medium skillet. Remove from the heat.

In a medium bowl, whisk the egg and the milk with salt and pepper. Sift the flour and baking powder on top and mix well. Add the grated cheeses and the melted butter, the grated potato, chives, and thyme, and stir well.

Heat the same medium skillet with a touch of butter or vegetable oil over moderate heat. Add a heaping tablespoon of batter to the hot skillet and cook the pancakes 2 minutes on each side. Keep warm in a 250 degree oven, or serve them up as you cook them. Serve hot with any of the toppings.

Makes 8 pancakes

Leek, Mushroom, and Asparagus Risotto

Risotto is a dish that requires love, time, and care. It's a dish to make when someone you really like comes over to spend time with you in the kitchen. You need to talk and stir the rice . . . and talk and stir the rice . . . and finally you'll have the most gorgeous, irresistible dish imaginable.

Think of this as a master recipe that can be made with endless variations. I love the combination of mild sweet leeks, earthy cremini mushrooms, and sweet asparagus with lots of fresh basil and Parmesan cheese. Use what you have, but make sure to use the finest ingredients: Arborio rice, real Parmigiano Reggiano, fresh herbs, and fresh vegetables.

1 tablespoon olive oil

1 leek, cleaned and cut into ½-inch pieces, or 1 small onion, chopped

About 5 tablespoons shredded fresh basil

Salt and freshly ground pepper

6 cremini mushrooms, quartered (or shiitake, portobello, morels, or porcini)

4 stalks asparagus, ends trimmed and cut on the diagonal into 1½-inch pieces

1½ cups Arborio rice

⅓ cup dry white wine

3 cups chicken or vegetable stock

About ⅓ cup freshly grated Parmesan cheese

In a heavy-bottomed, medium saucepan, heat the oil over moderately low heat. Add the leek and sauté about 6 minutes, or until softened but not brown. Add a tablespoon of the basil, salt, pepper, the mushrooms, and asparagus, and sauté another 4 minutes, stirring frequently. Raise the heat to moderate and add the rice, and let cook 1 minute, stirring constantly. Add the wine and let it simmer about 1 minute. Add 2 tablespoons of the remaining basil and 1 cup of the stock, stirring frequently. When the rice appears to have absorbed the liquid, add another cup of stock and continue stirring. Add the last cup of stock and stir until the rice is still moist, but thoroughly cooked. Remove from the heat and sprinkle with half the cheese. Serve hot, sprinkled with the remaining 2 tablespoons basil and the remaining cheese.

Makes 4 servings

You Can Also Add . . .

- $\frac{1}{4}$ cup chopped pancetta or prosciutto for a meatier flavor. Add with the mushrooms and asparagus.
- Fresh peas instead of asparagus.
- A combination of wild mushrooms.

Rigatoni in Creamy Walnut-Pea Sauce

Use rigatoni or any shape of pasta you have on hand, grab a bag of peas from the freezer, and chop a few walnuts. This creamy sauce cooks while the pasta boils leaving you with an incredibly comforting, colorful dish that takes under fifteen minutes to prepare.

1 pound rigatoni, or your favorite pasta shape
1 tablespoon olive oil
2 cloves garlic, finely chopped
2½ cups frozen peas
1½ cups walnuts, chopped
A generous pinch of salt and freshly ground pepper
½ cup chicken or vegetable broth, or dry white wine
½ cup heavy cream, or evaporated milk
Freshly grated Parmesan cheese, optional

Bring a large pot of salted water to boil. Add the rigatoni and cook for 10 to 12 minutes, or until almost cooked, or al dente. Drain.

Meanwhile, in a large skillet heat the oil over moderate heat. Add the garlic and cook 1 minute, stirring frequently, being careful not to let the garlic burn. Add the peas and cook for 1 minute. Add the walnuts, salt, and pepper and stir together for another minute. Reduce the heat to low and add the broth and cream and let simmer, uncovered, for about 6 minutes, or until slightly thickened. Taste for seasoning and add more salt and pepper if needed.

Toss the drained rigatoni with the sauce in a large serving bowl. Sprinkle with cheese, if using.

Makes 4 servings

You Can Also Add . . .

- Fresh peas instead of frozen: Sauté with the walnuts for only 1 minute and proceed.
- Frozen carrots or corn.
- 2 tablespoons of fresh minced chives; add with the cream.

- 2 tablespoons chopped ripe tomatoes; add raw when you toss the sauce with the pasta.
- Almonds, pine nuts, hazelnuts, or pecans can be substituted for the walnuts.
- 2 tablespoons chopped sun-dried tomatoes; add with the peas.
- 2 tablespoons prosciutto, smoked ham, or smoked bacon, cut into thin cubes; add with the peas.
- 4 anchovy fillets; add with the peas and let them dissolve into the sauce (be careful to reduce the amount of salt you add to the recipe).

Summer Tomato and Basil Linguine

Fresh vine-ripened tomatoes and pungent basil leaves are tossed with hot linguine, pine nuts, roasted garlic, and caramelized onions to create a dish that is the very essence of a summer garden. If you roast the garlic, make the basil oil, and caramelize the onions ahead of time, you can throw the dish together in the time it takes to boil the water and cook the pasta.

Serve the pasta with good crusty bread, garlic bread (see page 84), or focaccia (see page 172), a summer salad, and a crisp, light white wine. Any leftovers are delicious served cold the next day.

5 tablespoons good-quality olive oil
1 cup fresh basil leaves, stemmed and very thinly sliced into julienne strips
Salt and freshly ground pepper
2 medium onions, very thinly sliced
2 cloves garlic, finely chopped
½ cup pine nuts
1 head roasted garlic (see page 143), cloves removed from skin
1 pound linguine, spaghetti, or your favorite pasta shape
3 large, ripe summer tomatoes, preferably red and yellow, chopped
Freshly grated Parmesan cheese

In a small bowl, mix 4 tablespoons of the oil with ¼ cup of the basil. Add salt and pepper and let sit for at least 15 minutes, or overnight.

In a medium skillet, heat the remaining 1 tablespoon olive oil over low heat. Add the onions, 2 cloves chopped garlic, salt, pepper, and 1 tablespoon of the remaining basil and sauté over low heat for 15 to 20 minutes, stirring frequently, or until golden brown and tender. Add the pine nuts and cook for about 2 minutes, or until the nuts are fragrant and just beginning to turn a deeper golden brown. Set aside.

Place the roasted garlic cloves in a small bowl and set aside.

The dish can be made 24 hours ahead of time up to this point. Cover and refrigerate the onions and pine nuts, the roasted garlic cloves, and the basil oil.

If you are making the onions and garlic ahead of time, place the onion mixture and the roasted garlic cloves in a skillet and warm over moderately low heat for about 5 minutes, or until warm.

Bring a large pot of salted water to a rolling boil over high heat. Add the linguine and cook for 9 to 11 minutes, or until al dente, or just tender. Drain the pasta in a colander.

Place the basil oil in the bottom of a large serving bowl or plate. Chop the tomatoes and set aside.

Add the hot, drained pasta to the serving bowl with the basil oil. Add the roasted garlic, the cooked onions and pine nuts, and toss well. Top with the chopped tomatoes and remaining basil and serve hot, with the grated cheese on the side.

Makes 4 servings

You Can Also Add . . .

- ¼ cup caperberries or capers to the pasta when you toss in the tomatoes.
- ¼ cup pitted green or black olives to the sauce when you add the tomatoes.
- 1 or 2 shallots to the onion mixture and cook until soft and tender.
- ⅛ pound chopped prosciutto or pancetta to the sauce and cook with the onions for a meaty flavor.
- ¼ pound sliced wild mushrooms to the onion mixture and cook for 15 minutes.
- ¼ cup cooked, sliced artichoke hearts to the onion mixture and cook for just 5 minutes.
- ½ cup cooked asparagus, cut into 1-inch pieces on the diagonal, and added with the tomatoes.
- Other fresh herbs like oregano, thyme, parsley, chives, or rosemary to substitute for half of the basil.
- Roasted red, green, or yellow bell pepper strips.
- A teaspoon of red wine or balsamic vinegar and serve the pasta (or any leftovers) cold or at room temperature.

Tan Tan Noodles

I first tasted this spicy noodle dish years ago at an amazing Szechuan restaurant in Hong Kong. It was just one small part of a huge banquet and, even though the other dishes were more elaborate and demanded far more mastery of Chinese cuisine, I found myself dreaming about this dish long after the banquet was over. When I got back home I learned how to make the rich, peanut- and chile-based sauce and Tan Tan Noodles instantly became a new comfort food for me.

If you make the sauce ahead of time, the whole dish can be prepared in under ten minutes—perfect for an impromptu dinner. Don't mix the sauce with the noodles until the last minute or they will soak up the sauce.

This dish should definitely have a spicy bite, but you can make it as mild or potent as you choose by varying the amount of chile paste and hot chile oil.

Serve as a first course, as part of a Chinese or Asian meal, or as a light lunch or dinner dish. Serve with a stir-fried vegetable and a cucumber and mint salad.

1 tablespoon vegetable or peanut oil
3 tablespoons chopped gingerroot
4 cloves garlic, finely chopped
1½ teaspoons sesame oil
1 teaspoon hot chile oil, optional
4 tablespoons Chinese fermented black beans, rinsed and chopped*
3 scallions, chopped, green and white parts
½ to 1 teaspoon Chinese chile paste*
½ to 1 teaspoon Chinese chile paste with garlic, optional *
2½ tablespoons soy sauce or tamari
3 tablespoons peanut butter
2 tablespoons tahini
4 cups chicken broth, vegetable broth, or water
12 ounces Japanese-style somen wheat noodles*

FOR GARNISH:
3 scallions, chopped
½ cup cilantro, finely chopped

*Available in Asian or specialty food shops.

In a medium saucepan, heat the oil over moderate heat. Add the ginger and garlic and cook about 3 minutes, or until they begin to turn golden brown. Add the sesame oil and chile oil and the black beans and cook 1 minute, stirring constantly. Add the scallions and cook 2 minutes. Stir in the chile paste, chile paste with garlic (if using), and soy sauce to create a smooth sauce. Add the peanut butter and tahini, again stirring to create a smooth paste. Cook 1 minute, stirring constantly. Add the broth and reduce the heat to low. Let the sauce simmer for 10 to 15 minutes, or until very flavorful and somewhat thickened. Taste for spiciness; add more chile paste if needed. The "heat" of the sauce will dissipate when it's mixed with the noodles. The sauce can be made 24 hours ahead of time; cover and refrigerate. To reheat, place over low heat for about 10 minutes until piping hot.

Just before serving, bring a large pot of water to a boil. Gently stir in the somen noodles to make sure they don't stick together, and cook for 3 to 5 minutes, or until tender. Drain the noodles and divide between four deep soup or noodle bowls. Ladle the sauce on top and garnish with the scallions and cilantro.

Makes 4 servings

You Can Also Add . . .

- Tofu cubes. Heat a wok or large skillet with 1 tablespoon vegetable or peanut oil over high heat. Add 1 tablespoon minced gingerroot and 1 package firm or extra-firm tofu cut into 1-inch cubes, and cook 2 minutes. Gently flip the tofu over and cook another 2 minutes. Add 1½ tablespoons soy sauce and cook another minute. Gently place the tofu on top of the finished noodles.
- 2 cups cooked fresh or frozen peas to the broth.
- 1½ cups cooked chicken, cut off the bone and into thin slivers, to the finished noodles.
- ½ pound grilled or cooked shrimp to the finished noodles.
- Stir-fried vegetables placed on top of the finished dish for a more substantial vegetarian meal.
- ⅓ cup chopped peanuts sprinkled over the finished dish.

Spicy Noodles with Ginger and Fresh Vegetables ☕ ☕

Thin julienne strips of carrots, zucchini, scallions, and ginger are stir-fried with coconut milk, red curry paste, and somen noodles to create this Thai-style dish.

2 carrots
1 large zucchini, ends trimmed
3 scallions
1 tablespoon vegetable oil
4 tablespoons gingerroot, in matchstick-sized strips
3 teaspoons garlic, chopped
1 teaspoon sesame oil
1¼ cups water
1 cup canned unsweetened coconut milk*
1 tablespoon low-sodium soy sauce
½ teaspoon Thai red curry paste*
9 ounces Japanese-style somen wheat noodles*
½ cup toasted peanuts, finely chopped
½ cup fresh mint leaves, finely chopped

Cut carrots, zucchini, and scallions into matchstick-sized strips.

Heat vegetable oil in large skillet or wok over high heat. Add half the ginger and garlic and sauté about 30 seconds. Add the carrots, zucchini, half the scallions, and sesame oil and sauté 2 minutes. Add the remaining ginger and garlic and sauté until vegetables are crisp-tender, about 1 minute longer. Use a slotted spoon to transfer the vegetables to a bowl.

Reduce heat to medium and add the water, coconut milk, soy sauce and curry paste to the wok or skillet. Stir until smooth. Simmer until sauce is reduced to 1¼ cups, about 6 minutes. Add sautéed vegetables and remaining scallions.

Meanwhile, cook the somen noodles in large pot of boiling water until just tender, 3 to 5 minutes. Drain. Place noodles in a large bowl and add the vegetable mixture and toss well. Sprinkle with the nuts and mint.

Makes 4 servings

*Available at Asian and specialty food shops and in the Asian food section of some supermarkets.

Grilled Salmon with Dill and Lemon

This salmon is superb cooked over a hot grill (charcoal, gas, or wood fire), but can also be cooked under a hot, preheated broiler. Serve with Yogurt "Cheese" with Mint, Scallions, and Cucumbers (see page 64), Sautéed Baby Spinach with Garlic (see page 150), and orzo or your favorite pasta dish.

1 large bunch fresh dill sprigs, about 1 cup
One 3-pound salmon fillet
1 lemon, cut in half
1½ tablespoons good-quality olive oil
1 lemon, cut into thin slices
Freshly ground pepper

In a nonreactive broiler pan or shallow casserole, place half the bunch of fresh dill on the bottom of the pan. Place the salmon on top, skin-side down, and squeeze the juice from the two lemon halves on top. Drizzle on the olive oil and place the lemon slices on top of the fish. Sprinkle generously with pepper. Chop the remaining dill and sprinkle on top. Let marinate, covered and refrigerated, for about 15 minutes and up to 1 hour. If you want to marinate the fish longer, do not add the lemon juice or lemon slices until 1 hour before cooking or it will prematurely "cook" the salmon.

Heat the fire until red-hot. Alternatively, preheat the broiler with the rack about 2 inches from the heat. Place the dill sprigs directly on the fire (don't worry if they burn; the dill will infuse the fish with a wonderful flavor and aroma) or place at the bottom of a broiler pan and place the salmon and marinade on top. Cook for 15 to 20 minutes, depending on the thickness of the fish, or until cooked through. If you are cooking on an open fire or a grill, create a tent over the fish using a piece of aluminum foil to make sure the fish cooks through. The fish is ready when it's no longer opaque in the thickest part when tested with a small sharp knife. Serve hot straight from the grill, or at room temperature, with the thin lemon slices.

Makes 6 servings

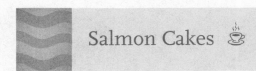

Salmon Cakes

The miracle of these fish cakes is that they are made with canned salmon. There's no reason to tell anyone, because they'll never guess. Serve hot with Spanish Chopped Salad (see page 71), Quick Tartar Sauce (see page 67), Pickled Red Onions (see page 146), or Yogurt "Cheese" with Mint, Scallions, and Cucumbers (see page 64).

1 tablespoon olive oil
¼ cup finely chopped sweet Vidalia or red onion
1 small red, green, or yellow bell pepper, finely chopped
Salt and freshly ground pepper
One 14¾-ounce can salmon, drained
¼ cup fresh parsley, finely chopped
3 tablespoons fresh dill, finely chopped
Juice of 1 large lemon
¼ cup heavy cream
½ to ¾ cup dry or fresh bread crumbs
Dash hot pepper sauce
About 1 to 2 tablespoons vegetable oil

THE GARNISHES:
Lemon and lime wedges
Sprigs of fresh dill

In a large skillet place the olive oil over a moderately low heat. Add the onion and sauté for 3 minutes, stirring frequently. Add the bell pepper, salt, and pepper and sauté another 5 minutes, stirring frequently to prevent browning.

In a large bowl, separate the salmon into flakes using a fork. Add the parsley, dill, and lemon juice. Add the sautéed vegetables and the cream and stir to mix. Add enough bread crumbs to hold the mixture together. Taste for seasoning and add additional salt, pepper, or hot pepper sauce. The mixture can be made only 1 to 2 hours ahead of time. Cover and refrigerate until ready to cook.

Preheat the oven to 250 degrees.

In a large skillet place 1 tablespoon of the vegetable oil over moderately high heat. Using your hands, form 2½-inch cakes. Add the salmon cakes to the skillet, being careful not to crowd the pan, and gently press down with a spatula to flatten. Cook 3 minutes, gently flip the cake, flatten again, and cook another 2 minutes. Remove to an ovenproof plate and keep warm in the oven. Repeat with the remaining mixture, adding more oil as needed. Serve hot with lemon and lime wedges, and top with a sprig of dill. Serve with the sauce of your choice.

Makes about 14 salmon cakes

Roast Haddock with Roasted Garlic, Tomato, and Capers ☕☕

For years I believed that haddock (and other thick, white-fleshed fish like halibut, scrod, and cod) were members of the "Boring Family." That is until I discovered this method for roasting fish using strong, assertive flavors. Use a good, dry white wine that you will drink with dinner. Chill and open it just before serving and splash on the fish six minutes before it's ready.

Serve with (or on top of) Roast Garlic Mashed Potatoes (see page 154) with sprigs of fresh thyme on top. The dish can be prepared, but not roasted, several hours ahead of time and popped into the oven about twenty minutes before serving.

3 pounds fresh haddock fillets*
1 tablespoon olive oil
1½ tablespoons fresh thyme, chopped
2 cloves garlic, very thinly sliced
3 tablespoons shredded fresh basil
1½ cups chopped ripe tomato (1 to 2 large tomatoes), or 1 cup canned whole
    tomatoes, drained and chopped
2 tablespoons capers, drained
2 tablespoons very finely chopped red onion
1 head roasted garlic (see page 143), cloves removed from skin
Freshly ground pepper
½ cup dry white wine (see headnote)
2 tablespoon bread crumbs, fresh or dry

Place the fish fillets in a large broiler pan, making sure not to crowd the pan. (If you must, use two pans or use ovenproof skillets.) Drizzle the fish with half the oil, flip over and drizzle with the remaining. Sprinkle the thyme over the fish and press the garlic slices into the flesh. Sprinkle on 2 tablespoons of the basil. Top with the tomatoes, capers, and onion equally scattered over the fish fillets.

Place the roasted garlic cloves over the fish along with any oil remaining in the pan that you roasted the garlic in. Sprinkle with the remaining tablespoon of basil and a grinding of pepper.

*You can also use scrod, cod, halibut, or any other thick, firm white-fleshed fish.

The dish can be made about 6 hours ahead of time up to this point. Cover and refrigerate until ready to proceed.

Preheat the oven to 450 degrees. Roast the fish on the middle shelf for 10 minutes. Remove from the oven and add the wine. Roast another 6 minutes, or until just tender.

Preheat the broiler. Sprinkle the dish with the bread crumbs and broil for 2 to 4 minutes, or until golden brown.

Makes 6 servings

Green Curry Chicken with Peas and Basil

A quick curry made with ginger, coconut milk, curry paste, basil, and cilantro with sautéed chicken strips. Serve with steamed jasmine rice, and for dessert try mango sorbet topped with canned lychees.

1½ cups white, jasmine, or basmati rice
1 teaspoon vegetable oil
Salt
2 teaspoons olive oil
1 cup chopped onion
2 teaspoons minced gingerroot
1 pound skinless boneless chicken breast halves, cut into strips
1 cup canned unsweetened coconut milk*
½ cup low-sodium chicken broth or homemade chicken stock
1 tablespoon Thai green curry paste*
4 tablespoons fresh basil, finely shredded
1 tablespoon cilantro, chopped
1½ cups snow peas, stringed
½ cup thinly sliced scallions, white and green parts
Freshly ground pepper

Place the rice and 3 cups cold water in a medium saucepan. Add the vegetable oil and a pinch of salt and bring to a boil over high heat. Stir the rice well, reduce the heat to low, and cover. Cook about 10 minutes, or until the rice has absorbed all the water.

Heat the olive oil in a large skillet over medium-high heat. Add the onion and 1 teaspoon of the ginger; sauté about 1 minute, stirring frequently. Add the chicken and sauté until golden brown on both sides, about 3 minutes. Using a slotted spoon, transfer the mixture to a bowl.

Add the coconut milk, broth, and curry paste to the skillet. Stir until smooth. Add 2 tablespoons of the basil, the cilantro, and the remaining teaspoon of the ginger and bring to a boil. Reduce the heat; simmer until the sauce thickens, about 7 minutes. Return the chicken mixture to the skillet. Add the snow peas and scallions and

*Available at Asian and specialty food shops and in the Asian food section of some supermarkets.

simmer until the chicken is cooked through, about 5 minutes. Season with salt and pepper.

Spoon the rice onto plates or bowls. Spoon the curry on top and sprinkle with the remaining basil.

Makes 4 servings

You Can Also Add . . .

- Asparagus cut on the diagonal into 1-inch pieces instead of the peas.
- Dash of hot pepper sauce or chopped fresh chile peppers during the last 5 minutes of cooking for a spicier dish.

African Chicken, Spinach, and Peanut Stew

Boneless chicken breasts are simmered in a delicious peanut butter–based sauce with spinach, fresh ginger, and scallions to create this quick-cook stew. You'll be amazed at the rich, complex flavors; it tastes as though the stew has been simmering all day. The stew can be made in under an hour (or it can be done ahead of time and simply reheated before serving). Serve with couscous and small bowls of peanuts, chopped scallions, and a hot pepper sauce. Ice cold beer is a great accompaniment.

THE STEW:
1½ tablespoons olive oil or vegetable oil
3 cloves garlic, chopped
2½ tablespoons chopped gingerroot, or 2 teaspoons dried ginger
2 pounds boneless skinless chicken breasts, cut into thick strips
Freshly ground pepper
1 medium onion, very thinly sliced
3 cups chicken broth
3 tablespoons peanut butter, smooth or chunky
2½ tablespoons soy sauce
1 tablespoon rice wine, balsamic, or wine vinegar
1½ teaspoons sesame oil
Dash hot pepper sauce or chile paste
2 scallions, chopped
2 cups fresh spinach, stemmed and coarsely sliced

THE COUSCOUS:
Salt
1 tablespoon olive oil
One 10-ounce box plain couscous

THE GARNISHES:
¾ cup chopped peanuts
2 scallions, chopped
Hot pepper sauce or chile paste

In a large, deep skillet, place half the oil over moderately high heat. Add half the garlic and ginger and heat for 10 seconds. Add the chicken breasts and sauté for 2 minutes, or until golden brown. Season with pepper and flip the chicken over and sauté another 2 minutes on the other side, or until golden brown. Remove the chicken from the pan and set aside. Reduce the heat to low and add the remaining oil. Sauté the onion for about 5 minutes, stirring frequently to prevent browning. Add the remaining garlic and ginger and cook 2 minutes and sprinkle with pepper. Place the browned chicken breasts on top of the onions and add the chicken broth. Let simmer 5 minutes.

In a small bowl, mix the peanut butter, soy sauce, vinegar, sesame oil, hot pepper sauce, and scallions to create a thick paste. Add about 4 tablespoons hot broth from the skillet and stir until smooth. Add to the pan and simmer another 10 minutes.

Add the spinach, stirring it into the sauce so it is thoroughly covered and simmer 5 minutes, or until the spinach is soft and tender.

Meanwhile, cook the couscous by boiling 2 cups water in a medium saucepan. Add a pinch of salt and the tablespoon of oil. Add the couscous, stir, and cover. Remove from the heat and let sit 5 minutes. Fluff the couscous with a fork to prevent clumps.

Divide the couscous between four dinner plates or large soup bowls. Serve the hot stew on top of the couscous.

Makes 4 servings

Chinese-Flavored Fried Chicken with Ginger Dipping Sauce

This crisp chicken is accented with the flavors of ginger and sesame oil, and served with a simple dipping sauce made with soy, cilantro, scallions, and ginger. The chicken and dipping sauce can both be made several hours to a day ahead of time. The chicken needs to marinate in the egg mixture for two hours, or overnight, in the refrigerator, before being cooked, so plan your time accordingly.

THE CHICKEN:
3 eggs
2 tablespoons soy sauce
2 teaspoons sesame oil
One 4- to 4-½ pound chicken, cut into 12 pieces*
1 quart vegetable oil or peanut oil
About 1 cup flour
3 tablespoons ground ginger
Salt and freshly ground pepper
Two 1-inch pieces gingerroot, halved lengthwise

THE DIPPING SAUCE:
½ cup low-sodium soy sauce
½ cup scallions, thinly sliced
2 tablespoons cilantro, finely chopped
1½ teaspoons gingerroot, finely chopped
1½ teaspoons hot chile sesame oil, or sesame oil and a dash of hot pepper sauce

*Ask your butcher to cut the chicken into 12 small pieces or buy a precut chicken.

Whisk the eggs, soy sauce, and sesame oil in a large bowl to blend. Add the chicken to the egg mixture, turning to coat. Cover; chill at least 2 hours or overnight in the refrigerator.

Whisk all the ingredients for the dipping sauce in a small bowl; cover and refrigerate the sauce.

Heat the vegetable oil in a wok or large, heavy skillet over medium-high heat until hot. (You'll know it's hot enough when you drop a dash of flour into it and it sizzles. If it doesn't sizzle right away it's not hot enough.) Mix the flour, ground ginger, salt, and pepper in another bowl. Remove the chicken from the marinade. Add the chicken thighs and drumsticks to flour mixture and turn to coat.

Add the ginger to the hot oil. Fry the chicken thighs and drumsticks in hot oil until golden and cooked through, about 10 minutes on each side. Using tongs, transfer the chicken to paper towels; drain. Coat the chicken breasts and wings with the flour mixture. Fry until golden and cooked through, about 6 minutes. Let stand at room temperature and serve within 3 hours with the dipping sauce.

Makes 4 servings

Grilled Chicken Done Two Ways

I invited a small group of friends and their children to dinner one autumn evening and decided to grill chicken. I began marinating the chicken in olive oil, garlic, lemon juice, and fresh herbs from the garden when my daughter said, "Can you please make the kids chicken with your special barbecue sauce?" I generally don't make separate "kids' food," but this seemed simple enough. I marinated a second chicken in this deliciously sweet, ketchup-based barbecue sauce, and everyone was happy. You can make both these marinades and offer everyone a choice of chicken.

Serve with Grilled Zucchini with Lemon (see page 147), corn on the cob, Roasted Potato Wedges (see page 153), Tomato, Avocado, and Red Onion Salad (see page 88), and a loaf or two of good crusty bread.

BARBECUE SAUCE:
1 cup ketchup
2 tablespoons soy sauce
1 tablespoon Worcestershire sauce
2 tablespoons maple syrup or honey
1 tablespoon gingerroot, finely chopped, or ½ teaspoon ground ginger
Hot pepper sauce

LEMON-GARLIC-HERB MARINADE:
2 tablespoons olive oil
4 cloves garlic, chopped
3 tablespoons fresh basil, chopped, or 1½ teaspoons dried
2 tablespoons fresh rosemary, chopped, or 1 tablespoon dried
1 tablespoon fresh thyme, chopped, or 1 teaspoon dried
Freshly ground pepper
Juice of 1 large lemon

THE CHICKEN:
2 roasting chickens, about 2 to 3 pounds each, cut into quarters

In a large bowl mix all the ingredients for the barbecue sauce. Add half the chicken and coat well on all sides. Marinate for at least 1 hour, or overnight. Cover and refrigerate until ready to cook.

In a second large bowl, prepare the Lemon-Garlic Marinade by mixing the oil, garlic, herbs, and pepper. If marinating for more than 1 hour do not add the lemon juice. Add the chicken and coat well on all sides. Let marinate for at least 1 hour, or overnight. Cover and refrigerate until ready to cook. Add the lemon juice to the bowl with the garlic-herb chicken and let marinate about 30 minutes before cooking.

Heat a charcoal or gas grill until very hot. Remove the chicken from the marinades and place on the grill skin-side down. Cook about 10 minutes, covered, making sure the chicken doesn't burn. Brush the chicken with the marinades from the bowls. Carefully flip the chicken over and cook another 10 to 15 minutes, or until the chicken is cooked through and there are no signs of pinkness, basting the chicken with the remaining marinade. Serve hot or at room temperature.

Makes 6 servings

Grilled Flank Steak with Fresh Corn-Tomato-Basil Sauté ☕ ☕

A simple dish ideal for a warm summer night that celebrates the fresh flavors of the season. The entire dish can be put together in about thirty minutes. Serve with Roasted Summer Beans with Sesame-Soy Glaze (see page 151), Garlic Bread (see page 84), and baked potatoes or Roast Garlic Mashed Potatoes (see page 154).

THE MEAT:

2 pounds flank steak

1 tablespoon olive oil

2 tablespoons soy sauce

2 cloves garlic, finely chopped

Freshly ground pepper

FRESH CORN-TOMATO-BASIL SAUTÉ:

4 ears fresh corn

1 tablespoon olive oil

2 cloves garlic, minced

½ cup chopped scallions, white and green parts

2 tablespoons fresh basil, shredded

2 ripe tomatoes, chopped

Salt and freshly ground pepper

Place the meat in a nonreactive pan such as ceramic and pour on the oil, soy sauce, garlic, and pepper. Marinate for at least 1 hour, or overnight.

Prepare a grill until red-hot.

Remove the meat from the marinade and cook 6 minutes. Flip the meat over with tongs, being careful not to pierce it, and brush with the marinade. Cook another 5 to 7 minutes, depending on how well-done you like it. Remove the meat from the heat and let sit for a minute or two before slicing on the diagonal.

Meanwhile, using a sharp knife cut the kernels off the corn and set aside in a bowl. In a large skillet heat the oil on moderate. Add the garlic and scallions and cook 2 minutes, stirring frequently. Add the corn kernels and half the basil and cook about 4 minutes, stirring frequently. (The idea is for the corn to be *just* cooked, and not mushy.) Remove from the heat and place in a serving bowl. Add the tomatoes and remaining basil, season with salt and pepper, and serve hot with the grilled meat.

Makes 4 servings

Braised Oriental-Style Short Ribs

Beef short ribs are the meaty ends of a standing rib roast. Because they don't contain the "prime" section of a rib roast they are usually very reasonably priced. But don't let their low cost fool you—short ribs are bursting with flavor.

In this dish the ribs are browned and then braised in a delicious broth full of fresh gingerroot, Chinese chile paste, hoisin sauce, sesame oil, and beef stock. Chunks of scallions, carrots, and celery fill out the stew. Serve over polenta, Roast Garlic Mashed Potatoes (see page 154), or White Rice with Scallions and Sesame (see page 158). Plan on letting the ribs simmer for almost two hours; they are best made a day ahead of time if possible.

1 cup flour
Salt and freshly ground pepper
4 pounds beef short ribs, about 8 to 10 ribs
1½ teaspoons vegetable oil
1½ teaspoons olive oil
2½ tablespoons finely chopped gingerroot
10 scallions, cut into 2-inch pieces, white and green parts
4 carrots, cut into 2-inch pieces
4 ribs celery, cut into 2-inch pieces
1½ teaspoons Chinese chile paste*
2½ tablespoons hoisin sauce*
3 tablespoons soy sauce
½ cup Chinese rice wine*
3½ cups beef or chicken broth
3 scallions, very finely chopped, white and green parts, for garnish

On a plate or in a plastic bag, mix the flour with salt and pepper. Dredge the ribs in the seasoned flour, making sure to coat all sides.

In a large, stovetop-safe casserole, heat the vegetable and olive oil on moderately high. Add the ribs and half the ginger and brown on all sides, 6 to 8 minutes. Remove the ribs and set aside. Remove all but 1 teaspoon of the fat from the pan and reduce the heat to low. Add the remaining ginger, scallions, carrots, and celery and cook for

*Available at Asian and specialty food shops.

about 3 minutes, stirring frequently. Stir in the chile paste and then the hoisin sauce, making sure the vegetables are coated. Add the soy sauce, rice wine, and broth and bring to a simmer. Add the ribs back into the pan, spooning the vegetables on top and around the beef, and cover. Simmer over a very low heat for about 2 hours, or until the beef is completely tender. If making ahead of time, let the stew return to room temperature, cover, and refrigerate. When removing from the refrigerator use a spoon to pull off any fat congealed on the top of the casserole. Place over low heat until hot, about 10 minutes. Let stand, covered, about 5 minutes before serving. Serve hot, sprinkled with the chopped scallions.

Makes 4 servings

You Can Also Add . . .

- $1/2$ cup peeled and quartered fresh or canned water chestnuts.
- $1/2$ cup fresh or canned bamboo shoots.
- 1 leek, cut into thin slices along with the scallions.
- 3 to 4 baby bok choy, cored and cut in half lengthwise along with the vegetables.
- 2 tablespoons chopped cilantro as a garnish with the scallions.
- Chopped fresh Mandarin oranges or tangerines as a garnish.

Ma Po Dofu
(Spicy Szechuan-Style Tofu Stew)

Simmering tofu with ginger and garlic in a chile-flavored broth is an old Szechuan recipe. This version combines tofu with ground sirloin, cilantro, and aromatic Chinese herbs to make a hearty one-dish dinner. Even people who claim to hate tofu fall in love with this dish. My youngest daughter says the dish tastes like "Chinese sloppy joes." If you're serving young kids, you can always make a milder sauce by adding little or no chile paste. Afterward you can mix the chile paste into the wok, or serve a tiny bowl of chile paste at the table.

Serve the tofu over White Rice with Scallions and Sesame (see page 158) and pass small bowls of chopped cilantro and scallions for everyone to sprinkle on top.

1 tablespoon vegetable oil
2 tablespoons minced gingerroot
3 cloves garlic, minced
6 scallions, white and green parts, thinly sliced
½ to 1 tablespoon Chinese chile paste, or hot pepper sauce*
4 tablespoons cilantro, chopped
2 tablespoons low-sodium soy sauce
½ pound ground sirloin, or ground round
2 tablespoons Chinese fermented black beans, rinsed and chopped, optional*
2 cups chicken broth, homemade or canned
1 pound firm tofu (bean curd), drained and cut into 1½-inch cubes
1 tablespoon cornstarch

In a wok or large, heavy skillet, heat the oil on high. Add half the ginger, garlic, scallions, chile paste, and cilantro, and cook about 30 seconds. Add half the soy sauce and cook another 30 seconds. Add the ground meat and black beans, and stirring frequently, cook for about 4 minutes, or until the meat is no longer pink. Add the remaining soy sauce, ginger, garlic, chile paste, and the chicken broth and bring to a boil.

Gently slide in the tofu, reduce the heat to moderately low, and simmer about 3 minutes. Meanwhile, place the cornstarch in a small bowl. Add about ¼ cup of the hot

*Available at Asian and specialty food shops.

liquid from the wok and stir to create a smooth paste. Slowly add the paste to the wok and simmer about 1 minute, until slightly thickened. The stew should be slightly spicy, but remember that the rice will offset the spiciness. Add a touch more chile paste if you want a spicier dish.

Serve hot over bowls of white rice and pass the remaining scallions and cilantro in small bowls separately.

Makes 4 servings

You Can Also Add . . .

- Ground turkey or finely chopped boneless skinless chicken breasts instead of the beef.
- Vegetable broth and omit the beef for a vegetarian version.

Turkish Lamb Kabobs

Kabobs are served throughout Turkey—from wooden carts with primitive charcoal and wood fires that line the streets of small villages to some of Istanbul's most sophisticated restaurants. Kabobs are made from lamb, chicken, or beef and can be marinated simply with a splash of lemon juice or more elaborately with spicy, thick pastes. This kabob—made with lamb chunks cut from a leg of lamb—is marinated in yogurt, mint, chile paste, olive oil, and lemon juice. Marinate overnight for incredibly tender, flavorful meat—but even an hour of marinating provides great flavor. Serve with a Middle Eastern–style rice pilaf (see page 155), Yogurt "Cheese" with Mint, Scallions, and Cucumber (see page 64), Sautéed Baby Spinach with Garlic (see page 150), and a variety of warm flat bread or pita bread. A platter of sliced cucumber, peppers, onions, and tomatoes makes a nice accompaniment.

2½ pounds boneless lamb, cut into 1½-inch cubes*
2 tablespoons olive oil
3 tablespoons plain, low-fat yogurt
5 cloves garlic, finely chopped
1 lemon (juice squeezed over the lamb) and the remaining lemon
    cut into small chunks
1 teaspoon dry mint
1 teaspoon dry thyme
1 teaspoon chile paste†
Coarsely ground pepper

THE GARNISHES:
1 lemon, cut into wedges
Fresh mint leaves

Place the lamb in a large bowl. Add the oil, yogurt, garlic, lemon juice and lemon wedges, mint, thyme, chile paste, and pepper and stir well to coat the meat thoroughly. Cover and refrigerate.

*Ask your butcher to cut the meat into 1½- to 2-inch cubes from a leg of lamb.
†*Aci Biber Sosu,* available in Middle Eastern stores, or substitute with Chinese chile paste or 1 teaspoon tomato paste mixed with a good splash of hot pepper sauce.

Light a charcoal or wood fire until red-hot. Clean the grill and lightly oil.

Remove the meat from the marinade. Divide the meat among 4 or 5 large skewers, placing a few chunks of lemon onto each skewer between the lamb. Grill the lamb 10 minutes, covered. Baste the meat with the marinade and flip the skewers over. Grill another 10 to 12 minutes on the other side, or until the meat is cooked through and just pink inside. Remove a piece of meat from the end and test it. (The meat should be just slightly pink in the middle for medium-rare lamb.) Remove the skewers from the heat and serve the meat on a platter scattered with fresh lemon wedges and mint.

Makes 4 servings

You Can Also Add . . .

- Bay leaves between every second or third piece of meat to infuse the lamb with a bay essence. Be sure to remove before serving.
- Thin slices of zucchini, eggplant, and cherry tomatoes between each piece of meat.
- Thin slices of red onion between each slice of meat; rub the onion with lemon juice before grilling.
- Mint leaves between each piece of meat.

Grilled Steak with Provençal Herbs

By adding a few herbs, pepper, and garlic, you can transform an ordinary grilled steak into something truly special. Cook over a hot charcoal, wood, or gas flame. The steaks can be marinated with the oil and herbs for several hours ahead of time; cover and refrigerate until ready to grill.

For a quick summer meal, serve the steak with the Spanish Chopped Salad (see page 71), Grilled Zucchini with Lemon (see page 147), Glenn's Tuscan Focaccia (see page 172), and lemonade, limeade, or iced tea with fresh mint.

Four 1½-inch-thick 12-ounce New York (top loin) or Delmonico steaks
1 tablespoon olive oil
2 cloves garlic, minced
1 tablespoon fresh rosemary, minced, or 1 teaspoon dried, crumbled
1 tablespoon fresh thyme, minced, or 1 teaspoon dried, crumbled
1 tablespoon fresh basil, finely chopped, or 1 teaspoon dried, crumbled
Freshly ground pepper

Place the steaks in a shallow dish. Rub both sides with the oil, garlic, and herbs. Season with pepper and let stand 10 minutes, or overnight.

Prepare the barbecue over high heat or preheat the indoor broiler. Cook the steak to desired doneness, 4 to 7 minutes per side for rare to medium-rare. Let sit 5 minutes, loosely covered, before slicing on the diagonal.

Makes 4 servings

Greek Lamb Burgers

A combination of ground lamb, fresh mint, pine nuts, and crumbled feta cheese, these burgers taste equally good grilled outside on an open fire, or inside in a hot skillet. The feta keeps the burgers moist and cheesy. Serve with Yogurt "Cheese" with Mint, Scallions, and Cucumbers (see page 64), warm pita bread, and Sautéed Baby Spinach with Garlic (see page 150) for a quick Greek-style feast.

1 pound ground lamb
Salt and freshly ground pepper
¼ cup pine nuts, finely chopped
2 tablespoons fresh mint, chopped
3 tablespoons crumbled fresh feta cheese
1 teaspoon olive oil, optional

In a bowl, mix the lamb, salt, pepper, pine nuts, mint, and feta, making sure the cheese and nuts are fully incorporated into the meat. Form the mixture into 4 large burgers or 6 smaller ones.

Light a charcoal or wood fire and allow it to burn until red-hot. Alternatively, heat a heavy cast-iron skillet over moderate heat. Add 1 teaspoon olive oil to the skillet. Cook burgers about 6 minutes on each side, until cooked through and crusty brown on the outside.

Makes 4 to 6 servings

You Can Also Add . . .

- Caramelized onions as a topping. Thinly slice 2 medium onions and cook over low heat with 1 tablespoon olive oil for about 15 minutes. Add 1 teaspoon balsamic vinegar and a pinch of sugar and cook another 10 to 15 minutes, or until golden brown and caramelized.

Quick Sausage and White Bean Stew

I was in the mood for comfort food—something soothing, satisfying, yet simple. I had a few fresh sausages, a can of white beans, an onion, and a handful of baby spinach and kale. With friends arriving in less than an hour, I browned the sausages with onions and garlic, threw in the beans, a splash of wine, a few herbs and tomatoes, and the spinach and kale. When we all sat down to eat (miraculously it was done in under an hour), we had a thick, hearty stew that tasted like it had been simmering all day. Served with linguine and crusty bread, this dish makes a completely satisfying meal.

1½ teaspoons olive oil

2 medium onions, thinly sliced

Salt and freshly ground pepper

1 tablespoon fresh thyme, chopped, or 1 teaspoon dried

1 tablespoon fresh rosemary, chopped, or 1 teaspoon dried

2 cloves garlic, minced

1 pound sweet or hot fresh sausage, cut into 2-inch chunks

One 19-ounce can white cannellini beans, drained

¼ cup dry white or red wine

¼ cup chicken broth

2 tomatoes, cored and cubed, or 1 cup peeled canned tomatoes

Hot pepper sauce

2 cups packed spinach, kale, or chard, stemmed and coarsely chopped

In a large skillet, heat the oil over moderate heat. Add the onions, salt, pepper, half the herbs, and half the garlic, and cook, stirring frequently, for 4 minutes.

Meanwhile, add the sausage to another skillet and cover with ½ cup water. Cook over high heat until the water evaporates, 8 to 10 minutes. Remove the sausage from the skillet with a slotted spoon and add to the skillet with the onions. Cook about 4 minutes to allow the sausage to brown lightly on both sides. Add the beans, wine, broth, tomatoes, a dash of hot pepper sauce, and the remaining herbs and garlic. Reduce the heat and simmer 4 minutes. Add the spinach and cook another 6 minutes, until the sauce is somewhat thickened, the greens tender, and the sausage is thoroughly cooked.

Makes 4 servings

You Can Also Add . . .

- Boneless, skinless chicken breasts, cut into 2-inch pieces instead of the sausage. Brown the chicken chunks with the onions for 4 minutes on each side and make the whole dish in one skillet.
- Chicken or turkey sausage instead of pork sausage.

Pork Chops with Caramelized Apples and Onions ☕ ☕

Homey comfort food elevated to a new status, these pork chops are panfried with herbs and served on top of caramelized apple and onion slices and then topped with a simple cream sauce made in the pan. Serve with Roasted Potato Wedges (see page 153), Sautéed Baby Spinach with Garlic (see page 150), a mixed green salad, and country bread.

1 tablespoon plus 1 teaspoon olive oil
2 medium sweet onions, thinly sliced
Salt and freshly ground pepper
1½ tablespoons fresh sage, chopped, or 1 teaspoon dried
1½ tablespoons fresh thyme, chopped, or 1 teaspoon dried
1½ tablespoons fresh rosemary, chopped, or 1 teaspoon dried
2 large tart apples, peeled and thinly sliced
1 tablespoon butter
1 tablespoon sugar
4 center cut pork chops, about 2 pounds, each about ½ inch thick
¼ cup chicken broth
¼ cup heavy cream

In a large, heavy-bottomed skillet heat the tablespoon of oil on moderately low. Add the onions, salt, pepper, ½ tablespoon of each of the herbs and cook, stirring frequently for 6 minutes. Add the apples, butter, and sugar and cook another 6 minutes.

Meanwhile, in another large skillet, heat the 1 teaspoon of the olive oil on moderately high. Add the chops and sprinkle with ½ tablespoon of each of the herbs, and a generous grinding of pepper. Cook 6 minutes. Flip the chops over and sprinkle the other side with the remaining ½ tablespoon of each of the herbs. Cook another 6 to 8 minutes, or until the pork is golden brown, and no longer has any visible signs of pink inside, or has reached an internal temperature of 137 degrees. Drain the chops on a paper towel.

Transfer the onion/apple mixture to a gratin dish or ovenproof skillet attractive enough to serve the chops in. Place the (drained) chops on top of the onion/apple mixture, and cover.

Meanwhile, remove all the grease from the bottom of the pork chop skillet. Over high heat, add the broth, the cream, salt, and pepper, and simmer for about 4 minutes, scraping up any bits clinging to the bottom of the pan. The sauce is ready when it's considerably thickened (enough to coat the back of a spoon), about 5 minutes. Pour on top of the pork chops.

Makes 4 servings

You Can Also Add . . .

- Pears instead of apples.
- Thinly sliced leeks and shallots instead of, or in addition to, the onions.

Maple-Glazed Ham Steaks

Serve these sweet, glazed ham steaks with fried eggs, toast, jelly, and good, strong coffee, hot cider, or cocoa for brunch, or a cozy dinner with a close friend.

1 tablespoon butter
2 ham steaks, about 1 inch thick (ask your deli to cut a ham steak from your favorite
    brand of smoked ham)
2 tablespoons grade A maple syrup

In a large skillet, melt the butter over moderate heat. Add the ham steak and cook about 3 minutes. Flip the ham over and drizzle with half the syrup. Lower the heat to prevent the syrup from burning and cook 2 minutes. Carefully flip the ham again and drizzle with the remaining syrup. Cook 2 minutes, or until the ham is golden brown and nicely glazed.

Makes 2 to 4 servings

Roasted Garlic

When you roast garlic, the assertiveness you find when garlic is raw is eliminated. The cloves become mellow and sweet. You can use roasted garlic with pasta dishes, as part of an antipasto platter, in salads and salad dressings, as a topping for pizza or sandwiches, and with rice dishes. You can also spread the roasted garlic cloves on grilled bread and serve as an appetizer or with salads.

1 head garlic
1 tablespoon olive oil
Salt and freshly ground pepper

Preheat the oven to 400 degrees. Cut the very tip off the head of garlic, to just expose the cloves. Place the garlic in a small, ovenproof skillet or a small gratin dish and drizzle with the olive oil, salt, and pepper. Roast for 15 to 20 minutes or until tender when tested with a small knife or fork. Remove from the oven and let cool for a minute or two before squeezing the garlic out of its skin and setting aside.

Makes about ⅓ cup roasted garlic

You Can Also Add . . .

- 1½ tablespoons chopped fresh herbs, or 1½ teaspoons dried herbs.
- Herb-flavored oil instead of olive oil.
- The garlic-infused oil from the pan to flavor pasta or to sauté vegetables, fish, poultry, or meat dishes.

White Beans Provençal

Canned white beans, cooked with garlic, herbs, tomatoes, and a dash of wine, are transformed into a buttery, herb-infused dish worthy of any meal. Serve with roasted or grilled poultry, meats, or fish, or serve as a first course with spicy greens (like arugula) and good bread.

1 tablespoon olive oil
1 medium onion, finely chopped
2 cloves garlic, finely chopped
1 tablespoon fresh rosemary, chopped, or 1 teaspoon dried
1 tablespoon fresh thyme, chopped, or 1 teaspoon dried
Salt and freshly ground pepper
2 cups canned white beans, rinsed and drained
1 large ripe tomato, cored and finely chopped
¼ cup dry white wine
⅓ cup finely chopped parsley

In a large skillet, heat the oil on moderately low. Add the onion and half the garlic, and sauté for 8 minutes, stirring frequently. Add half the herbs, the salt and pepper, and cook 1 minute. Add the beans and stir well to coat the beans with all the other ingredients. Stir in the tomato and raise the heat to high. Add the remaining garlic and herbs and the wine. Cook 2 minutes. Reduce the heat to low and simmer 5 minutes. Sprinkle with the parsley and serve hot.

Makes 4 servings

You Can Also Add . . .

- ¼ cup freshly grated Parmesan cheese sprinkled over the top and place the dish under the broiler until the cheese is golden brown.
- 2 tablespoons chopped marinated sun-dried tomatoes instead of the fresh tomatoes.
- 2 to 3 tablespoons pesto sauce instead of the rosemary and thyme. Add with the beans for a basil-infused flavor and a beautiful green color to the beans.
- ¼ cup chopped roasted pepper instead of the tomatoes.
- ¼ cup chopped arugula with the tomato toward the end of the cooking time.
- 1 tablespoon heavy cream with the wine for a richer, even creamier dish.

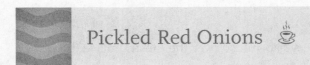

Pickled Red Onions

These thin strips of pickled red onions can transform the most ordinary sandwich into a special treat. I love to put these on a cheese sandwich, roast beef, smoked turkey, or any kind of wrap sandwich. They are also an excellent accompaniment to curries and stews.

You can also try this recipe using sweet Vidalia onions, but you'll miss the rosy red color.

1 medium red onion
½ cup good-quality cider vinegar
⅓ cup water

Peel the onion and slice thinly. Separate the rings and place in a medium bowl. Cover with boiling water, let sit for 1 minute, and drain. Place the onion back into the bowl.

Combine the vinegar and the ⅓ cup water in a saucepan and bring to a boil. Pour over the onions and let cool. Cover and refrigerate for at least 4 hours. Serve cold within a week.

Makes 1 cup

You Can Also Add . . .

- 1 to 2 teaspoons of peppercorns, mustard seeds, cilantro seeds, fennel seeds, or dried red chile peppers to the onions for a varied flavor.

Grilled Zucchini with Lemon

Try to serve this deliciously simple dish when zucchini is plentiful and you have the grill on for some other dish.

4 medium zucchini
2 tablespoons olive oil
Juice of 2 lemons
3 cloves garlic, finely chopped
Salt and freshly ground pepper

Cut off the ends of the zucchini. Slice the zucchini lengthwise into thin strips, like strips of lasagna pasta. Place in a shallow broiler pan or casserole and coat with the oil, lemon juice, garlic, and salt and pepper; let marinate for 5 minutes, or up to several hours refrigerated.

Preheat a charcoal or gas grill until quite hot. Place the zucchini strips over the heat and grill for about 3 minutes. Carefully flip the strips over, basting them with the oil/lemon/garlic mixture left over in the pan. Grill another 2 to 4 minutes, or until the zucchini is just tender.

Makes 4 to 8 servings

Panfried Summer Tomatoes

When you fry fresh summer tomatoes in a hot pan with a touch of olive oil and butter, you taste the very best of summer. These are a favorite treat in our house, a traditional weekend summer breakfast or brunch. Serve the tomatoes with toast, fried eggs, home-fried potatoes, a platter of fresh fruit, iced tea, and iced coffee. Or serve the tomatoes as a side dish with grilled or roasted foods.

1 cup flour
Salt and freshly ground pepper
4 large ripe summer tomatoes, cored and cut into ½-inch thick slices
1 tablespoon olive oil
1 tablespoon butter

Place the flour, salt, and pepper in a bowl or on a plate. Lightly coat the tomatoes on both sides, making sure the flour sticks.

In a large, heavy-bottomed skillet (cast iron is ideal), heat half the oil and butter on moderately high. When the oil is hot, add half the tomatoes, being careful not to crowd the pan, and cook for 2 to 3 minutes. Using a spatula, carefully flip the tomatoes and cook another 3 to 4 minutes, or until they have a golden brown crust and are soft but not falling apart. Repeat with the remaining tomatoes, adding additional oil and butter as needed.

Makes 4 servings

You Can Also Add . . .

- A pinch of ground ginger to the flour mixture.
- Chopped fresh basil, thyme, oregano, or rosemary sprinkled over the tomatoes as they cook.
- A teaspoon of your favorite dried herbs to the flour mixture.
- Chopped fresh parsley, chives, or cilantro (or a combination of all) sprinkled over the finished tomatoes.

- Chopped and pitted green and black olives over the finished dish.
- Capers and chopped red onions to sprinkle on the finished dish.
- Edible flowers sprinkled over the finished dish.
- Thin slices of garden fresh zucchini instead of, or in addition to, the tomatoes. Use the exact same technique, cooking them for 4 to 5 minutes on each side, or until tender and golden brown.

Sautéed Baby Spinach with Garlic

This is one of the simplest recipes in the book. But when properly made it's one of the greatest vegetable dishes of all time. Use the tenderest, freshest spinach you can find, preferably baby spinach. Serve with any lamb dish, grilled fish, chicken, or meat. The spinach also makes a great topping for pasta, or you can spread it on grilled slices of French bread as an appetizer or side dish.

1½ tablespoons olive oil
2 to 3 cloves garlic, finely chopped
1 pound baby or young spinach or regular spinach, thoroughly cleaned, dried and
    stemmed*
Salt, preferably sea salt

In a large, heavy-bottomed skillet, heat the oil on moderately-high. Add the garlic and cook, stirring, about 10 seconds, being careful not to let it burn. Add the spinach in handfuls, and cook over high heat, stirring constantly, for about 4 minutes, or until wilted and just cooked. Sprinkle liberally with salt and serve hot, immediately.

Makes 2 to 4 servings

You Can Also Add . . .

- 2 to 4 tablespoons heavy cream and a generous grinding of freshly grated nutmeg to the spinach. Let cook 4 to 5 minutes, or until the cream is slightly thickened for a fabulous creamed spinach dish.

*If your spinach is large or not particularly tender you may want to steam it for just a minute or two before sautéing. Baby spinach can be found in many specialty food shops.

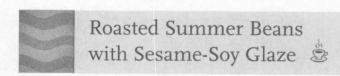

Roasted Summer Beans
with Sesame-Soy Glaze

Fresh summer beans are roasted with a splash of sesame oil and soy sauce in a hot oven. That's the recipe—the whole thing. These beans make a great accompaniment to grilled foods, particularly steak. Any leftovers are delicious served the next day as a cold salad with chopped tomatoes.

1½ pounds fresh green beans, ends trimmed*
1 tablespoon sesame oil
2½ tablespoons soy sauce, or low-sodium soy sauce

Preheat the oven to 400 degrees.

In a large ovenproof skillet, broiler pan, or large gratin dish, mix the beans, oil, and soy sauce. Toss well to coat the beans thoroughly. Roast for 15 to 20 minutes (depending on the thickness of the beans), tossing the beans once or twice. The beans are cooked when they are tender, glazed, and golden brown. They shouldn't be limp or overcooked. Keep in mind that they will continue to cook after you've taken them out of the oven.

Makes 4 servings

You Can Also Add . . .

- 1 tablespoon finely chopped gingerroot.
- 1 tablespoon butter during the last 2 to 3 minutes of roasting time to create a buttery glaze. Toss once after the butter melts.
- ¾ cup chopped wild mushrooms. Try a combination of cremini, portobellos, and shiitake added to the beans.

*Try to use beans of equal thickness so they cook evenly. Choose beans that are not paper-thin or very thick and tough.

Roasted Winter Root Vegetables

Root vegetables have a natural sweetness that shines through when roasted in a hot oven. In this dish I've combined parsnips (an off-white carrot-shaped vegetable, full of earthy flavor), turnips (white with a purple crown), rutabagas (also called Swede turnips), sweet carrots, leeks, and rosemary. This dish can be served as a main course with crusty bread and a hearty salad, or as a side dish with virtually any type of meat, poultry, or fish. Feel free to experiment with different root vegetables.

3 leeks
3 small parsnips, peeled and cut into 1½-inch pieces
1 medium turnip, peeled and cut into 1½-inch pieces
1 rutabaga, peeled and cut into 1½-inch pieces
2 cups carrots, peeled and cut into 1½-inch pieces, about 2 large carrots
1½ tablespoons olive oil
Salt and freshly ground pepper
2 tablespoons crushed fresh rosemary

Preheat the oven to 425 degrees. Cut the leeks down the middle lengthwise. Rinse the leeks under cold running water, separating the layers to remove any hidden dirt. Cut the leeks into 1½-inch long pieces. Place the leeks into a medium roasting pan. Add the parsnips, turnip, rutabaga, and carrots and drizzle with the olive oil. Sprinkle with the salt, pepper, and rosemary and toss to coat all of the vegetables. Roast for 45 minutes to 1½ hours, occasionally tossing the vegetables to brown them evenly. The vegetables are done when they feel tender when tested in the middle with a small, sharp knife.

Makes 4 servings

You Can Also Add . . .

- Beets (trimmed and left whole if small, or cut in half or in quarters if large).
- Celery root or celeriac (cut into wedges).
- Red or white onions (peeled and cut in half or left whole if small).
- Baby potatoes, cut in half, or large baking potatoes, cut into 1½-inch cubes.
- Fennel bulbs cut in quarters.
- 10 garlic cloves, peeled and left whole.

Roasted Potato Wedges

My daughters call these "pretend french fries," which may not sound like a compliment, but it most surely is. I call them healthful, satisfying "french fry wannabes," and I love making them with blue (or purple) potatoes, but you could easily use red bliss, Yukon gold, or any good white or yellow baking variety.

8 medium blue, purple, red, yellow, or white potatoes
2 tablespoons olive oil
Salt and freshly ground pepper

Preheat the oven to 400 degrees. Cut the potatoes in half lengthwise. Cut each half into 4 long wedges making a total of 8 wedges per potato. Place the potatoes on a baking sheet and drizzle with the oil. Sprinkle liberally with salt and pepper and any other herbs and spices (see below) and toss to coat the potatoes. Bake for 8 minutes. Flip the potatoes over and bake another 8 minutes or until crisp outside and tender inside and golden brown.

Makes 4 to 6 servings

You Can Also Add . . .

- Cayenne for spicy potato wedges.
- Fresh or dry herbs (such as thyme, oregano, basil, rosemary, chives, cumin, lemon verbena).
- Herb-flavored olive oil instead of regular olive oil.
- Salsa and sour cream to the potatoes and serve them as an appetizer.
- A variety of red, white, and blue potatoes and serve at a summer picnic or barbecue.
- Sweet potatoes instead of white potatoes.

Roast Garlic Mashed Potatoes

> *A whole head of garlic is roasted until golden brown and tender and then stirred into mashed potatoes for a rich, earthy flavor. They can be made a day ahead of time.*
>
> 10 large potatoes, peeled and cut in half*
> 4 tablespoons butter (½ stick)
> 2 cups milk†
> ¼ cup heavy cream, optional†
> Salt and freshly ground pepper
> 1 head roasted garlic (see page 143)

Bring a large pot of water to a boil. Add the peeled potatoes and cook for about 25 minutes or until tender when pierced with a small, sharp knife. Drain the potatoes thoroughly and place back into the pot. Using a potato masher, mash the potatoes with the butter, milk, and cream (if using), until almost smooth and fluffy. (Don't get obsessed with lumps; they are an inevitable part of mashed potatoes). Add salt and pepper to taste and stir in the roasted garlic cloves. Serve hot. If you make the dish ahead of time, cover and refrigerate until ready to serve. Heat on low, stirring to make sure all the potatoes are piping hot before serving. If the potatoes seem dry and flaky, stir about ¼ cup milk or cream into them until hot, soft and fluffy.

Makes 8 servings

You Can Also Add . . .

- 1½ tablespoons grated horseradish for a spicy flavor. Add with the salt and pepper.
- 1 to 2 tablespoons chopped fresh rosemary, thyme, oregano, basil, or any herb, or 1½ teaspoons dried.
- 1 tablespoon herb-flavored oil drizzled over the top just before serving.
- 2 to 3 tablespoons crème fraîche or sour cream instead of the heavy cream for a tart, creamy flavor.

*You can use your favorite variety—yellow, Yukon gold, red bliss, or any good white potato variety.
†You can make these potatoes as light or rich and creamy as you like. I have made them with great success using nothing but skim or 2% milk. You can use whole milk or low-fat milk and add as much or as little as you like, or use no cream at all.

Rice Pilaf

A simple yet elegant Middle Eastern–style rice dish, rich with spices and onion. Serve with grilled meats, fish, or chicken.

1 tablespoon olive oil
1 medium onion, finely chopped
1 scallion, trimmed and finely chopped, white and green parts
1½ teaspoons dried thyme
1 teaspoon dried oregano
½ teaspoon turmeric
Dash paprika
1½ cups basmati or short-grained white rice
2 tablespoons dry white wine, optional
3 cups chicken broth, vegetable broth, or water
⅓ cup slivered almonds

In a heavy-bottomed medium saucepan, heat the oil on moderately low. Add the onion and sauté about 6 minutes, stirring frequently, until soft and just golden brown. Add the scallion, thyme, and oregano and cook 2 minutes. Sprinkle in the turmeric, paprika, and the rice and cook, stirring, for 1 minute to coat the rice grains thoroughly. Raise the heat to high, add the wine (if using) and the broth or water, and bring to a boil. Stir the rice well to prevent it from sticking. Reduce the heat to low, cover, and cook until the rice has absorbed all the liquid and is cooked through. Gently stir in the almonds.

Makes 4 servings

You Can Also Add . . .

- ¼ cup golden raisins with the almonds.
- ¼ cup sun-dried cranberries or cherries with the almonds.
- Chopped pistachio nuts, pine nuts, or walnuts instead of almonds.
- A few flakes of saffron with the broth for color and flavor.
- ½ teaspoon ground cumin with the scallions.

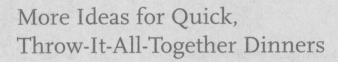

More Ideas for Quick, Throw-It-All-Together Dinners

- Bake potatoes and look into the deep recesses of your refrigerator for filling ideas: Bake white and/or sweet potatoes until tender—about 45 minutes to 1 hour and 15 minutes, depending on the size. Fill the hot, steaming potatoes with goat cheese (it melts like butter and adds much more flavor and creaminess), olive puree, flavored olive oil and fresh pepper, grated cheeses, chopped herbs, or dried spices.

- Make a quick quesadilla: Place grated cheese or a variety of cheeses on tortillas and cook over low heat until the cheese melts and is bubbling. Add any or all of the following, depending on what you have in the refrigerator and pantry: chopped avocado, salsa, chopped olives, chopped cilantro, chopped chile peppers, cooked sausage slices, thinly sliced mango, chopped tomatoes, roasted garlic cloves, sour cream, chopped scallions, sliced sun-dried tomatoes. Top with another warmed tortilla and cut into quarters. Make a variety of quesadillas and serve.

- Heat one can of anchovies with the oil from the can and cook over low heat until the anchovies "melt" into a paste. Add a clove of chopped garlic and ¼ cup chopped parsley and any fresh or dried herbs and heat 5 minutes. Toss with 1 pound of linguine or shaped pasta.

- Add chopped garlic, thyme, basil, oregano, chopped olives, and capers to your favorite tomato sauce. Simmer 5 minutes over moderate heat. Toss with shaped pasta and grated Parmesan cheese.

- Make a quick frittata: Sauté onion, peppers, mushrooms, or any combination of vegetables you have on hand in 1 tablespoon olive oil in a heavy, ovenproof skillet for 10 minutes. Vigorously whisk 5 eggs and season with salt, pepper, and herbs. Pour eggs over vegetables and cook 1 minute. Sprinkle 1/3 cup grated cheese over the eggs and bake on the middle shelf of a 450 degree oven until puffed and golden, about 15 minutes.

- Tacos and burritos can be put together by warming corn or wheat tortillas and filling with grilled (or warmed leftover) chicken, beef, or fish. Let guests choose their own toppings by setting out bowls of salsa, sour cream, chopped cilantro, olives, grated cheese, chopped avocado, chopped chiles, chopped fresh tomatoes, chopped red or white onions, and scallions.

- Make a chopped salad using diced carrots, celery, tomatoes, peppers, scallions or onions, cucumbers, and any other vegetables you may have on hand. Toss with a few tablespoons of red wine vinegar and olive oil, salt, pepper, and any fresh chopped herbs. Sprinkle with chopped blue cheese or feta. Leftover bread can be cut into small cubes, toasted, and added on top of the salad.

White Rice with Scallions and Sesame

This is a simple way to cook rice with a decidedly Asian twist. Serve with grilled foods, seafood of any kind, or a stew with Asian flavors.

1½ cups short-grained white rice
Salt
1 teaspoon vegetable or peanut oil
3 tablespoons very thinly sliced scallions, white and green parts
1½ teaspoons sesame oil or sesame oil with chile

Place the rice and 3 cups water in a medium saucepan and bring to a boil. Add a pinch of salt and the vegetable oil. Reduce the heat to low, stir well, cover, and cook about 10 minutes, or until the rice is cooked through and the liquid has been absorbed.

Divide the hot rice between four serving bowls. Sprinkle the top of each bowl with the scallions and a drizzle of sesame oil.

Makes 4 servings

You Can Also Add . . .

- 1 tablespoon sesame seeds that have been lightly toasted in a dry skillet over moderate heat for 5 minutes.
- 1 tablespoon chopped cilantro.
- Dash Chinese chile oil for a spicy bite.

6

Celebrations!

Soups, Breads, Salads, Elegant Meals, and Sides

Rouille (Red Pepper and Garlic Sauce)

Tomato, Basil, and Garlic Soup with Rouille

Vichyssoise

Corn Chowder with Bacon and Thyme

Turkish Lentil and Vegetable Soup

Cuban-Style Black Bean Soup

Glenn's Tuscan Focaccia

Roasted Spring Asparagus Salad with Dill Vinaigrette and
    Crumbled Feta

Mediterranean Couscous Salad with Roasted Vegetables

Roasted Beet and Fennel Salad

Prosciutto-Wrapped Asparagus Bundles with
    Garlic Butter

Cabbage Salad with Blue Cheese and
    Honeyed Walnuts

Rouille (Red Pepper and Garlic Sauce)

A simple adaptation of the traditional French sauce rouille, *this sweet, garlicky paste adds great flavor to Tomato, Basil, and Garlic Soup (see page 162), to a fish stew or soup, or as a dip for steamed or grilled shrimp, grilled meats or chicken, or raw or steamed vegetables.*

You can make the sauce a day ahead of time. Bring to room temperature and stir until smooth before serving.

1 large red bell pepper
One 2-inch-thick slice crusty French or Italian bread
4 cloves garlic, peeled
2½ tablespoons good-quality olive oil
About ¼ teaspoon cayenne
Salt and freshly ground pepper

Place the pepper under the broiler or over a gas flame turning it until the skin is blackened on all sides. Place in a paper bag for about 2 minutes to steam and release the skin and then peel the skin off. Remove the seeds and ribs, and chop the pepper. Soak the bread in water to soften and then squeeze out all the moisture (like squeezing a sponge). Place the garlic and pepper in the container of a food processor and puree until almost smooth. Add the bread and process for 5 seconds. With the machine running, slowly add the olive oil. Season to taste with the cayenne, salt, and pepper and process until very smooth. Cover and refrigerate until ready to serve.

Makes about 1 cup

Tomato, Basil, and Garlic Soup with Rouille

Every spring I plant dozens of tomato plants, some eight to ten varieties, and never consider all the work I'll have come August when they all seem to ripen during the exact same week. That's when I get out my Mason jars and cook up huge batches of pasta sauce and salsa, canning all day. Then as a reward for all that work, I make this soup for my family and myself. Tomato and garlic soup is the essence of summer, sun, and earth and the sheer tomato-ness of tomatoes. Anyone who has grown tomatoes knows exactly what I mean.

The soup and the rouille can be made a day ahead of time.

THE SOUP:

4 pounds fresh vine-ripened tomatoes, plum or your favorite variety, or two
    16-ounce cans whole tomatoes
4 tablespoons butter
2 tablespoons olive oil
2 large onions, chopped
2 ribs celery, chopped
¼ cup fresh basil, shredded
5 cloves garlic, chopped
1 clove garlic, peeled and left whole
6 cups chicken broth, homemade or canned
Salt and freshly ground pepper

THE GARNISHES:

Rouille (see page 161)
Croûtes or croutons (see page 85 for recipes for making croûtes)
¼ cup fresh basil, shredded

Bring a pot of water to a boil and have a bowl of ice-cold water ready. Place the tomatoes in the boiling water for about 15 seconds, then place them immediately in the cold water for about 30 seconds. Remove and peel. If you hate seeds in your soup this is also the time to remove the seeds from the tomatoes: Slice the tomatoes in half and squeeze them out into a bowl. Quarter the tomatoes.

In a large pot, heat the butter and oil over moderate heat. Add the onions, celery, half the basil, the chopped and whole garlic, and sauté about 8 minutes, or until soft. Add the tomatoes and stir to coat, then add the broth and the remaining basil and simmer, covered, for 15 minutes. Remove from the heat and puree in the container of a food processor or blender. Cover and refrigerate until ready to serve; reheat over low until simmering. Serve topped with the rouille, croûtes, and fresh basil.

Makes 6 to 8 servings

Vichyssoise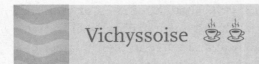

On a hot summer night there are few dishes that are more satisfying and refreshing than this cold, creamy soup made from leeks and potatoes. When the weather turns cold the soup is transformed into a hot leek and potato soup that is excellent served with a drizzle of cold cream and a sprinkling of fresh chives. Serve as a first course or as a main course for a summer lunch, accompanied by a variety of salads and breads.

In order to chill the soup properly, plan on making it at least five hours ahead of time, or preferably the night before.

4 medium to large leeks
1 tablespoon olive oil
1 teaspoon butter
5 medium potatoes, peeled and cut into 8 wedges
Salt and freshly ground pepper
8 cups chicken or vegetable broth
½ cup heavy cream

THE GARNISHES:
About 3 tablespoons minced fresh chives
Heavy cream

Trim all the green off the leeks and discard or save for a stock. Cut the whites of the leeks down the middle lengthwise and clean thoroughly under cold running water. Chop the leeks into 1-inch pieces.

In a large soup pot heat the oil and butter on moderately low. Add the leeks and cook, stirring frequently, for about 15 minutes, or until softened but not brown. If the leeks begin to burn, reduce the heat to low. Add the potatoes, salt, and pepper and cook 1 minute. Raise the heat to high and add the broth. Bring the broth to a boil, reduce the heat, and cook, partially covered, for about 15 minutes, or until the potatoes are tender and the broth is flavorful. The potatoes need to be fully tender, but not falling apart.

Working in batches, place the soup and the cream in the container of a food processor or blender and blend until smooth. (This takes special care; you want to avoid any potato lumps in the soup.) Taste for seasoning and add more salt or pepper as needed. Place the soup in a large serving bowl and chill for at least 5 hours, or preferably overnight. Serve ice cold, garnished with a sprinkling of chives and swirl of heavy cream in each bowl, if desired. To serve hot: Simply heat the soup until piping hot and garnish.

Makes 6 servings

Corn Chowder with Bacon and Thyme

Make this chowder in August when corn is fresh and ripe. Even if you use frozen corn (don't even try to use canned—at best it will taste like canned chowder) you'll be impressed with the results. This chowder makes a great first course, but it's also hearty enough to be a main course served with biscuits or the Double Corn Muffins with Chives and Cheddar (see page 82), a salad or two, and red wine.

Assuming you have fresh corn on the cob, be sure to finish the chowder at least one hour, or preferably several hours, before serving to let the cobs soak in the broth and infuse the soup with its corn essence.

6 strips bacon, preferably thick slab
1 teaspoon butter
1 medium onion, finely chopped (about 1 cup)
1 yellow, green, or red bell pepper, finely chopped
1½ tablespoons chopped fresh thyme, or 1 teaspoon dried
Salt and freshly ground pepper
3 medium potatoes, peeled and almost finely chopped, about 3 cups
6 ears fresh corn on the cob, or 2½ cups frozen corn
4 cups milk, whole or low fat
Dash of hot pepper sauce
½ cup heavy cream

THE GARNISHES:
Sweet paprika
2 tablespoons fresh chopped thyme (do not substitute with dried)

In a large soup pot, cook the bacon strips over moderately low heat until crisp on both sides, about 5 minutes per side. Remove the bacon and drain on a paper towel. Remove all but 1 tablespoon of the bacon fat and heat with the butter over low heat. Add the onion and cook about 5 minutes, stirring frequently. Add the bell pepper, thyme, salt, and pepper and cook another 3 minutes. Add the potatoes and cook 3 more minutes.

Meanwhile, husk the corn and remove the silk. Using a sharp knife and working over a large bowl, scrape the corn kernels off the cob by cutting down the sides of the corn cob and catching the kernels and any juice in the bowl. *Don't throw away the cobs.* You should have 2 to 2¹/₂ cups corn.

Add the corn to the potatoes and vegetables and cook 1 minute. Crumble or chop 2 strips of the bacon and add to the pot along with the milk. Bring to a simmer over moderately high heat. Add the corn cobs (they will infuse the soup with more corn flavor). Reduce the heat, season with the pepper sauce to taste (you only want a small bit), and simmer, covered, for 15 to 20 minutes or until the potatoes are *just* tender but not falling apart; the potatoes will continue to cook as the chowder sits. Remove from the heat and let sit, covered and refrigerated. Place the remaining strips of bacon into an airtight bag or wrap in foil and set aside until ready to serve the chowder.

Using tongs, remove the corn cobs from the chowder and scrape off any bits of corn or vegetables clinging to them. (Discard the cobs.) Add the cream and heat the chowder on low until steaming hot.

To serve, ladle out each bowl of chowder and top with a very modest dusting of paprika and thyme. Crumble the remaining bacon and sprinkle on top.

Makes 6 servings

You Can Also Add . . .

- Chopped roasted chile pepper for a spicy bite to the chowder. Roast a chile pepper over a gas flame or under the broiler until blackened. Steam in a paper bag for a few minutes. Remove and peel off the blackened skin and discard the seeds. Chop the roasted pepper flesh and sprinkle over the soup.
- Olive oil to the pan and omit the bacon if you want to make a vegetarian soup. Instead of the bacon, simply sauté the onion in 1 tablespoon olive oil and 1 teaspoon butter.
- Lobster meat. Chop cooked lobster and add to the soup with the cream for a delicious lobster-corn chowder.
- Sautéed scallops as a luxurious garnish. Sauté 6 sea scallops in a hot pan with 1 tablespoon olive oil and 2 cloves chopped garlic. Brown for 2 minutes on each side, or until just cooked through. Add the hot sautéed scallops and the garlic from the pan on top of the soup.

Turkish Lentil and Vegetable Soup

I first tasted this soup at Asitane Restaurant in Istanbul, which is famous for recipes dating from the Ottoman Empire. The traditional way to serve the soup is topped with a splash of pomegranate vinegar, which adds a tart finish to the rich flavors in the soup; you can easily substitute balsamic or red wine vinegar. The soup can be made a day ahead of time.

4 sprigs thyme
4 sprigs parsley
4 peppercorns
1 bay leaf
1½ pounds lamb shank
8 cups water
3 cups chopped onion
2 cups dried lentils
2 cups thinly sliced celery
2 cups thinly sliced carrots
1 cup chopped leek
1 cup dry red wine
1 tablespoon fresh thyme, chopped, or 1 teaspoon dried
Salt and freshly ground pepper
⅛ teaspoon crushed red pepper
8 teaspoons fresh mint, chopped
8 teaspoons pomegranate vinegar or red wine vinegar*

Place the thyme, parsley, peppercorns, and bay leaf in a piece of cheesecloth and tie it up securely.

In a large pot, place the cheesecloth bag, lamb shank, water, onion, lentils, celery, carrots, leek, wine, chopped thyme, salt, pepper, and red pepper and bring to a boil over high heat. Reduce the heat and simmer, uncovered, for about 2 hours, or until the lamb is tender and almost falling off the bone. Remove

*Pomegranate vinegar can be found in Middle Eastern specialty shops.

the lamb from the pot and cut the meat from the bone, discarding the bone. Cut the meat into bite-sized pieces and stir into the soup. The broth should be flavorful and the lentils and vegetables tender; bring to a vigorous simmer if the soup tastes weak, and reduce until the soup has intensified in flavor. Remove the cheesecloth bag and discard. Cover and refrigerate the soup until ready to reheat. Spoon into bowls and sprinkle each serving with 1 teaspoon mint and 1 teaspoon vinegar.

Makes 8 servings

Cuban-Style Black Bean Soup

Rich, thick, and full of cumin, thyme, and onion, this hearty soup can make a meal. The fun of this soup is serving it with a wide variety of garnishes and then inviting each guest to create his or her own custom-made dish.

For the broth, I use a combination of four cups chicken broth and three cups of the water that I have soaked the beans in. You can also use all stock—vegetable or chicken—or just the soaking water from the beans. The beans need to soak for eight to twelve hours, so plan your time accordingly. The soup can be made a full day ahead of time.

THE SOUP:
3 cups dry black beans
1½ tablespoons olive oil
2 medium onions, chopped
4 cloves garlic, chopped
2 ribs celery, chopped
2 tablespoons fresh thyme, chopped, or 2 teaspoons dried
1 teaspoon cumin
Salt and freshly ground pepper
7 cups broth or water
¼ cup dry sherry or red wine, optional
2 cups white rice
1 teaspoon vegetable oil
Salt

THE GARNISHES:
1 large onion, finely chopped
½ cup fresh parsley, chopped
1 green bell pepper, cut into small pieces
1 red bell pepper, cut into small pieces
1 hot chile pepper, seeded and very finely chopped
1 lime, cut into wedges
Hot pepper sauce

Place the beans in a large bowl or pot and cover with at least 7 cups water. Soak overnight.

In a large soup pot, heat the oil on moderately low. Add the onions and half the garlic and cook 10 minutes, stirring frequently. Add the celery, thyme, cumin, salt, and pepper and cook another 5 minutes. Remove the beans from the bowl using a slotted spoon (making sure to save the water the beans have been soaking in) and add the beans to the soup pot. Add the remaining garlic and 7 cups of liquid (the broth and/or soaking water; see headnote). Add the sherry or wine, raise the heat to high, and bring to a boil.

Reduce the heat to low, cover, and simmer for $1^{1}/_{2}$ to 2 hours, or until the soup has thickened and the beans are tender and buttery. Cover and refrigerate until ready to reheat.

Cook the rice: Place the 2 cups rice and 4 cups water in a large saucepan. Add the vegetable oil and a pinch of salt and bring to a boil. Stir the rice, reduce the heat to low, cover, and let cook until all the water has been absorbed, about 10 minutes.

Chop the garnishes and set each one out in a small bowl. Serve the soup piping hot, accompanied by the rice and garnishes and let everyone add what they like.

Makes 6 to 8 servings

Glenn's Tuscan Focaccia

Don't be scared off by the idea of using yeast, letting dough rise, and making your own fo-caccia. I adore this chewy, pizzalike bread and its infinite possibilities for creative top-pings, but thought it would be too much of a commitment to make my own. Friend and caterer Glenn Smith sent me his recipe. I tried it once, and now I'm a make-your-own fo-caccia convert. Try the basic recipe or try any of the topping ideas listed below.

The dough can be made ahead of time, toppings prepared and placed on the dough and set in the pan, up to eight hours ahead of time.

2 cups water
½ cup milk
2 packages dry yeast, ¼ ounce each
1 tablespoon sugar
1 tablespoon kosher salt
⅓ cup good-quality olive oil, plus 1 tablespoon, plus oil for greasing the bowl
6 to 7 cups flour
About ½ cup cornmeal

Heat the water and milk to 104 degrees on a candy thermometer—warm to the touch, but not simmering.

In a large mixer bowl, combine the warm water and milk, yeast, sugar, salt, the ⅓ cup of olive oil, and 3 cups of the flour. Mix with a hook or a mixing paddle for about 2 minutes. Let rise in the bowl for about 10 minutes, or until bubbles appear and the dough has visibly risen a bit. Gradually add the remaining flour and mix on low for about 10 minutes, scraping down the sides occasionally. The dough is ready when you poke it with your finger and it leaves a dent.

Turn out the dough and knead by hand on a floured surface for a few minutes. Lightly oil a large bowl and place the dough in the bowl, tossing it once to coat with the oil. Cover the dough with a clean tea towel until doubled in size, about 40 minutes. Punch down the dough with your fist, divide in half, and place each half in a well-oiled half-sheet or broiler pan. Using your fingers, stretch and spread the dough until it is half the size of the pan. Sprinkle each batch with half the cornmeal and flip the dough over. Spread the dough to the edges of the pan, stretching it out so it covers the entire pan. Drizzle with the 1 tablespoon of olive oil and the topping of your choice, if desired, and cover.

After you sprinkle the topping over the dough, let the dough rise until doubled in thickness, 15 to 20 minutes. Use your fingertips to make indentations throughout the dough. You can cover the dough and let it sit for several hours up to this point.

Preheat the oven to 450 degrees. Bake on the middle shelf until light golden brown, 15 to 20 minutes, turning the pan a half turn halfway through baking. Cut into thin strips or large squares, depending on what else you're serving.

Makes about 12 servings

You Can Also Add . . .

- Caramelized onions: In a skillet, heat 1 tablespoon olive oil over moderately low heat. Add 2 medium onions, thinly sliced, and cook about 15 minutes, or until golden brown. Season with salt, pepper and fresh rosemary and spread on top of the dough. Sprinkle with ⅓ to ½ cup freshly grated Parmesan cheese.
- Anchovies: Scatter about 12 anchovies on the dough, placing two of them into an "X" set about 1 inch apart all over the focaccia.
- Olive puree or chopped olives and fresh thyme.
- Chopped fresh rosemary, kosher salt, and a drizzle of olive oil and pepper.
- Chopped fresh sage and thin, seeded slices of roma tomatoes, salt, and pepper.
- Sliced red onion, oil-cured olives, and fresh herbs.
- Halved red and green grapes, melted butter, and a sprinkling of brown sugar.
- 1 cup grated cheese(s). Mix a variety of hard and soft cheeses, like grated Parmesan, crumbled fresh ricotta or goat cheese, and shredded fresh mozzarella.

Roasted Spring Asparagus Salad with Dill Vinaigrette and Crumbled Feta

Asparagus is the ultimate spring food. There's nothing better than snapping fresh stalks from the garden. If you're buying asparagus from a farmer's market or grocery store always look for unblemished, bright green stalks with a closed compact tip. The ends should be moist and not look dried out. Try to choose asparagus of uniform size so they all require the same cooking time.

The dish can be made several hours ahead of time; cover and refrigerate until ready to serve.

THE ASPARAGUS:
1 pound asparagus
1 teaspoon olive oil

THE VINAIGRETTE:
½ teaspoon mustard
Salt and freshly ground pepper
1 tablespoon fresh dill, chopped
1 tablespoon fresh lemon juice
1½ tablespoons wine vinegar or balsamic vinegar
1½ tablespoons olive oil
About ¼ cup crumbled feta cheese

Preheat the oven to 400 degrees. Trim the asparagus by snapping off the very tough end or trimming the ends with a sharp knife. (Save the trimmed ends for a vegetable broth or soup.) Place the asparagus on a large sheet of aluminum foil and drizzle with the teaspoon of oil. Wrap tightly and bake on the middle shelf for 20 to 40 minutes, depending on the thickness of the asparagus stalks. The asparagus is done when tender, but *not* falling apart. (It should still have a "bite," as it will continue to cook after coming out of the hot oven.)

To make the vinaigrette, mix the mustard, salt, pepper, and dill in a small bowl. Add the lemon juice and the vinegar and slowly whisk in the oil.

Remove the asparagus from the oven and place on a serving plate. Spoon the vinaigrette and the feta over the warm asparagus and serve warm, at room temperature, or chilled.

Makes 4 servings

You Can Also Add . . .

- 1 small red bell pepper, finely chopped.
- 1 hard-boiled egg, very finely chopped.
- Spoonful of salmon caviar instead of the feta.
- Chopped walnuts, almonds, pine nuts, pistachios, or pecans.
- Thinly sliced shallots.

Mediterranean Couscous Salad with Roasted Vegetables ☕ ☕

This meatless salad combines couscous with roasted eggplant, zucchini, red bell pepper, and leeks. It is hearty enough to be served as a main course on a cool evening. Serve with garlic bread (see page 84) or foccacia (see page 172). It can be made a day ahead of time.

1 to 1¼ pounds eggplant, cut lengthwise into 8 wedges
2 medium zucchini, cut lengthwise and into 4 wedges
3 large leeks, halved lengthwise, cut crosswise into 2½-inch pieces
1 red bell pepper, cut into ½-inch-wide strips
10 cloves garlic, unpeeled
3½ tablespoons plus ¼ cup olive oil
2 tablespoons balsamic vinegar
1 tablespoon fresh thyme, chopped
1 tablespoon fresh rosemary, chopped
Salt and freshly ground pepper
2½ cups water
1 teaspoon salt
One 10-ounce box couscous
1 cup pitted black olives, such as kalamata, halved
6 tablespoons fresh lemon juice
3 tablespoons capers, drained
3 tablespoons fresh basil, thinly sliced

Preheat oven to 400 degrees. Place the eggplant, zucchini, leeks, bell pepper, and garlic in a large roasting pan and brush the vegetables with 3 tablespoons of the olive oil and the vinegar. Sprinkle the thyme and rosemary on top and season with salt and pepper. Roast until tender, turning occasionally, about 45 minutes. Cool. Remove and discard peels from garlic and coarsely chop. Cut roasted vegetables into ¾-inch pieces and set aside.

Bring the 2½ cups of water, the teaspoon of salt, and ½ tablespoon of the oil to a boil in medium saucepan. Stir in the couscous. Remove from the heat, cover, and let

stand until water is absorbed, about 5 minutes. Fluff couscous with a fork and transfer to a large bowl.

Gently mix the roasted garlic and vegetables, the remaining $1/4$ cup oil, olives, lemon juice, capers, and basil into the bowl with the couscous. Season with salt and pepper. Cover and refrigerate. Let stand 30 minutes at room temperature before serving.

Makes 6 servings

You Can Also Add . . .

- Toasted pine nuts or pistachios.
- Shallots and red onions cut in half to the roasting pan.
- Fennel bulbs cut into quarters and roasted with the other vegetables.
- $1/2$ to 1 cup cooked sausage, cut into bite-sized pieces.

Roasted Beet and Fennel Salad

If you have never understood the appeal of beets, you need to try this recipe. Roasting beets (as opposed to steaming them and leeching away their flavor and many of the nutrients) brings out their earthiness and natural sweetness. The fresh, bracing anise flavor of raw fennel really wakes up the flavor of the beets. You can make most of the salad a day ahead of time.

3 medium beets, red or golden
¼ cup pine nuts
1 teaspoon Dijon mustard
Salt and freshly ground pepper
2 to 3 tablespoons balsamic vinegar
About ¼ cup good-quality olive oil
1 large bulb fennel

Preheat the oven to 350 degrees. Trim off the stems and wrap each beet individually in aluminum foil. Roast for about 30 minutes to an hour, depending on their size and thickness, or until a knife or skewer inserted in the middle of the beet feels tender, but not soft. The beets will continue to cook after they're removed from the oven.

Meanwhile, place the pine nuts on a baking sheet or ovenproof skillet and bake in the 350 degree oven for about 5 minutes, being careful that they don't burn.

Let the beets sit and, when cool enough to handle, peel them using your hands, a vegetable peeler, or small knife.

Meanwhile in a small bowl, mix the mustard, salt, and pepper; whisk in the vinegar and oil. Wrap the beets in plastic. Place the pine nuts in a plastic bag. Cover the bowl containing the vinaigrette. Refrigerate all until ready to serve.

Cut the beets into thin slices and place on a serving platter or bowl.

Core the fennel and cut off the dill-like fronds. Reserve a bit of the dill-like fronds and chop finely, about 1 tablespoon. Thinly slice the fennel bulb and arrange around the beets. Sprinkle the pine nuts over the beets and fennel. Serve the vinaigrette on top, or on the side, of the salad.

Makes 4 servings

Prosciutto-Wrapped Asparagus Bundles
with Garlic Butter ☕☕

The idea behind this dish is simple: Asparagus is steamed and then wrapped in "bundles" using thin slices of prosciutto as the "wrapper." The bundles are placed in a baking dish, topped with garlic butter, and then lightly dusted with Parmesan cheese. The entire dish can be made a day ahead of time and simply heated in the oven at the last minute. Serve as a first course, side dish, or main course with linguine (tossed with more garlic and oil) and good crusty bread to mop up all the juices.

You can use thick or thin asparagus in this dish, but make sure they are all of uniform size.

2 pounds fresh asparagus, of uniform size, ends trimmed
2 to 3 tablespoons butter
2 to 3 cloves garlic, finely chopped
¼ pound prosciutto, thinly sliced
1 tablespoon olive oil
¼ cup freshly grated Parmesan cheese
Freshly ground pepper

Fill the bottom of a steamer with about 2 inches of water, or fill a large skillet with 2 inches of water, and bring to a boil over high heat. Steam the asparagus for 6 to 10 minutes, depending on the thickness and freshness, or until they are just cooked—slightly al dente. Drain the asparagus and refresh under cold running water to stop the cooking. Drain again.

Meanwhile, in a small skillet melt the butter over low heat. Add the garlic and cook about 4 minutes, making sure the garlic doesn't brown.

Place the cooled asparagus on a work surface. Gather 4 asparagus into a bundle and trim the ends so they are all the same length. Place a slice of prosciutto on a work surface and place an asparagus bundle in the middle of the ham. Wrap the prosciutto around the asparagus, rolling it up like a fat cigar.

Using the oil, grease the bottom of a large gratin dish or a large ovenproof skillet or baking dish. Place the wrapped asparagus bundles in the dish. Drizzle the garlic butter on top and sprinkle on the cheese. Season with the pepper. Cover and refrigerate until ready to cook.

Preheat the oven to 350 degrees. Bake the asparagus on the middle shelf for 10 to 12 minutes, or until it is hot and the cheese is melted and bubbling.

Makes 6 servings

Cabbage Salad with Blue Cheese and Honeyed Walnuts

An ideal salad for autumn, the combination of thinly sliced red cabbage, creamy blue cheese, and caramelized honeyed walnuts goes well with just about anything—grilled or roasted meats (particularly a pork roast), fish, or poultry. The salad is hearty enough to be the main course, surrounded by an assortment of crusty breads. It's ideal to bring to a potluck. The dish can be made several hours ahead of time. Cover and refrigerate until ready to serve.

THE MUSTARD VINAIGRETTE:
1½ tablespoons Dijon mustard
Salt and freshly ground black pepper
½ pound Roquefort or good-quality blue cheese
¼ cup plus 1 tablespoon red wine vinegar
¾ cup olive oil

THE SALAD:
1 large red cabbage, about 2½ pounds
1 tablespoon olive oil or vegetable oil
1 teaspoon butter
1 cup walnut halves
Salt and freshly ground pepper
3 tablespoons honey

In the bottom of a large salad bowl, mix the mustard, salt, and pepper. Add 1 or 2 tablespoons of the Roquefort and mash to create a paste. Add the vinegar and stir well. Add the olive oil and stir to create a smooth sauce.

Core the cabbage and cut in half. Using a food processor or a sharp knife, cut into very thin slices and place on top of the dressing in the bowl.

In a medium skillet, heat the oil and butter over moderate heat. Add the walnuts, salt, and pepper and cook about 5 minutes, stirring frequently. Be careful not to let the nuts burn. Drizzle the honey over the nuts, stir well, and cook another 2 to 3 minutes, or until all the nuts are coated in the honey. Remove from the heat.

Sprinkle the honeyed walnuts and the remaining Roquefort over the cabbage and toss well. Taste for seasoning and add more salt and pepper, if needed. If you have a particularly large cabbage you may want to make the salad moister by adding 1 tablespoon vinegar and 1 to 2 tablespoons oil. Serve at room temperature.

Makes 6 to 8 servings

You Can Also Add . . .

- ¹/₂ pound pancetta or thick slab bacon. In a large skillet, cook the pancetta or bacon until crisp. Drain on paper towels and sprinkle onto the salad with the Roquefort.
- Thinly sliced peeled pears or apple slices, about 1 cup.
- Almonds, pecans, or pistachios instead of the walnuts.
- White and red cabbage for added color. Use 2 small cabbages, one white and one red, instead of one large red.

Vidalia Onion Tart

Sweet, mild Vidalia onions are grown in southeastern Georgia. Some people find them so sweet they eat them like an apple. I prefer to thinly slice them, sauté them long and slow, and place them in this creamy, thyme-infused tart. The tart is ideal for a picnic, to serve with grilled or roasted foods, or simply as a luxurious snack.

You'll need either a round or rectangular tart pan with a removeable bottom. If you're pressed for time you can always use a premade piecrust from the grocery store and whip the filling together in about fifteen minutes.

THE PASTRY:
2 cups flour
Pinch salt
1½ sticks unsalted butter, ice cold and cut into cubes
About ¼ cup ice cold water

THE FILLING:
1 tablespoon olive oil
2 large Vidalia onions, or sweet, mild onions, very thinly sliced
Salt and freshly ground pepper
4 tablespoons chopped fresh thyme
½ cup heavy cream
2 eggs
⅓ cup freshly grated Parmesan cheese

To make the pastry, place the flour and salt in the container of a food processor and pulse once or twice. Add the butter and pulse about 20 times, or until the butter is the size of peas. Add the water and process until the dough begins to pull away from the sides of the machine. You may need to add more water; add a teaspoon at a time. Place the dough in aluminum foil, wrap tightly, and form into a ball. Refrigerate for at least 2 hours, or overnight.

Preheat the oven to 400 degrees.

In a large skillet, heat the oil over low and add the onions, salt, pepper, and 1 tablespoon of thyme. Sauté the onions for about 15 minutes, stirring frequently to prevent browning. The onions are ready when they are very soft, tender, and golden brown.

Meanwhile, place the cream and 2 tablespoons of thyme in a small saucepan. Place over moderate heat and simmer about 10 minutes, or until thickened and somewhat reduced.

In a bowl, whisk the eggs with the remaining tablespoon of thyme, salt, and pepper. Add the cheese and whisk well. Add the reduced cream and whisk.

Roll out the dough on a lightly floured work surface. Place the dough in a tart pan with a removable bottom—preferably a 10-inch round. Trim the edges.

Place the sautéed onions on the bottom of the crust, and top with the egg/cream mixture. Bake on the middle shelf for 50 minutes to an hour, or until golden brown and set. Serve hot or at room temperature.

Makes 4 servings

Spinach Tart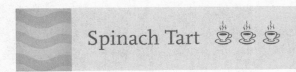

Serve this fresh spinach tart as a first course, lunch dish, or part of dinner, surrounded by a variety of salads. The tart makes ideal picnic food. Make the tart ahead of time and serve at room temperature, or prepare the filling and pastry and assemble and bake one hour before serving.

If you're pressed for time you can always use a premade piecrust from the grocery store and put the filling together in about fifteen to twenty minutes.

THE PASTRY:
2 cups flour
Pinch salt
1½ sticks very cold butter, cut into small cubes
About ¼ cup ice water

THE FILLING:
1 tablespoon olive oil
2 cloves garlic, chopped
1½ pounds fresh spinach, stemmed, cleaned, and dried
Salt and freshly ground pepper
Ground nutmeg
8 ounces heavy cream
1 tablespoon fresh thyme, or 1½ teaspoons dried
3 eggs
½ cup plus 2 tablespoons freshly grated Parmesan cheese

To make the pastry, blend the flour and salt in a food processor. Add the butter and pulse about 15 times or until the butter is the size of large bread crumbs. With the motor running, add the water until the dough begins to pull away from the sides of the machine. It will still be crumbly. Add a tablespoon or two more water if needed. Wrap the dough in aluminum foil and form into a large ball. Refrigerate for 2 hours, or overnight.

Start making the filling by heating the oil in a large skillet over moderate heat. Add the garlic and sauté 10 seconds. Add the spinach and cook, stirring constantly, for about 5 minutes, or until the spinach is soft and tender. Season with salt, pepper, and a pinch of ground nutmeg. Remove from the heat and let cool. Using your hands, squeeze any excess liquid from the spinach. Chop the spinach and garlic coarsely and set aside.

Add the cream to the skillet you cooked the spinach in along with the thyme and a pinch of nutmeg. Place over moderate heat for about 7 minutes, or until simmering and somewhat thickened. The herbs will infuse the cream.

In a large bowl, whisk the eggs, the $\frac{1}{2}$ cup of cheese, salt, and pepper. Add the cream and whisk. Add the spinach and mix well. Sprinkle with the remaining 2 tablespoons cheese. The filling can be made several hours ahead of time. Refrigerate and cover until ready to use.

Preheat the oven to 400 degrees.

Remove the dough from the refrigerator. Working on a well-floured surface, roll the dough out to fit a 10-inch round or an 11-×-8-inch rectangular tart pan with a removable bottom. Trim the dough and freeze any remaining dough for another time.

Place the filling in the pastry and place the tart on a baking sheet. Bake on the middle shelf for 20 minutes. Reduce the temperature to 350 degrees and bake another 30 to 40 minutes, or until the tart has puffed up and a toothpick inserted in the center comes out clean. Remove and let cool a few minutes before cutting. Serve hot or at room temperature.

Makes 4 to 6 servings

You Can Also Add . . .

- Crumbled feta instead of the Parmesan cheese.
- White or red chard instead of the spinach.

Eggplant and Tomato Gratin

Although you can make this delicious dish year-round, it's superb toward the end of the summer when eggplant and tomatoes are fresh and plentiful in the garden and at local farmers' markets. The eggplant is prebaked and then sliced and layered with ripe tomatoes, fresh basil, and fresh mozzarella slices, dusted with Parmesan cheese, and baked until crisp and golden. The whole dish can be assembled several hours ahead of time and baked just before serving.

You can serve this as a main course with crusty bread and your favorite pasta mixed with olive oil and garlic (the juices from the gratin are delicious spooned over the pasta). It is also delicious served with mashed or roasted potatoes.

2 medium eggplant, ends trimmed, about 1 to 1½ pounds each
2 tablespoons olive oil
4 large, ripe tomatoes, about 1½ pounds, cut into 18 slices
1½ pounds fresh mozzarella, cut into 18 slices
18 fresh whole basil leaves
1 cup chopped ripe tomatoes
2 tablespoons fresh basil, finely chopped
Salt and freshly ground pepper
4 cloves garlic, minced
⅓ cup freshly grated Parmesan cheese
2 tablespoons good-quality dry bread crumbs

Preheat the oven to 400 degrees. Tightly wrap each eggplant in a large piece of aluminum foil. Bake on the middle shelf for 45 minutes to an hour, or until the eggplant is just soft when pierced with a small, sharp knife. It shouldn't be mushy, but cooked through. Let cool slightly and, using your hands or a small, sharp knife, peel off the skin. Cut each eggplant into 9 slices.

Grease the bottom of a large gratin dish or shallow casserole with ½ tablespoon of the oil. Place a slice of eggplant creating a row on one side of the dish. Lay on a slice of tomato, a slice of mozzarella, and a basil leaf. Repeat with 8 additional slices of eggplant, tomato, cheese, and basil, leaning the row up against the dish so it lies on the diagonal. Repeat with the remaining eggplant, tomatoes, mozzarella, and basil by creating a second row. Place the chopped tomato and basil in the middle. Sprinkle the entire dish with salt, pepper, and the chopped garlic. Sprinkle on the cheese and then the bread crumbs. Drizzle the entire dish with the remaining 1½ tablespoons olive oil. Cover and refrigerate until ready to bake.

Preheat the oven to 350 degrees. Bake for about 30 minutes, or until the cheese is melted, bubbling, and golden brown. Place under the broiler for 3 to 4 minutes for an even crisper golden brown.

Makes 4 to 6 servings

You Can Also Add . . .

- Anchovy fillets to the top of the eggplant. After you've prepared the eggplant rows, crisscross 10 to 12 anchovy fillets on top of the eggplant before sprinkling with cheese and bread crumbs.

Double-Dipped Chicken Parmesan

My friend Ronnie Maddelena is as passionate about food as I am. This recipe of hers is the real thing—the kind of chicken Parmesan you imagine being served by an Italian mama in a red-checkered apron. This dish—where the chicken is dipped in egg and then bread crumbs not once, but twice, and then baked in a homemade tomato sauce and sprinkled liberally with Parmigiano Reggiano—is guaranteed not to disappoint.

Serve with linguine tossed with olive oil, salt, and pepper, sautéed broccoli rabe (or escarole), and roasted balsamic portobello mushrooms. Accompany the meal with a robust Chianti and, as Ronnie says, "You are in business."

7 cups Simple Tomato Sauce with Herbs, (see page 218), or your favorite tomato sauce
2 pounds boneless skinless chicken breasts
4 eggs
Salt and freshly ground pepper
About 3 cups good-quality bread crumbs, seasoned or plain
¼ cup olive oil
½ cup freshly grated Parmigiano Reggiano cheese
⅓ cup minced fresh parsley, optional

Make the sauce and simmer until warm.

Divide each whole chicken breast in half.

Place the eggs in a bowl and whisk with salt and pepper. Place the bread crumbs on a large plate.

Dip the chicken in the egg and then dredge in the bread crumbs. Redip in the egg a second time and then dredge in the bread crumbs again.

In a large, heavy skillet, heat the olive oil over moderate heat. Brown the double-dipped chicken in the hot oil for 3 to 4 minutes on each side, or until golden brown. Remove the chicken and drain on paper towels. You can make the sauce and the chicken up to this point a day ahead of time. Wrap the chicken in foil and refrigerate. Place the sauce in a covered jar and refrigerate.

Preheat the oven to 350 degrees. Pour about 2 cups of the sauce in the bottom of a large gratin dish or large glass, ovenproof baking dish. Place the browned chicken breasts on top of the sauce and cover with half or all of the remaining sauce. (I like it with lots of sauce poured on top of the chicken. If you like a less saucy chicken, only add half.) Sprinkle with the cheese and bake on the middle shelf for 45 minutes, or until the sauce and cheese are bubbling. Serve hot, and sprinkle with parsley, if using.

Makes 4 to 6 servings

Sue's Meatballs and Spaghetti

Spaghetti and meatballs may not sound like traditional party food, but wait until you taste these extraordinary meatballs. My friend Sue Schardt grew up in Syracuse, New York, where she shared many meals with her neighbors and friends. She credits a small circle of women for inspiring these incredibly flavorful meatballs: Antoinette Mucci, Josephine Cotroneo, Rita Cua, Marisa D'Augustino, and Jeanette Reale. This recipe doesn't really belong to any one of these women; rather it's a synthesis of different tricks and ingredients they've each taught Sue and that she's adapted over the years. Try the meatballs on their own, or simmer them in a tomato sauce (see page 218), and serve on top of spaghetti or linguine. You will never think of meatballs in the same way.

THE MEATBALLS:
12 slices day-old French or Italian bread, cut into ½-inch slices
2 cups milk
1½ pounds ground beef, no leaner than 80%
¾ pound ground pork
5 cloves garlic, very thinly sliced
2 eggs
1 packed cup fresh basil, cut into very thin strips, or 2 tablespoons dried
½ cup parsley, very finely chopped
1½ to 2 cups freshly grated Romano or Parmesan cheese
1 tablespoon salt
Generous grinding of freshly ground pepper
1½ cup dry bread crumbs
About ¼ to ⅓ cup olive oil

THE SAUCE AND PASTA:
7 cups Simple Tomato Sauce with Herbs (see page 218)
2 pounds spaghetti or linguine
Freshly grated Romano or Parmesan cheese

Put the bread slices into a bowl and cover with 1 cup of the milk, so the bread is thoroughly soaked. Let sit for 3 to 5 minutes until the milk becomes absorbed into the bread.

Meanwhile, in a large bowl, mix the ground beef and pork with the garlic and knead it with your hands until it's well integrated. Add the eggs, the remaining 1 cup of milk, the basil and parsley. Mix well with your hands; the consistency will be loose. Mix in the cheese.

Pick up about 6 slices of the bread and squeeze out all the milk. Crumble it into the meat mixture, "kneading" all the ingredients together. Add salt and pepper and knead the mixture again. To test if the mixture is ready, form a small fist–size meatball and drop it on the counter. It should hold its shape. If the mixture doesn't hold together, add a few more bread slices and crumble it into the mixture until it holds together. Do the counter test again.

The mixture should give you between 20 and 24 small fist–sized meatballs. You can make the meatballs an hour or two ahead of time; cover and refrigerate until ready to cook.

Place the bread crumbs on a large plate or a flat bowl. Roll the meatballs in the bread crumbs, coating them on all sides.

Fill one or two large, deep skillets with half an inch of olive oil and place over moderate heat. When the oil is hot (drop a bread crumb into the oil; if the bread sizzles, the oil is hot enough), gently add the meatballs without crowding the pan. Brown them thoroughly, letting them cook about 15 minutes, turning them gently to make a nicely uniform "crust" on all sides. Remove one meatball and cut in half; there should be no sign of pinkness. Taste for seasoning and sprinkle with more salt and pepper if needed. Remove the finished meatballs to make room for new ones. The meatballs are best served hot, straight from the pan. If you want to make them ahead of time, keep them in the pan and reheat them on low for about 10 minutes or until hot.

Serve the meatballs plain or heat them in the tomato sauce. Remove all the oil from the skillet and add the tomato sauce. Add the browned meatballs and let simmer for 30 to 45 minutes, or until cooked through. The sauce can also be made several hours ahead of time and reheated over a gentle simmer. Serve on top of spaghetti or linguine and pass the cheese separately.

Makes 20 to 24 meatballs

Stuffed Turkish Peppers

When green bell peppers are stuffed with this aromatic mixture of basmati rice, fresh mint, cumin, cinnamon, pine nuts, and currants the results are worthy of any party. This vegetarian dish can be served as a main course or side dish. There are several steps involved in preparing these peppers, but they can be made a full day before serving. If you prepare them ahead of time, reheat them in the oven or on the stove and serve them hot, smothered in the hot tomato sauce they cook in. You can also cook the peppers a day ahead of time and serve them at room temperature. Cut the cooled peppers in half and drizzle with olive oil and lemon juice and garnish with sprigs of fresh mint. Fresh mint is vital to the flavor of this dish.

1½ cups basmati or short-grained white rice
3 cups water
Salt
1 teaspoon vegetable oil
6 medium-large bell peppers, green, red and/or yellow (a combination of colors is nice), or 8 small bell peppers
3 tablespoons olive oil
3 cloves garlic, minced
2 large onions, chopped
2 tablespoons fresh oregano, chopped, or 1 tablespoon dried
½ cup fresh mint, chopped
2 tablespoons fresh thyme, chopped, or 2 teaspoons dried
1½ teaspoons cumin
1½ teaspoons cinnamon
½ teaspoon turmeric
Freshly ground pepper
Hot pepper sauce
½ cup pine nuts
3 tablespoons chopped fresh chives
1 cup currants, golden raisins, or plain raisins
2 scallions, finely chopped, white and green parts
1 bay leaf

4 cups Simple Tomato Sauce with Herbs (see page 218) or good-quality bottled sauce
About 1 cup water

In a medium saucepan, mix the rice, water, salt, and vegetable oil and bring to a boil over high heat. Stir well, reduce the heat to low, cover, and cook for another 10 minutes, or until all the water has been absorbed and the rice is cooked through. Remove from the heat and let cool.

Meanwhile, cut about ⅛ inch off the top of the peppers. Remove and discard the ribs, core, and seeds. Finely chop the pepper slice you just cut and set aside. Make sure the pepper sits absolutely flat on a work surface; if it wobbles or falls over, carefully slice off the smallest possible amount from the bottom to make sure it sits evenly and flatly on the surface.

In a large skillet, heat 1½ tablespoons of the olive oil over low heat. Add the garlic and onions and sauté, stirring frequently, for 10 minutes, or until the mixture is golden brown. Add the chopped, reserved pepper and cook another 5 minutes. Stir in the oregano, half the mint, the thyme, cumin, cinnamon, turmeric, salt, pepper, and a dash of hot pepper sauce. Add the pine nuts and cook for 2 to 3 minutes, or until the mixture is fragrant.

Place the slightly cooled rice in a large bowl, making sure to separate the rice so it doesn't clump together. Add the onion/spice mixture to the rice and stir well. Stir in the remaining mint, the chives, currants, and scallions. Taste for seasoning; add salt, pepper, and hot sauce as needed. (The rice filling should be *very* flavorful, as the flavors will be incorporated as it cooks.)

Place the peppers in a large casserole or saucepan, making sure they sit on the bottom without wobbling or tipping over. Trim the bottom again if needed to make sure the peppers sit flat. Using a spoon or your hands, stuff each of the peppers, pressing down to get as much filling in each one as possible without making them burst. Place the bay leaf in the bottom of the pan and cover the peppers with the tomato sauce. Pour the water into the bottom of the pan. Cover and refrigerate until ready to cook.

Place the casserole over low heat and let the peppers cook for about 1½ hours, basting them every 15 minutes or so with the tomato sauce at the bottom of the pan. If the sauce seems to be drying out, lower the heat and add another ½ cup of water. The peppers are ready when they are tender to the touch and the filling is hot. If cooking ahead of time cover and refrigerate. Reheat over low flame until hot throughout. Remove bay leaf before serving. Serve hot or at room temperature (see headnote).

Makes 6 servings

Roast Duck with Thyme-Honey-Mango Sauce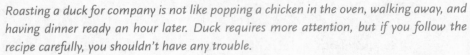

Roasting a duck for company is not like popping a chicken in the oven, walking away, and having dinner ready an hour later. Duck requires more attention, but if you follow the recipe carefully, you shouldn't have any trouble.

The duck is marinated in honey, thyme, fresh ginger, and unsweetened pineapple juice. It is then roasted until crisp on the outside and juicy and tender inside. The duck is finished with a simple sauce made in the pan using the marinade, stock, and slices of fresh mango. You can marinate the duck and prepare the stock several hours or a day ahead of time.

Duck is extremely rich, and a little bit goes a long way. Think about serving it with Roasted Potato Wedges (see page 153) or Roast Garlic Mashed Potatoes (see page 154), and Sautéed Baby Spinach with Garlic (see page 150) or the Leek Gratin (see page 216), and a green salad. A bottle of red wine should warm you up sufficiently.

THE DUCK AND THE MARINADE:
One 4- to 6-pound duck, totally thawed if frozen
1 cup good-quality honey
½ cup unsweetened pineapple juice
½ cup dry red wine
1 tablespoon soy sauce
2 tablespoons fresh thyme, chopped
1 tablespoon minced gingerroot
Freshly ground pepper

THE STOCK AND SAUCE:
Neck and heart from the duck
½ large carrot, chopped
1 rib celery, chopped
1 small onion, halved
1 bay leaf
4 peppercorns
Pinch salt
2 ripe mangoes, peeled and cut into thick slices

Using a fork, pierce the duck in several places over the breast and thighs. Place the duck in a medium roasting pan, large bowl, or a large resealable plastic bag. Cover with the honey, pineapple juice, wine, soy sauce, thyme, ginger, and pepper. Cover and refrigerate for at least 1 hour and up to 24 hours.

Make the stock by placing the neck and heart from the duck in a medium saucepan. Add the carrot, celery, onion, bay leaf, peppercorns, and salt and add about 4 cups water. Bring to a boil, reduce the heat, partially cover, and simmer about 1½ hours, or until reduced and flavorful. If you make the stock ahead of time, cover and refrigerate until ready to roast the duck.

Preheat the oven to 400 degrees. Remove the duck from the marinade and place the marinade in a small saucepan. Place the duck, breast side up, in a large roasting pan. Use a roasting rack if you have one, otherwise it's fine to place the duck directly in the pan. Pour 1 cup of water around the duck (this prevents the fat from burning while the duck is roasting) and pour about 2 to 3 tablespoons of the marinade on top of the duck. Roast for 15 minutes. Carefully flip the duck over, breast side down, and reduce the oven to 325 degrees. Roast another 45 minutes, basting the bottom of the bird with another few tablespoons of the marinade. Flip the duck over again, and, using a baster or a spoon, remove all the fat from the bottom of the pan. Baste the duck with the marinade and continue roasting another 20 to 30 minutes. If the juices appear to be burning in the bottom of the pan, add another ⅓ cup water. The duck should roast for a total of about 1½ hours; it's done when the juices run clear yellow and not pink when an inner thigh is pierced.

Remove the duck from the oven and pour any juices from the duck's cavity into the remaining marinade. Place the duck on a carving board and cover loosely with aluminum foil for about 10 minutes.

Remove all the fat or pieces of burned fat from the bottom of the roasting pan. Strain 1 cup of the reduced stock into the pan. Whisk in any of the reserved marinade and bring to a boil over high heat. Add the mango slices, reduce the heat, and simmer 10 minutes. Carve the duck and serve with the mango slices and sauce drizzled on top.

Makes 4 servings

A Provençal-style stew rich with garlic, fresh herbs, buttery leeks, and tart olives. Like most stews this one can be made a day ahead of time and reheated over a low flame. Serve with egg noodles, Roast Garlic Mashed Potatoes (see page 154), or risotto (see page 106), and crusty bread for sopping up the juices.

1 to 2 tablespoons olive or vegetable oil

3 leeks, ends trimmed, with white and 1 inch of green part sliced lengthwise and then cut into 1-inch pieces

3 large carrots, halved lengthwise and cut into 2-inch pieces

3 cloves garlic, minced

2 tablespoons thyme, or 2 teaspoons dried

1 cup fresh parsley, minced

1 cup flour

Salt and freshly ground pepper

2 cups boneless or bone-in veal stew meat, cut into about 1-inch chunks

3 cloves whole garlic

1 tablespoon fresh rosemary, chopped, or 1 teaspoon dried

1 cup dry red wine

1½ cups chicken broth, homemade or canned

½ teaspoon tomato paste

1 bay leaf

½ to 1 cup pitted black or green olives (good French olives), halved if large

In a large casserole or saucepan, heat half the oil over moderate heat. Add the leeks and sauté for 5 minutes, stirring frequently to prevent browning. Add the carrots, 3 cloves minced garlic, half the thyme, and half the parsley and sauté 5 minutes, stirring frequently. Transfer the vegetable to a plate or the lid of the pan and set aside.

Place the flour, salt, pepper, and remaining thyme on a plate or in a plastic bag. Dredge the meat in the seasoned flour, coating each side well.

Raise the heat to high and add the remaining oil to the casserole or saucepan. Brown the meat on both sides, working in

batches if necessary. Add the reserved sautéed vegetables, the whole cloves of garlic, rosemary, and the red wine. Reduce the heat to a low simmer and add the chicken broth, tomato paste, bay leaf, salt, and pepper. Cover the pot and let simmer for 1 hour. Add the olives and remaining parsley and let simmer 5 minutes, uncovered. Remove from heat and let sit 5 minutes before serving. Taste for seasoning, and adjust as needed.

Makes 4 servings

Lamb Stew with Ginger

Soothing and hearty, this main-course stew should be made one or two days ahead of time, if possible. Serve with crusty bread, Roasted Potato Wedges (see page 153), Roast Garlic Mashed Potatoes (see page 154), or White Rice with Scallions and Sesame (see page 158), Leek Gratin (see page 216), and Grated Carrot and Sun-Dried Cranberry Salad (see page 87).

1 cup plus 1 tablespoon flour
Salt and freshly ground pepper
2½ pounds lamb stewing meat, cubed
2 tablespoons vegetable oil
5 cloves garlic, minced
2 tablespoons chopped gingerroot
2 large onions, sliced
3 leeks, sliced lengthwise and then into 2-inch pieces
5 carrots, cut into 1-inch pieces
2 tablespoons rosemary, or 2 teaspoons dried
1 tablespoon thyme, or 1 teaspoon dried
1 tablespoon tomato paste
1 cup dry red wine
2 cups chicken broth, homemade or low-sodium canned
1 tablespoon soy sauce or tamari
1 bay leaf

Place the 1 cup of flour on a large plate and add a generous amount of salt and pepper. Dredge the meat on all sides, coating well.

In a large casserole, heat 1 tablespoon of the oil over moderate heat. Add half the coated meat, along with a handful of garlic and ginger. Brown the meat on all sides. Drain with a slotted spoon and transfer the meat to a plate. Repeat with the remaining oil and meat.

Remove all but 1 teaspoon of the oil in the pan using a paper towel or spoon. Heat the remaining oil over low heat and add the onions and leeks, and sauté, stirring frequently, for 5 minutes. Add the carrots, half the remaining garlic and ginger, the rosemary and thyme, and cook another 2 minutes, stirring. Add the 1 tablespoon of flour and stir well to coat all the vegetables. Add the tomato paste and cook for 1 minute. Raise the heat to moderately high and add the wine. Simmer and add the chicken broth, remaining garlic and ginger, soy sauce, a grinding of pepper, and the bay leaf. Add the browned meat and bring to a boil.

Preheat the oven to 350 degrees. Remove the casserole from the heat, cover, and place on the middle shelf of the oven. Cook for 1½ to 2 hours, or until the meat is tender and almost falling off the bone. Taste for seasoning. Before serving, warm the stew over low heat, or in a 300 degree oven until simmering.

Makes 4 servings

Braised Lamb Shanks with Five Onions

Lamb shanks are a relatively unknown cut of meat, which is a real mystery considering their low cost, buttery texture, and rich, full flavor. The shanks are browned and then simmered with leeks, onions, shallots, garlic, and scallions until they just about fall off the bone. Try to braise the shanks several hours before serving, or preferably a day ahead of time.

Serve the rich, meaty shanks with Roast Garlic Mashed Potatoes (see page 154) or Layered Sweet and White Potatoes with Maple-Sage Cream (see page 209), Eggplant and Tomato Gratin (see page 186) or Leek Gratin (see page 216), and Roasted Pear and Mixed Green Salad (see page 86).

1 cup flour
Salt and freshly ground pepper
3 tablespoons fresh rosemary, finely chopped, or 2 teaspoons dried
3 tablespoons fresh thyme, finely chopped, or 2 teaspoons dried
1 tablespoon vegetable oil
2 tablespoons olive oil
6 lamb shanks, about 8 pounds
4 cloves garlic, finely chopped
5 leeks, cut lengthwise and into 2-inch pieces
1 large onion, quartered
6 shallots, peeled and left whole, halved if large
6 scallions, cut into 2-inch long pieces, white and green parts
12 cloves garlic, peeled and left whole
1 tablespoon tomato paste
3 cups good-quality dry red wine
2 cups beef or chicken broth
1 Turkish bay leaf
1 cup fresh parsley, finely chopped

Preheat the oven to 300 degrees.

On a large plate or in a plastic bag, mix the flour, salt, pepper, and 1 tablespoon of the rosemary and thyme. Dredge the lamb in the seasoned flour, making sure it is coated on all sides.

In a large casserole, heat half the vegetable oil and $\frac{1}{2}$ tablespoon of the olive oil over moderately high heat. Brown half the lamb shanks on all sides, about 6 minutes. Remove and set aside. Brown the remaining shanks with the remaining vegetable oil and another $\frac{1}{2}$ tablespoon olive oil if needed; set aside. Use a paper towel and remove all the fat from the bottom of the pan.

Heat the casserole over moderately low heat and add the remaining tablespoon of the olive oil. Add the chopped garlic and cook 1 minute, stirring frequently. Add the leeks, onion, shallots, and scallions and cook 3 minutes, stirring frequently. Add the whole garlic cloves, remaining rosemary and thyme, and the tomato paste and stir well to coat the onion mixture. Add the wine and bring to a boil. Add the broth, bay leaf, and the lamb, making sure the meat is covered with the liquid. Spoon some of the onion mixture on top of the meat.

Let the lamb cook on the middle shelf of the oven for 2 to $2\frac{1}{2}$ hours, or until the lamb is very tender and just about falling off the bone. Spoon off any fat that is sitting on the surface of the stew. Taste for seasoning; remove the bay leaf. Remove any fat that has hardened on top of the stew. Bring to room temperature and then refrigerate. To reheat, place in 300 degree oven or place over moderately low heat until hot and the sauce is bubbling, about 15 minutes.

Sprinkle the stew with the parsley and serve bubbling hot.

Makes 6 servings

Marinated Grilled Butterfly of Lamb

Ideal for a picnic or barbecue, this lamb is so full of flavor that you don't need much to serve with it. Try warm pita bread, a variety of fresh salads, and the Yogurt "Cheese" with Mint, Scallions, and Cucumber (see page 64).

Be sure to marinate the lamb for at least two hours, or preferably overnight and up to forty-eight hours. The longer it marinates the more the flavors will permeate and tenderize the meat. Fresh mint, rosemary, and ginger really make a difference in this dish.

1 butterflied leg of lamb, about 6 pounds*
1 cup dry red wine
¼ cup low-sodium soy sauce or tamari
2 tablespoons olive oil
1 cup fresh mint, coarsely chopped
3 cloves garlic, chopped
2 tablespoons fresh rosemary, chopped, or 1 teaspoon dried
1 tablespoon chopped gingerroot, or 1 teaspoon ground ginger
2 scallions, white and green parts, chopped
2 tablespoons fresh mint leaves, chopped
1 cup fresh mint leaves for garnish

Place the lamb in a large, nonreactive bowl (ceramic or stainless steel) or use a resealable plastic bag. Add all the remaining marinade ingredients and stir well to make sure the meat is thoroughly coated on both sides. Cover with plastic wrap and let marinate, flipping the meat over once or twice during the marinade time.

Preheat a charcoal or gas grill, or an oven broiler. Remove the meat from the marinade, letting all the juices run off. Place the marinade in a small saucepan and simmer over moderate heat for about 20 minutes, or until reduced and flavorful. Place the meat on the hot grill, cover, and cook for about 5 minutes. (If using a broiler, place in a shallow broiler pan and cook the meat about 2 inches from the heat.) Flip the meat over and grill another 5 minutes. Place the meat away from the direct flame and continue cooking for 10 to 15 minutes, or until it is pink, but not raw. You can cook it

*Ask your butcher to butterfly, or remove the bone from, a leg of lamb. Keep the bone for making soups and stocks.

longer if you like your lamb well-done. Remove from the heat and let sit for 5 to 10 minutes before carving the meat on the diagonal.

Serve the lamb with a few tablespoons of the reduced marinade juices drizzled on top and serve the remaining marinade on the side. Garnish with the fresh mint leaves.

Makes 8 servings

Sautéed Sea Scallops with Shallots and Vermouth ☕ ☕

I often find that scallops cooked in restaurants are overcooked, so I prefer to cook them myself at home. Scallops need only about two minutes of cooking on each side, until they are just cooked through. Because scallops are so naturally sweet and meaty they don't need a lot of strong flavors. In this dish the scallops are lightly dredged in a seasoned flour, then sautéed in a very hot pan with fresh garlic, shallots, thyme, and parsley. Then an instant sauce is created by deglazing the pan with dry vermouth and lemon juice. Serve with crusty bread, pasta, risotto, polenta, or as a first course.

1½ pounds very fresh sea scallops*
1 cup flour
Salt and freshly ground pepper
2 to 2½ tablespoons olive oil
2 shallots, very finely chopped
4 cloves garlic, finely chopped
2 tablespoons fresh thyme, chopped
½ cup fresh parsley, finely chopped
½ teaspoon paprika
⅓ cup dry vermouth
Juice of 1 lemon, about 3 tablespoons
1 lemon, cut into wedges or thin slices, for garnish

Pat the scallops dry using paper towels or a tea towel.

On a large plate or in a plastic bag, mix the flour with a *generous* dash of salt and pepper. Add the scallops and dredge on both sides. Remove the scallops from the flour, making sure there aren't any clumps of flour clinging on.

In a large, heavy-bottomed skillet, heat 1 tablespoon of the oil over a moderately low heat. Add the shallots and half the garlic and cook, stirring constantly, for about 5 minutes, or until golden brown and quite soft. Remove the shallot mixture to a plate and set aside.

*Be sure to buy your scallops from a reputable fish market. Unfortunately, some fishermen and fish shops are selling fake scallops by stamping out perfect, scallop-size rounds from skate or ray wings. Look for the real thing by finding scallops that are irregular sizes and range in color from a pale ivory to a coral pink. Avoid frozen scallops; if the scallops are sitting in a milky white liquid it's a sign that they've been frozen.

If you sauté the shallots and garlic and prepare all the other ingredients ahead of time, the final dish can be put together in about 10 minutes.

Raise the heat to high and add 1 tablespoon of the oil to the pan. When the oil is hot, but not smoking, add the scallops. Sprinkle with 1 tablespoon of the thyme, 1 tablespoon of parsley, the remaining garlic, and half the paprika. Cook 2 minutes. Using tongs (you want to be very careful not to pierce the delicate scallops) flip the scallops over. If the pan appears dry, add another teaspoon of oil. Sprinkle the scallops with the reserved shallot mixture, the remaining tablespoon thyme, 1 tablespoon parsley, and the remaining paprika. Cook 2 minutes. Add the vermouth and lemon juice to the hot pan and let it simmer for 1 minute. Remove the scallops to a serving plate. Cook the sauce in the pan another minute, scraping up any bits clinging to the bottom of the pan. Pour the sauce over the scallops, sprinkle with the remaining parsley and the lemon wedges, and serve immediately.

Makes 4 servings

Roast Salmon on Garlic Spinach
with Cherry Tomatoes and Mushrooms

Some dishes are meant to be admired with the eye before being devoured, and this is one of them. A bright orange fillet of fresh salmon is placed on a bed of sautéed spinach (heavily laced with garlic) and surrounded with red and yellow cherry tomatoes and slices of cremini mushrooms. The dish is sprinkled with fresh chives and popped into the oven to roast. The result: perfect party food. Bright, colorful, fresh flavors—not to mention an entire dish in one pan. Serve with orzo, Roasted Potato Wedges (see page 153), or linguine.

1 tablespoon olive oil, plus 1½ teaspoons

3 cloves garlic, thinly sliced

2 pounds spinach, preferably baby spinach, well cleaned, or regular spinach, stemmed

Salt and freshly ground pepper

One 2-pound fillet of fresh salmon

2½ tablespoons fresh chives, minced

1 cup red cherry tomatoes

1 cup yellow pear mini cherry tomatoes (if you can't find them, double up on the regular red cherry tomatoes)

1½ cups cremini mushrooms, quartered (you can also substitute shiitake or portobello mushrooms)

1 tablespoon soy sauce or low-sodium soy sauce

1 lemon, cut into wedges

In a large ovenproof skillet or a large gratin dish or shallow casserole, heat 1 tablespoon of the oil over moderate heat. Add 2 cloves of the sliced garlic and sauté about 20 seconds. Add the spinach, salt, and pepper and cook, stirring frequently, for about 5 minutes or until the spinach is *just* wilted and *just* cooked. Remove from the heat; remove any excess liquid from the spinach by blotting it up with a paper towel. Place the salmon fillet on top of the spinach, skin side down. Press the remaining slices of garlic into the salmon flesh. Sprinkle the salmon with pepper and half the chives. Surround the fish with the two types of tomatoes and the mushrooms, alternating a red tomato with a yellow tomato and

then a mushroom wedge. Drizzle the soy sauce over the vegetables and then sprinkle them with the remaining chives, salt, and pepper. Drizzle the remaining 1½ teaspoons of olive oil over the fish. The dish can be made several hours ahead of time up to this point; cover and refrigerate until ready to cook.

Preheat the oven to 400 degrees.

Place the fish on the middle shelf of the oven and roast for 15 to 20 minutes, depending on the thickness of the salmon, or until the fish is cooked through and the vegetables are tender. Surround with lemon wedges.

Makes 4 servings

Roast Swordfish with Horseradish-Thyme Sauce

A thick slab of fresh swordfish is one of the great treats from the sea. This recipe always sounds odd when I first describe it, but once you taste it you'll understand the appeal. The swordfish is "marinated" in milk and/or cream and then a very simple horseradish-thyme sauce is place on top. The fish is then roasted until tender and finally placed under the broiler for just a minute. The milk acts as a kind of tenderizer for the fish and creates a delicious, creamy sauce. Serve with Roast Garlic Mashed Potatoes (see page 154), Roasted Potato Wedges (see page 153), or Rice Pilaf (see page 155). The Stuffed Tomatoes Provençal (see page 214) or Sweet Onions with Roasted Chile and Feta Stuffing (see page 210) would also be delicious.

One 2-pound swordfish steak
1 cup milk, or ½ cup milk and ½ cup heavy cream
Freshly ground pepper
2 tablespoons butter
1 tablespoon fresh thyme, chopped, or 1 teaspoon dried
1 tablespoon horseradish
1 lemon, cut into wedges

Preheat the oven to 400 degrees. Place the swordfish in a large roasting or broiler pan and pour the milk and cream (if using) on top. Add a grinding of pepper to the fish. Marinate for at least 15 minutes, or up to several hours. Cover and refrigerate.

In a small saucepan, melt the butter over moderate heat. Add the thyme and horseradish and stir to create a smooth sauce. Spoon evenly over the fish.

Bake the swordfish on the middle shelf for 12 to 15 minutes, depending on the thickness of the fish. Test by gently inserting a small, sharp knife or fork into the center. The knife should go in easily, with little resistance. Place the fish under the broiler for 1 to 2 minutes, or until the milk is bubbling and turning golden brown and the fish is completely cooked. Serve hot, surrounded by lemon wedges.

Makes 4 servings

Layered Sweet and White Potatoes with Maple-Sage Cream ☕ ☕

This is my version of an outrageous sweet potato and maple syrup dish I tasted at Arrows restaurant in Ogunquit, Maine. Chefs Mark Gaier and Clark Fraser had a special New England Wild Game Dinner late one fall. I decided to try a simple version combining sweet potatoes, white potatoes, fresh sage, maple syrup, and cream. This dish would be ideal for a Thanksgiving feast, or served with roasted foods, or when you simply crave hearty comfort food for the soul.

3 tablespoons butter, cut into cubes, plus 1 teaspoon butter
5 medium white potatoes, peeled and thinly sliced
Salt and freshly ground pepper
3 tablespoons maple syrup
3 large sweet potatoes or yams, peeled and thinly sliced
1½ tablespoons chopped fresh sage
½ to 1 cup heavy cream, depending on how creamy you want the dish

Grease the bottom of a 9 x 13-inch baking dish, either metal, Pyrex, or pottery, with the 1 teaspoon butter. Add half the white potatoes, to create a layer along the bottom, overlapping the potatoes slightly. Sprinkle with 1 tablespoon of the butter cubes and sprinkle liberally with salt and pepper. Drizzle with 1 tablespoon of the maple syrup. Top with half the sweet potatoes, overlapping slightly. Top with 1 tablespoon butter cubes, salt, pepper, half the sage, 1 tablespoon syrup, and half the cream. Place the top layer of potatoes by alternating the remaining white and sweet potatoes, overlapping the slices slightly. Scatter the top with the remaining tablespoon of butter, salt, pepper, sage, maple syrup, and cream. The dish can be covered and refrigerated for up to 24 hours before baking.

Preheat the oven to 400 degrees. Bake on the middle shelf, loosely covered with aluminum foil, for 30 minutes. Reduce the heat to 350 degrees, remove the foil, and bake another 30 to 35 minutes, or until the potatoes are tender and the cream and maple syrup have caramelized the top of the potatoes.

Makes 8 servings

Sweet Onions with Roasted Chile and Feta Stuffing ☕ ☕ ☕

I had a bushel of beautiful sweet onions from my garden one year and decided to try stuffing them. Roasted jalapeños, bread crumbs, and creamy feta cheese combined to make an incredibly flavorful counterpoint to the mild onions. Try serving these with roasted or grilled meats, lamb, or chicken, or simply accompanying them with a big vegetable salad and good bread.

Although there are several steps involved in making these onions, you can prepare the whole dish a day ahead of time and simply heat the dish in the oven forty minutes before serving.

4 jalapeños or other fresh chile peppers
2½ tablespoons olive oil
4 medium sweet onions
1 teaspoon butter
½ cup fresh parsley, finely chopped
¼ cup heavy cream
Salt and freshly ground pepper
½ cup plus 4 teaspoons feta, crumbled
½ cup fresh bread crumbs
¾ cup vegetable or chicken stock

Preheat the oven to 500 degrees. Place the chiles on a baking sheet, making a small slit in the side of each pepper, to prevent it from exploding. Roast 10 minutes, or until blackened on all sides. Remove the chiles and reduce the oven to 400 degrees. Wrap the peppers in aluminum foil for a few minutes, then peel and remove the seeds, being careful not to touch your eyes. Puree the pepper in a food processor with 1½ tablespoons of the oil and set aside.

In pairs, wrap the onions in foil and bake for 45 minutes. Remove from the oven and let cool slightly. When the onions are cool enough to handle, strip off their skins. Carefully slice off the root end at the base. Slice off the stem end about ¼ of the way down the onion. Scoop out the interior of the onion, using a melon baller or a small, sharp knife. Reserve the insides of the onion. You want 4 hollow onion shells with sides about ¼ inch thick and the bottoms intact.

Finely chop the reserved onion and measure out ¾ cup. In a medium skillet, heat

the remaining tablespoon of oil and the butter over moderate heat. Add the onion and cook 5 minutes, stirring frequently. Add 1 to 1½ teaspoons of the pureed chile pepper, the parsley, and cream and cook another 2 minutes. Remove from the heat and cool slightly, about 2 minutes. Season with salt and pepper, add ½ cup of the feta and the bread crumbs. Taste for spiciness. You want the stuffing to have a bite; stir in more pepper puree if needed.

Divide the stuffing among the 4 onions, pressing down to pack the onion shells and doming the stuffing on top. Place the stuffed onions in a shallow casserole or medium gratin dish and pour the stock around the onions. Cover and refrigerate until ready to bake.

Place the onions in a preheated 400 degree oven. Bake for 30 minutes, basting the onions once or twice. Sprinkle 1 teaspoon of the remaining feta on top of each onion, baste, and bake another 10 minutes, or until the cheese is melted and bubbling.

Makes 4 servings

The Morning After

Having weekend guests is a mixed blessing. It's wonderful to share a whole weekend with friends or family. You can have a full day together, cook and eat a big meal, blow out the candles and know you can keep talking and catching up the next morning. But cleaning up from Saturday night's dinner can leave you exhausted, and the last thing you want to think about is getting ready for Sunday morning's breakfast. And what about lunch?

When friends stay overnight I always try to shop for a few simple but special foods to have on hand for breakfast. For me, the best breakfasts are made up of a table full of seasonal foods. You can put together the breakfast listed below in about ten minutes, with almost no cooking involved.

- Plain, low-fat yogurt (served plain or mixed with honey and chopped nuts)
- Granola, or an assortment of healthful cereals
- Fresh seasonal fruits (in the summer, ripe peaches, nectarines, and an assortment of fresh berries; in the fall and winter, fresh figs, melon, apples, bananas, and pears)
- Bagels, croissants, muffins, warm French bread for toast
- An assortment of jellies and marmalades
- Cream cheese (plain or mix your favorite brand of cream cheese with chopped olives, or chopped chives, or chopped sun-dried tomatoes, or chopped nuts and raisins—serve a selection of several)

- Platter of assorted cheeses
- Assorted olives
- Capers (great for sprinkling on bagels)
- Smoked salmon or smoked fish
- A platter of tomatoes, thinly sliced cucumbers, and red or sweet Vidalia onions
- A plate of dried apricots, figs, currants, and raisins (for sprinkling into cereals, on toast or bagels, or to serve with cheese)
- And, of course, fresh OJ, good, strong coffee with a pitcher of steamed or warm milk, hot tea with lemon slices and honey, cold or hot cider, or hot cocoa, depending on the weather.

Stuffed Tomatoes Provençal

Garden-ripe tomatoes are stuffed with olive puree, sautéed onion, and garlic and Provençal herbs. Serve with any roasted or grilled foods, or as an accompaniment to seafood. A really interesting and unusual vegetarian treat is serving an entire meal of stuffed vegetables hot from the oven or at room temperature. Try these tomatoes with the Stuffed Turkish Peppers (see page 192) and the Sweet Onions with Roasted Chile and Feta Stuffing (see page 210). Serve with good crusty bread and a salad.

You can stuff the tomatoes ahead of time and heat them in the oven fifteen minutes before you're ready to eat.

4 medium ripe tomatoes
1 tablespoon olive oil
1 medium onion, finely chopped
2 cloves garlic, minced
¼ cup parsley, chopped
¼ cup fresh basil, cut into thin strips
1 tablespoon fresh thyme, chopped
3 tablespoons olive puree*
Salt and freshly ground pepper
¼ cup fresh bread crumbs
4 teaspoons basil-flavored olive oil or olive oil
Fresh basil leaves for garnish

*Olive puree, or tapenade, is available at specialty food shops. You can also puree good-quality pitted black olives with a touch of good olive oil as a substitute.

Stem the tomatoes and cut them in half widthwise. Use a small knife or a spoon to remove about 2 tablespoons of pulp from each half. Chop the pulp finely and reserve. Place the tomatoes in a shallow roasting pan.

Pour the olive oil into a medium skillet over moderate heat. Add the onion and garlic and cook, stirring, for 3 minutes. Add the reserved tomato pulp, half the parsley and basil strips, and the thyme and cook another 3 minutes. Add $1\frac{1}{2}$ tablespoons of the olive puree, stir well, and remove from the heat. Add the remaining parsley and basil strips and season with salt and pepper.

Using a spoon or a pastry brush, spread $\frac{1}{2}$ teaspoon olive puree in the bottom of each tomato. Divide the stuffing among the 8 tomato halves and top each with $\frac{1}{2}$ teaspoon bread crumbs. Cover and refrigerate until ready to bake.

Preheat the oven to 400 degrees. Drizzle each of the tomatoes with $\frac{1}{2}$ teaspoon basil oil. Bake for 15 minutes and serve hot or at room temperature with a garnish of basil leaves.

Makes 4 servings

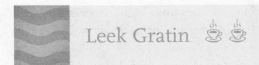
The trick to preparing leeks—with their sweet onion flavor and their ability to intensify other flavors mixed in with them—is to properly clean them. Leeks have multiple layers in which dirt can hide—and hide it does! To clean a leek, cut off the root end. Remove the tough green ends, at least one inch from the top, or more if they appear particularly tough or dried out. Then cut the leek down the middle lengthwise and clean under cold running water, separating the layers to reveal the dirt hiding inside. The leek can then be cooked whole or cut into smaller pieces.

Serve this rich, comforting gratin with roast chicken, meat, or grilled fish, or accompanied by crusty bread and a crisp salad. A full, fruity red wine would be an ideal complement.

1 tablespoon olive oil
2 cloves garlic, minced
1 medium-large onion, very thinly sliced
4 medium leeks, cleaned as described above, and cut into 1- to 1½-inch pieces
1 tablespoon fresh thyme, chopped, or 1 teaspoon dried
2 tablespoons fresh basil, cut into thin strips
Salt and freshly ground pepper
About ⅓ cup heavy cream
About ⅓ cup freshly grated Parmesan cheese

Bring a large pot of water to boil. Preheat oven to 350 degrees.

In an ovenproof skillet or gratin dish, heat the oil over moderate heat. Add the garlic and onion and sauté, stirring frequently, for about 8 minutes, or until turning golden brown.

Meanwhile blanch the leeks by placing them in the boiling water for about 30 seconds; remove with a slotted spoon. Run under cold water to stop the cooking and refresh the color; drain well. Add the blanched leeks to the skillet with the onion, the thyme, basil, salt, and pepper and cook about 2 minutes, stirring frequently. Add the cream and cover with aluminum foil or a lid and place in the oven. Bake for 30 minutes, or until the leeks are tender and the cream is thickened. Remove the foil and sprinkle with the cheese; bake another 5 minutes. Place the dish under the broiler for 1 to 2 minutes, or until the cheese is melted and bubbling.

Makes 4 servings

You Can Also Add . . .

- 2 large bulbs fennel, cored and sliced about ½ inch thick, instead of the leeks.
- Crème fraîche instead of heavy cream.

Simple Tomato Sauce with Herbs

This is a simple, fresh-tasting tomato sauce that's ideal for tossing with your favorite pasta, or to use with Sue's Meatballs and Spaghetti (see page 190), Double-Dipped Chicken Parmesan (see page 188), Stuffed Turkish Peppers (see page 192), or any dish that requires an exceedingly fresh tasting yet straightforward tomato sauce. The sauce can be made several days ahead of time and placed in a jar and refrigerated until ready to use. It can also be frozen in plastic freezer bags or an airtight container for up to two months.

3 tablespoons olive oil
4 cloves garlic, coarsely chopped
2 to 3 tablespoons chopped fresh thyme, or 2 teaspoons dried
½ to 1 teaspoon crushed red pepper flakes
Two 28-ounce cans good-quality Italian-style whole tomatoes
Salt and freshly ground pepper

In a large skillet, heat the oil on moderate. Add the garlic and cook for about 3 minutes, or until lightly browned. Do not let the garlic burn. Add the thyme and red pepper and cook 1 minute. Add the tomatoes, mashing them using your hands or a fork. Season with salt and pepper and reduce the heat to low. Simmer, uncovered, stirring frequently, for about 30 minutes. Taste for seasoning.

Makes about 7 cups

You Can Also Add . . .

- 1 tablespoon chopped fresh rosemary, basil, or oregano, or 1 teaspoon crushed dried.
- ⅓ cup chopped fresh parsley for the final 5 minutes of simmering.
- 1 bay leaf with the tomatoes and remove before serving.
- Pinch sugar if the tomatoes taste at all bitter.

7
Desserts

Nutty, Fruity, Chocolatey, and Altogether Satisfying

Kipferln (Nut Delights)

Almond Crisps with Amaretto-Glazed Almonds

Poached Pears with Caramelized Raspberry Sauce

Honeyed Bananas

Rhubarb Crumble

Shortcakes with Strawberry-Rhubarb Sauce

Plum and Nectarine Tartlets

Pineapple Upside-Down Cake

Lemon Tart

Lemon Poppy Seed Cake

Eve's Lemon Cheesecake

Pavlova

Apple Crostada

Pound Cake with Peach, Honey,
     and Rum Sauce

Panna Cotta

Kipferln (Nut Delights)

A variation on an old Austrian cookie, these nutty cookies are delicious when rolled in powdered sugar. You can make them with pecans, almonds, or walnuts, in a ball or crescent shape. This is a favorite cookie around Hanukkah.

1 cup butter, at room temperature
¼ cup brown sugar
Pinch salt
1 cup pecans, almonds, or walnuts, finely chopped
1 teaspoon vanilla extract or ½ teaspoon vanilla extract and ½ teaspoon
    almond extract
2 cups sifted flour
Confectioners' sugar

In a mixer, cream the butter and brown sugar until fluffy. Add the salt, chopped nuts, and vanilla extract and mix well. Add the sifted flour on top and thoroughly mix; the dough will still be crumbly. Place the dough on a sheet of aluminum foil or wax paper and form into a ball. Refrigerate for 1 hour.

Preheat the oven to 350 degrees.

Remove the dough from the refrigerator and let it come to room temperature. Using about 1 teaspoon of dough at a time, shape into balls. Place the balls on ungreased cookie sheets. Alternatively, use your hands to roll about a teaspoon of dough into a snake shape and then shape into a crescent. Bake about 15 minutes, or until golden brown.

Place the confectioners' sugar on a large plate. While still warm, roll the cookies in the confectioners' sugar. Let cool and roll again in the sugar; shake off excess.

Makes about 6 dozen cookies

Almond Crisps with Amaretto-Glazed Almonds

These thin, buttery cookies are delicious served with a fresh, seasonal fruit salad or fruit platter. They will keep for several weeks in an airtight container. The recipe doubles easily.

GLAZED ALMONDS:
1½ teaspoons unsalted butter
¾ cup slivered almonds (about 3 ounces)
1½ tablespoons Amaretto liqueur (or ½ teaspoon almond extract)

DOUGH:
1 cup flour
Pinch salt
1 stick butter, at room temperature
½ cup sugar
1 egg, at room temperature
2 teaspoons Amaretto liqueur or ½ teaspoon almond extract
Sugar
Confectioners' sugar, optional

To glaze the almonds, melt the butter in a small skillet over medium heat. Add the almonds and Amaretto and stir until the nuts are golden brown, about 5 minutes. Cool and drain on paper towels.

Preheat the oven to 350 degrees and lightly grease 2 large baking sheets.

Sift the flour with the salt into a small bowl. Using an electric mixer, the cream butter with the ½ cup sugar in large bowl until light and fluffy. Blend in the egg and Amaretto. Add the flour and mix until the dough binds; the dough will be sticky.

Divide the dough into 30 pieces. Using your hands roll each piece into a ball, dusting your hands with flour if needed. Set the balls on baking sheets, spacing about 2 inches apart.

Fill a small bowl with water. Mound the sugar on a plate. Dip the bottom of a 2½-inch round glass into the water and then into the sugar. Press the glass down onto one dough ball, flattening it out into a 2½- to 3-inch round. Repeat with the remaining dough. Sprinkle the rounds lightly with sugar.

Gently press several glazed almonds in a flower pattern into each round. Bake until the edges of the cookies are golden brown, 8 to 10 minutes. Cool on a rack. Just before serving, dust the cookies with confectioners' sugar, if using.

Makes about 30 cookies

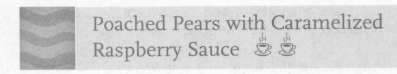

Poached Pears with Caramelized Raspberry Sauce

A festive, cooling dessert (ideal after a big meal) that can be made with white or red wine (or champagne if you have a bottle open from a previous celebration) or with plain water. Any way it's a beautiful dish, with a syrupy, caramelized raspberry sauce surrounding the delicately poached pears.

You can make the pears and sauce a day, or several hours, ahead of time in order to give it time to chill properly.

8 large, firm-ripe Bosc or Bartlett pears, peeled, cored and left whole with the stem
1 cup sugar
1½ cups water, red or white wine, or champagne
½ vanilla bean, split down the middle, or ½ teaspoon vanilla extract
1 cinnamon stick
1½ cups fresh raspberries

If the pears don't stand you may need to remove a thin slice from the bottom of the fruit so that it sits flat.

In a saucepan large enough to hold all the pears, mix the sugar, water, vanilla bean, and cinnamon stick. Bring to a boil over high heat. Reduce the heat to low and add the pears, standing up. Sprinkle ½ cup of the berries into the hot syrup.

Cover the pot and simmer for 20 to 25 minutes, gently turning the pears once or twice to make sure they are well coated with the sugar syrup. The pears are done when they feel tender throughout; gently test the pears with a small, sharp knife. Remove the pears with a slotted spoon and place in a large serving bowl or deep plate (you'll be adding the juices).

Taste the syrup (careful, it's still hot!); if it tastes sweet and concentrated, strain it over the pears. If the syrup tastes weak, simmer over low heat for another 5 to 15 minutes, until reduced and sweetened. Strain over the pears. Cool in the refrigerator for at least 2 hours, or overnight. Just before serving, sprinkle with the remaining cup of berries.

Makes 8 servings

Honeyed Bananas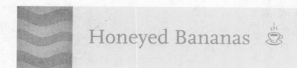

A dessert to make in a flash—all you need to have on hand is a banana or two, honey, and maybe a splash of rum.

1 tablespoon butter
½ tablespoon gingerroot, grated, or ½ teaspoon dried powdered ginger, optional
2 bananas, split lengthwise
2 tablespoons good-quality honey
2 tablespoons heavy cream, or about ½ cup vanilla ice cream, optional

In a large skillet, melt the butter over moderate heat. Add the ginger and cook 10 seconds. Place the bananas in the hot pan, flat side down. Cook for 1 minute. Drizzle the bananas with half the honey and cook 2 minutes. Gently flip over and drizzle with the remaining honey. Cook 1 minute. Serve hot, as is, or drizzle with heavy cream or top with a scoop of vanilla ice cream, if using.

Makes 2 to 4 servings

You Can Also Add . . .

- A touch of cinnamon or nutmeg sprinkled on the bananas for added spice.
- 1 tablespoon rum when you flip the bananas over. Raise the heat to high and cook for 1 minute to allow some of the alcohol to burn off.
- 1 tablespoon unsweetened coconut flakes sprinkled over the bananas when you remove them from the skillet.
- Ginger ice cream or coconut sorbet on top of the hot, finished bananas to highlight the ginger flavor.
- Maple syrup instead of honey.

Rhubarb Crumble

Come April when the first leaves of the rhubarb patch poke through the ground, I know there is hope for a new season—one that promises new, fresh flavors. Rhubarb is an odd-looking plant with huge, inedible leaves, and pinkish-red tinged stalks that look like celery. Exceedingly sour, it needs to be balanced with sweetness and this simple crumble does the trick. The whole recipe can be made in very little time, but try to leave at least half an hour to "marinate" the rhubarb slices in sugar to soften. Serve topped with vanilla ice cream, whipped cream, a drizzle of heavy cream, or a dollop of crème fraîche.

4 cups fresh rhubarb, cut into 1½-inch pieces
½ cup granulated sugar
1 teaspoon ground ginger
½ teaspoon cinnamon
½ cup flour
⅓ cup brown sugar
1 cup granola, preferably with nuts
1 stick butter, cut into cubes, plus 1 teaspoon for greasing the dish

THE TOPPINGS:
Vanilla ice cream, whipped cream, heavy cream, or a dollop of crème fraîche

Place the rhubarb in a bowl and sprinkle with the granulated sugar. Stir in half the ginger and cinnamon. Let "marinate" for at least 30 minutes, and up to 2 hours.

Meanwhile, mix the flour and brown sugar in a bowl. Add the granola and the remaining ginger and cinnamon. Add the cubes of butter and, using your hands or a pastry knife, break the butter into the mixture until it is the size of peas.

Preheat the oven to 350 degrees. Lightly butter the bottom of a pie plate or medium gratin dish with the remaining teaspoon of butter. Add the rhubarb chunks. Spoon the crumble on top and press down to form a crust. Make sure the butter isn't all in one clump, but distributed through the crust. Bake on the middle

shelf for 20 to 35 minutes, or until the rhubarb is soft and the fruit begins to bubble under the crust; the crust should be golden brown. Remove from the oven and serve hot or at room temperature with any of the toppings.

Makes 4 servings

You Can Also Add . . .

- 1 cup sliced strawberries with the rhubarb.
- A combination of fresh summer berries instead of the rhubarb; use 4 cups blueberries, raspberries, and/or blackberries.
- A combination of 4 cups of peeled, cored, and quartered apples.
- 4 cups peeled, cored, and quartered pears instead of the rhubarb, or try half apples and half pears.
- 1 tablespoon crystallized ginger, finely chopped, instead of ground ginger.
- ⅓ cup golden or regular raisins.

Shortcakes with Strawberry-Rhubarb Sauce

Fresh rhubarb simmered with a touch of sugar and water creates a sweet-and-sour sauce that is thickened with fresh sliced strawberries and then layered between flaky shortcakes, with vanilla-scented whipped cream and whole strawberries. If rhubarb is not available, try these seasonal variations instead: sautéed bananas with a touch of brown sugar in winter, peaches and berries in the summer, and figs and apricots in the fall.

SHORTCAKES:
2 cups flour
2 teaspoons double-acting baking powder
Dash salt
5 tablespoons butter, cut into pieces
½ cup milk

THE STRAWBERRY-RHUBARB SAUCE:
1½ cups rhubarb, chopped, about 3 stalks
1 cup water
3 to 4 tablespoons sugar
2 cups ripe strawberries, stemmed and sliced

THE WHIPPED CREAM AND STRAWBERRIES:
1 cup heavy cream
About 2 tablespoons sugar
½ teaspoon vanilla
About 20 ripe whole strawberries, stemmed

Make the shortcakes by sifting the flour, baking powder, and salt into a bowl. Add the butter and, using a pastry blender or your hands, blend until the mixture resembles coarse bread crumbs. Add the milk and stir into a ball of dough. Roll the dough out on a floured surface until it is ½ inch thick. (If you roll the dough out too thin the short-cakes won't rise properly.) Using an upside-down 3-inch-diameter glass, cut out 6 short-cakes. You may need to reroll the dough to get the last 2 shortcakes. Place on an ungreased baking sheet. Make these several hours ahead of time; cover and refrigerate.

Make the sauce by placing the rhubarb, water, and sugar in a saucepan and bring to a boil. Reduce the heat to low and simmer about 15 minutes, or until the rhubarb is completely soft. Remove from the heat and cool 5 minutes. Add the sliced strawberries and stir well. The sauce can be made several hours ahead of time; cover and refrigerate.

About 25 minutes before you want to serve the shortcakes (they are so good warm and fresh out of the oven), preheat the oven to 450 degrees. Bake the shortcakes on the middle shelf for 18 to 20 minutes, or until golden brown and puffed slightly.

Meanwhile, whip the cream until soft peaks form. Add the sugar and vanilla and whip until firm.

To assemble: Remove the hot shortcakes from the oven. Cut them in half crosswise. Pour a few tablespoons of the strawberry-rhubarb sauce over the bottom, add a dollop of whipped cream, and add the top half of the shortcake. Add another dollop of whipped cream, several whole strawberries and pour more sauce over or around the shortcakes. Serve additional sauce, whipped cream, and strawberries on the side.

Makes 6 servings

Plum and Nectarine Tartlets

You can make these fresh fruit tartlets using a variety of summer fruit, but the combination of nectarines and plums is a particularly good one. You'll need six 4½-inch-diameter tartlet pans with removable bottoms to make these. The pans are available at specialty food shops and in gourmet food catalogues. These tarts can be made a day ahead of time.

THE DOUGH:

2 cups flour
¼ cup sugar
Pinch salt
1½ sticks butter, chilled, cut into ½-inch pieces
About ¼ cup ice water

THE FILLING:

4 firm but ripe nectarines or peaches, halved, pitted, and cut into ⅓-inch-thick
    wedges
4 firm but ripe plums, halved, pitted, cut into ⅓-inch-thick wedges
3½ tablespoons sugar
½ cup plum jelly
6 blackberries, or blueberries or raspberries

To make the pastry, combine the flour, sugar, and salt in a food processor. Add butter and pulse the machine until the mixture resembles coarse cornmeal. Add ¼ cup water and process using on/off turns until moist and the dough just begins to pull away from the sides of the bowl. Add another teaspoon or two of water, if needed. Gather the dough together. Divide the dough into six equal pieces and, using the palm of your hand, flatten into disks. Wrap each disk in plastic and chill at least 1 hour, or overnight.

Preheat the oven to 400 degrees. Roll out each dough disk on a well-floured surface to a 5½-inch round. Transfer rounds to six 4½-inch-diameter tartlet pans with removable bottoms. Press the dough into pan bottom and up the sides. Place pans on baking sheet.

Toss the nectarines, plums, and sugar in a medium bowl. Arrange the fruit in the six crusts. Bake the tartlets on the middle shelf for 10 minutes. Reduce the heat to 350 degrees and bake another 40 minutes, or until the fruit is tender and beginning to bubble and crust is golden brown. Transfer the tartlets to a rack and cool completely.

Meanwhile, stir the jelly in a small saucepan over low heat until melted. Using a pastry brush or the back of a spoon, brush warm jelly over the tartlets. Place a berry in the center of each tartlet and serve at room temperature within 1 day of baking.

Makes 6 servings

You Can Also Add . . .

- About 4 cups fresh summer berries instead of the nectarines and plums.
- Apples and pears instead of the nectarines and plums.
- Raspberry, blackberry, blueberry, or apple jelly instead of the plum jelly.
- A large round or rectangular tart pan with a removable bottom instead of the six small tartlet pans.

Pineapple Upside-Down Cake

An old classic with a few new twists, this cake is flavored with ginger and toasted pecans and poured on top of pineapple slices that have been drenched in caramelized brown sugar and butter. This moist cake is best served warm, straight from the oven. However, it can be successfully made a day ahead of time; cover and refrigerate. Bring to room temperature at least two hours before serving.

THE TOPPING:
1 fresh ripe pineapple, or one 20-ounce can unsweetened pineapple slices
   in unsweetened pineapple juice
4 tablespoons butter
½ cup light brown sugar

THE CAKE:
½ cup pecan halves
4 tablespoons butter
½ cup light brown sugar
2 eggs
1 teaspoon vanilla
1 teaspoon gingerroot, very finely chopped, or ⅛ teaspoon ground ginger
½ cup unsweetened pineapple juice
1¼ cups flour
1½ teaspoons baking powder
½ teaspoon salt

Preheat the oven to 350 degrees.

If using a fresh pineapple, peel and core the pineapple. Cut about 10 slices of pineapple, each about ½ inch thick. Save any remaining pineapple for a garnish or other use.

In a 9-inch cake pan, melt the 4 tablespoons butter over low heat. Add the brown sugar and mix, stirring; let cook about 4 minutes until caramelized. Remove from the heat and add the 10 pineapple slices directly on top of the butter/sugar mixture, overlapping the slices slightly.

Place the pecans on a baking sheet or another cake pan and toast about 10 minutes, or until they begin to turn a golden brown and the room is filled with a nutty scent. Shake the pan once or twice to make sure the nuts aren't burning and that they are browning evenly. Chop the pecans. You can toast the nuts 48 hours ahead of time; cover until ready to use.

To make the cake batter, beat the butter in a mixer until soft. Add the brown sugar and beat until creamy. Add the eggs, one at a time, and then vanilla. Add the ginger and pineapple juice and beat until smooth. (Don't be concerned if the batter seems to separate at this stage.) Sift the flour, baking powder, and salt into the butter mixture and beat gently until incorporated, and smooth. Gently fold in the chopped nuts and pour the batter into the cake pan, smoothing it evenly over the pineapple slices.

Bake on the middle shelf for about 45 minutes, or until the cake springs back when pushed with your fingers in the center. Let cool about 10 minutes. Using a kitchen knife, loosen the cake around the edges. Place a large plate over the cake pan and invert it, tapping lightly on the bottom of the cake pan. Release the cake and serve warm or cover and refrigerate until ready to serve.

Makes 6 to 8 servings

You Can Also Add . . .

- Whipped cream flavored with a tablespoon or two of pineapple juice.
- Nutmeg, cardamom, or allspice instead of the ginger.

Lemon Tart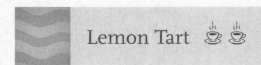

We all have desserts we can rely on time and time again. This fresh-tasting, lemony tart is my standard. The recipe comes from a great baker, my sister-in-law, Andrea Gunst. I make the tart when it's cold and winter taste buds need brightening and in the spring to reawaken tastes. I bake it throughout the summer surrounded by gorgeous seasonal fruit and in the fall with fresh figs and late raspberries. You won't go wrong serving this at the most elegant party (surround the tart with chocolate truffles) or at a casual potluck. You can make the tart a day ahead of time. Cover and keep refrigerated. Cut into squares just before serving.

THE CRUST:
1 cup flour
¼ cup confectioners' sugar
½ cup butter, softened and cut into small pieces

THE LEMON FILLING:
2 eggs
¾ cup plus 2 tablespoons sugar
½ teaspoon baking powder
¼ teaspoon salt
1½ tablespoons grated lemon peel
2 tablespoons fresh lemon juice

THE GARNISHES:
1 to 2 tablespoons confectioners' sugar
Fresh fruit or berries
Chocolate truffles or assorted chocolates

Preheat the oven to 350 degrees. Set aside an 8 × 8 × 2-inch tart pan with a removable bottom.

In a medium bowl, mix the flour and the ¼ cup confectioners' sugar. Add the butter and, using either your hands or a pastry cutter, mix well until the butter breaks down into small pea shapes. Press the crust (it will appear very dry and crumbly; don't despair) into the tart pan with your hands, building a half-inch edge up the sides. Bake on the middle shelf for 20 minutes.

Meanwhile, in a large bowl, beat the eggs with a whisk or an electric mixer. Add the sugar, baking powder, salt, lemon peel, and lemon juice and beat until light and fluffy, about 5 minutes.

Pour the mixture over the hot crust and bake another 25 minutes on the middle shelf. If the tart begins to brown, cover very loosely with a sheet of aluminum foil. The tart is done when no indentation appears when touched lightly in the center. Remove and let cool. Sift the tart with confectioners' sugar and surround with fruit or chocolates, if desired.

Makes 12 squares

Lemon Poppy Seed Cake

I first tasted this cake at our temple in Dover, New Hampshire. Eve Edelstein-Williams was shy when I asked who made the amazing lemon poppy seed cake, but I finally got her to own up to it and give me the recipe. It was well worth the effort. This cake is the perfect balance of lemon and poppy, light and fluffy. The orange glaze that is brushed over the top while the cake is still warm gives it an extra sweetness. The cake takes very little time or effort to put together considering what a show-off it is.

You will need a large Kaiser fluted tube pan or angel food cake pan with a removeable bottom. The cake can be made up to a day ahead of time.

THE CAKE:
Butter and flour for greasing the pan
3 cups flour
1 teaspoon salt
1½ teaspoons baking powder
2¼ cups sugar
4½ tablespoons poppy seeds
1⅓ cups canola oil
1½ cups milk
2½ teaspoons vanilla extract
2½ teaspoons lemon extract*
3 eggs

THE GLAZE:
1 cup confectioners' sugar
¼ cup orange juice
1½ teaspoons lemon extract*
1½ teaspoons vanilla extract

Grease and flour one large Kaiser fluted tube pan or angel food cake pan with a removable bottom.

Preheat the oven to 350 degrees.

*You can substitute 1 teaspoon grated lemon rind and 1 tablespoon lemon juice for the lemon extract.

Using a regular mixer or a handheld mixer, combine the flour, salt, baking powder, sugar, and poppy seeds in a large bowl. At medium speed, gradually add the oil, and then the milk and then the vanilla and lemon extracts. Increase the speed to high and mix about 1 minute. Add the eggs, one at a time, and mix well at medium-high speed. Pour the batter into the prepared pan and bake, on the middle shelf, for about 1 hour and 15 minutes, or until a toothpick inserted in the center comes out clean.

Meanwhile, to make the glaze, whisk together the sugar, orange juice, and extracts in a bowl until smooth. Set aside.

Let the cake cool just slightly on a rack. Invert the cake onto a serving plate and, using a pastry brush or the back of a spoon, brush the glaze onto the top and sides of the cake while still hot. Let cool thoroughly. When the cake is room temperature you should loosely cover it and refrigerate until 1 hour before serving time.

Makes 8 to 10 servings

Eve's Lemon Cheesecake

Dense, creamy, and subtly flavored with lemon juice and lemon zest, this cheesecake is a big hit at any party. It can be made a full day ahead of time and takes only about an hour and a half from start to finish.

THE CRUST:
Butter for greasing the pan
1 stick butter
1½ cups graham cracker crumbs*
½ cup sifted confectioners' sugar
1 teaspoon cinnamon, optional

THE CHEESECAKE:
2 pounds softened cream cheese
1¼ cups sugar
4 eggs, at room temperature
Juice of 1 lemon
Grated zest of 1 lemon
½ to 1 teaspoon vanilla extract

Grease the bottom and sides of a 10-inch springform pan.

In a small skillet, melt the stick of butter over low heat.

Prepare the crust by placing the crumbs, confectioners' sugar, melted butter, and cinnamon in a bowl and mixing until the crust comes together. Press the crust into the bottom of the prepared pan and chill for at least 15 minutes, or for several hours, before filling.

Preheat the oven to 350 degrees. In a mixer, cream the cream cheese until softened. Gradually add the sugar and then the eggs, one at a time, until the mixture is smooth, light, and fluffy. Add the lemon juice, zest, and vanilla and mix again.

*Crush a large packet of graham crackers by placing them in a tightly sealed plastic bag and crushing them with a rolling pin.

Pour the filling into the chilled crust and bake the cake for 1 hour. The cake is done when it is still soft in the center; when gently jiggled, the cake moves as one. The cake will firm up and continue to cook after it's removed from the oven. Let cool. Remove from the pan and place on a serving plate.

Makes 8 to 10 servings

You Can Also Add . . .

- A variety of fresh berries or seasonal fruit around the cake.
- Paper-thin lemon slices as a garnish.
- Thin slivers of candied ginger as a garnish.
- Caramelized lemon slices: Boil 1 cup sugar with $\frac{1}{2}$ cup water to create a sugar syrup. Add paper-thin lemon slices and cook until well coated with the sugar syrup and cooked, about 5 minutes. Carefully remove the lemon slices and dry on a plate. Roll in sugar and add to the sides of the cake.
- Orange juice and orange zest instead of the lemon for an orange-flavored cheesecake.

Pavlova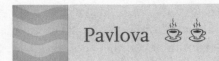

For this delicious dessert, a huge white swirl of meringue is baked until crisp and dry and then filled with whipped cream and fresh fruit. Don't attempt to make this on a humid day. The meringue will not hold together. Depending on the season you can fill this meringue with any variety of fruit: In the spring you could add strawberry-rhubarb sauce (see page 228) topped with fresh strawberries; in the summer a mixture of fresh berries or slices of ripe peaches; in the fall wedges of fresh figs, and in the winter slices of banana and apple, or red and green grapes.

THE MERINGUE:
5 egg whites
⅛ teaspoon cream of tartar
1¾ cups sugar
¾ teaspoon vanilla extract

THE CREAM AND FRUIT:
About 1 to 1½ cups heavy cream
2 to 4 tablespoons sugar
1 teaspoon vanilla extract
About 3 to 4 cups fruit (see headnote), cut into bite-sized pieces, or slices

Preheat the oven to 275 degrees. Grease a baking sheet liberally with butter and set aside.

In an electric mixer, whisk the egg whites until foamy. Add the cream of tartar and continue beating until the whites are just about stiff. Add the sugar, half a cup at a time, and then add the vanilla. Continue beating until the whites are very stiff with a shiny look, about 10 minutes.

Spoon the meringue onto the prepared baking sheet, mounding it into a large circle with raised edges—creating the look of a large, indented shell. Don't worry about making it perfect or even, but make sure to create an indentation in the middle that you will later fill with whipped cream and fruit. Bake in the center shelf for about 1½ hours, or until the meringue appears dry, and very lightly colored. Turn off the oven and let sit another 30 minutes. Remove from the oven and let cool completely. The

meringue can be made several hours ahead of time, or overnight. Keep in a cool, dry spot in a covered tin.

To serve: Whip the cream until almost thickened. Add the sugar and vanilla and beat until thick. Do not fill the shell with the cream until you are ready to serve.

Spoon the cream into the inside of the meringue shell, spreading it out evenly. Arrange the fruit along the outside of the meringue, with some fruit in the center. Serve immediately.

Makes 6 servings

You Can Also Add . . .

- Edible flowers (such as nasturtium, edible marigold blossoms, or violets) on top of the meringue.
- Thin shavings of white and dark chocolate.
- Thin slivers of crystallized ginger.
- A drizzle of chocolate sauce; see recipe on page 248.

Apple Crostada

This rustic pie is filled with a variety of fresh apples, a dash of cinnamon, and just a touch of sugar. It's a great way to celebrate fall. Be sure to look for a variety of local apples. Serve the crostada hot from the oven, or at room temperature with ice cream (vanilla or ginger are particularly good) and hot cider.

You can make the dough a day ahead of time, or freeze it for up to two months. Don't make the apple filling ahead of time because it will turn brown.

THE DOUGH:
2 cups flour
1 tablespoon sugar
2 sticks butter, ice cold and cut into 1-inch cubes
About ¼ cup ice cold water

THE FILLING:
About 4 medium tart apples, such as McIntosh, Winesap, Baldwin, or Cortland
¼ cup sugar or brown sugar
Pinch cinnamon
Pinch ground ginger, optional

To make the dough whirl the flour and sugar in a food processor. Add the butter and pulse the machine about 15 times, or until the mixture resembles coarse cornmeal. Add enough water to the food processor with the machine running until the dough *just* begins to pull away from the sides of the machine. Wrap the dough in aluminum foil for at least 2 hours, or overnight.

Peel and core the apples and cut each apple into 8 slices. Place in a bowl and toss with the sugar, cinnamon, and ginger.

Preheat the oven to 450 degrees.

Working on a floured surface, roll the dough out into a large circle (12 to 14 inches wide). Place on an ungreased baking sheet. Place the apple filling in the middle of the dough, leaving an outside border of 1½ to 2 inches. Drape the edges of the dough over the filling and press down lightly to crimp the edges. The dough won't cover the filling completely. Bake on the middle shelf for about 20 minutes, or until the dough is golden brown and the filling is tender when tested with a small, sharp knife. Serve hot, or at room temperature.

Makes 4 to 6 servings

Pound Cake with Peach, Honey, and Rum Sauce ☕

This is one of those quick, throw-it-together desserts you can rely on. Store-bought pound cake is doused with fresh fruit and a quick honey-rum sauce. You can use any type of fruit that is in season, but peaches or nectarines are particularly delicious.

4 ripe peaches or nectarines
¼ cup good-quality honey
¼ cup dark rum
1 drop vanilla extract
8 slices pound cake, butter cake, or angel food cake
Fresh mint leaves, optional

Blanch peaches in a large pot of boiling water for 15 seconds. Transfer to a bowl of ice water. Peel the peaches and cut into thin slices. Mix the honey, rum, and vanilla in a large bowl. Mix in the peach slices. Cover and refrigerate until ready to serve. The sauce can be prepared 1 day ahead of time.

Arrange a slice of pound cake on each plate. Spoon peach sauce on top and garnish with mint leaves.

Makes 6 to 8 servings

You Can Also Add . . .

- Fresh berries instead of, or in addition to, peach slices.
- Shaved slices of good chocolate over the dish just before serving.
- A pinch of ground cinnamon, ginger, or nutmeg to the sauce when you add the peaches.
- A sweet muscadet dessert wine to really impress your friends.

Panna Cotta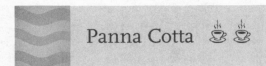

Talk about a sensual dessert—this Italian classic (whose name means "cooked cream") is so silky smooth that it should be considered an aphrodisiac. Flavored with vanilla and lemon, it can be served with a variety of fresh berries (strawberries and raspberries are particularly good) and strong cups of espresso.

For the creamiest consistency, serve the panna cotta four to six hours after cooking; the longer it chills, the firmer it becomes.

Butter for greasing the mold or cups
1 packet unflavored gelatin
¼ cup cold water
2 cups heavy cream
½ cup vanilla-flavored sugar (see page 36) or sugar
¾ teaspoon grated lemon zest
¼ teaspoon vanilla extract
About 3 cups berries

Lightly butter a 3-cup mold or 6 individual (¹/₃-cup) ramekins or custard cups.

Dissolve the gelatin and water in a small bowl and let sit for 10 minutes to soften.

Place the cream, sugar, lemon zest, and vanilla in a medium saucepan and bring to a boil, whisking to dissolve the sugar. Remove from the heat and whisk in the gelatin to blend thoroughly. Pour the mixture into the prepared mold, cover with aluminum foil, and refrigerate for at least 4 hours.

To remove the panna cotta, set the mold in a bowl of hot water for just a few seconds. Run a flat knife around the rim of the mold or the custard cups. Invert the mold onto a serving plate and release it. Surround with the berries.

Makes 6 servings

You Can Also Add . . .

- Orange or tangerine zest to the cream instead of the lemon.
- A few tablespoons of very strong espresso or a few coffee beans to infuse the cream.

- Buttermilk instead of cream for a lower fat dessert.
- A cinnamon stick and vanilla bean to the cream.
- A splash of rosewater to the cream.
- Honey instead of sugar.
- Candied orange peel as a sweet decoration.

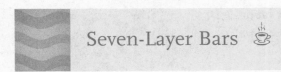
I found this in my grandmother's recipe file and thought it was too good to be true. Seven ingredients layered on top of each other and baked in a pan. That's it—no mixing, stirring, or whisking involved. The result: a sweet, barlike confection that is satisfying enough for any event.

1 stick butter or margarine
2 cups graham cracker crumbs*
One 12-ounce package semisweet chocolate chips
One 12-ounce bag butterscotch chips
1 cup chopped pecans
1 cup shredded coconut
One 14-ounce can sweetened condensed milk

Melt the butter in a small saucepan. Preheat the oven to 350 degrees.

In a 9 × 13-inch pan, add the melted butter. Sprinkle on the graham cracker crumbs, and then the chocolate chips, butterscotch chips, pecans, and coconut. Pour the condensed milk on top and bake on the middle shelf for 30 minutes. Remove from the oven and let cool about 15 minutes. Cut into 30 small squares.

Makes 30 bars

*Place graham crackers in a tightly sealed plastic bag and crush with a rolling pin.

Quick Chocolate Fondue with Cherries

All you need is a chocolate bar and a few tablespoons of cream to make this delicious fondue. Don't make the fondue ahead of time; it takes about five minutes to put together.

16 ounces semisweet chocolate, good quality, broken into small pieces, or good
    quality chocolate chips
About ¼ cup heavy cream
About 2 pounds Bing cherries

Place the chocolate in a small saucepan and set over *very low* heat. Whisk the chocolate into a sauce as it melts. Add the cream, 1 tablespoon at a time, whisking it into the chocolate until you have a soft, thick (but not too thick) sauce. You want to be able to dip the cherries into the chocolate. If the chocolate clumps together it has gotten too hot. Remove from heat and whisk in another tablespoon of cream. Serve the sauce in a pot surrounded by the cherries.

Makes about 1 cup (about 4 servings)

You Can Also Add . . .

- 1 teaspoon grated orange rind.
- Orange juice (preferably fresh-squeezed) instead of cream.
- A dash of your favorite liqueur, particularly orange-flavored.
- Peach, nectarine, melon, apple, or banana slices or fresh berries for dipping instead of, or in addition to, the cherries. Use fondue forks or wooden skewers to dip the fruit into the chocolate.
- Butter cookies to dip into the chocolate.
- A bowl of good ice cream and pour the chocolate fondue on top.

Birthday Meringues with Chocolate Sauce

I first made these treats—two deliciously crunchy meringue cookies sandwiched together with a rich chocolate sauce—for a good friend as an alternative to a traditional birthday cake. Sometimes you just want something sweet and celebratory without the fancy, multi-layered cake and those embarrassing candles.

Bake the meringues a day ahead of time; you can also freeze them for up to three weeks ahead of time and thaw them on the night of the party. Add the chocolate sauce a few hours before serving. (Do not attempt to make meringues when it is particularly humid; they will inevitably fall apart.)

THE MERINGUES
4 egg whites
Pinch salt
1 cup sugar

THE CHOCOLATE SAUCE
6 ounces good-quality bittersweet chocolate
4 tablespoons heavy cream

Make the meringues by preheating the oven to 200 degrees. Line two baking sheets with aluminum foil, laying the shiny side down.

Using an electric mixer, whisk the egg whites and salt in a large bowl until frothy. Increase the speed to high and whisk until the whites form a peak. Add the sugar, one tablespoon at a time, until the egg whites are glossy and stiff.

Spoon heaping tablespoons of the mixture onto the prepared baking sheet, spacing them about an inch or two apart from each other. (You should have 24 cookies.) Bake for 3 hours, or until the meringues are pale and dry and crisp throughout. Turn off the oven and let the cookies dry out in the oven for at least 1 hour and up to 12 hours. (If it is the least bit humid you will want to let them sit for several hours.) Gently peel the cookies off the foil and place in a cool, dry spot. (If you want to freeze them or keep them for

several days, place in an airtight cookie tin or plastic container with wax paper between the layers.)

Make the chocolate sauce at least an hour before serving: Melt the chocolate in a small saucepan over *very* low heat. Stir in the cream and whisk together until smooth. Add a good tablespoon of sauce to the bottom of a meringue cookie (the flat side) and sandwich it together by adding another cookie (again the flat side) onto the chocolate sauce. Let sit or refrigerate for about an hour before serving. Save any remaining chocolate sauce to drizzle over the tops of meringues, or save to serve on top of ice cream.

Makes 8 servings

Chocolate Rugalach

This Hanukkah favorite is made with a dough rich with cream cheese, sour cream, and butter, stuffed with chocolate and a sprinkling of sugar, and rolled into a delicious crescent. It is adapted from Joan Nathan's recipe for classic rugalach in her book The Jewish Holiday Baker. *The dough needs to be refrigerated for one hour.*

8 ounces cream cheese, softened
2 sticks butter
¼ cup sour cream
2 cups flour
1½ cups semisweet chocolate chips
About ¼ cup sugar
Confectioners' sugar for dusting

Make the dough by mixing the cream cheese, butter, and sour cream in an electric mixer until well incorporated and soft. Add the flour and mix until a soft dough comes together. Place in a sheet of aluminum foil or wax paper and refrigerate for at least 1 hour.

Preheat the oven to 350 degrees. Butter two baking sheets and set aside.

By hand or in a food processor, chop the chips until coarse.

Divide the dough in fourths and roll out one fourth on a well-floured surface. Roll the dough out to a circle about 9 inches wide and about ⅛ inch thick. Sprinkle the dough with a tablespoon of the sugar and sprinkle on a quarter of the chopped chocolate, and then another tablespoon of sugar. Press the chocolate and sugar down into the dough gently.

Imagine the dough round is a pizza and, using a flat knife, cut into 16 slices. Roll each slice working from the wide end and rolling toward the narrow center. Place the rugalach on the prepared cookie sheet. Repeat with the remaining 3 rounds of dough and the chocolate and sugar.

Bake the cookies on the middle and lower shelf for 13 minutes. Switch the baking sheets, moving the one on the middle shelf to the lower shelf and vice versa. Bake another 12 minutes, or until golden brown. Let cool thoroughly and sprinkle with confectioners' sugar.

Makes about 64 cookies

You Can Also Add . . .

- $^1/_2$ teaspoon ground cinnamon.
- $^1/_2$ cup finely chopped nuts or dried fruit to the filling with the chocolate and sugar.

Three-Layer Mint Brownies

These brownies offer a deliciously dense mint-flavored base, with a mint and chocolate layer on top—elevating the humble brownie to serve-at-any-occasion status. For a more regal presentation, serve a brownie square with fresh fruit salad, or top with mint sorbet or vanilla ice cream and a simple chocolate sauce (see page 248).

There are several steps involved in making these brownies, but they can be made up to eight hours ahead of time. Cover with foil and store at room temperature until ready to serve.

THE BROWNIES:
Butter for greasing the pan
1 stick butter
2 ounces unsweetened chocolate, chopped
2 eggs
1 cup sugar
½ cup flour
½ teaspoon peppermint extract
½ teaspoon vanilla extract
Pinch salt
½ cup chopped pecans

THE TOPPINGS:
1 cup sifted confectioners' sugar
4 tablespoons butter, at room temperature
1 tablespoon milk
¼ teaspoon peppermint extract
4 ounces semisweet chocolate, chopped

Preheat the oven to 350 degrees.

Lightly butter an 8 × 8 × 2-inch metal baking pan.

Stir the 1 stick butter and chocolate in a small saucepan over *very* low heat until melted and smooth. Using an electric mixer, beat the eggs and sugar in a large bowl until light and fluffy, about 5 minutes. Add the melted chocolate mixture, the flour, peppermint and vanilla extracts, and salt; stir until just blended. Mix in the nuts.

Transfer the batter to the prepared pan. Bake until a toothpick inserted in the center comes out moist with crumbs attached, about 25 minutes. Cool slightly.

For the toppings: Beat the confectioners' sugar, 2 tablespoons of the butter, milk, and peppermint extract in a bowl until creamy. Spread over the warm brownies. Chill until set; about 1 hour.

Stir the semisweet chocolate and the remaining 2 tablespoons butter in a small saucepan over very low heat until melted and smooth. Cool slightly. Pour over mint toppings, spreading evenly. Cover and chill until set, about 1 hour. Cut into 20 squares.

Makes 20 brownies

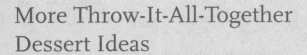

More Throw-It-All-Together Dessert Ideas

- Choose a few flavors of good-quality sorbet (or ice cream)—think about colors and flavors that will go together: lemon and raspberry, orange and lime, chocolate and strawberry. Place 2 small scoops of each sorbet in a bowl and top with thin slices of whatever fruit you have on hand: fresh berries, bananas, pears, melon balls, apples, and so on.

- Orange or grapefruit slices with shaved dark and white chocolate (to shave chocolate simply grate a good-quality chocolate bar with a regular cheese grater or vegetable peeler).

- Sprinkle orange slices or Mandarin orange wedges with toasted grated coconut. Place ½ cup unsweetened grated coconut in a dry skillet. Toast over moderately low heat for about 4 minutes, shaking the pan occasionally to keep the coconut from burning. It should just begin to turn a very pale golden brown. Sprinkle over slices of 1 peeled orange or Mandarin orange.

- Sprinkle fresh or thawed berries over vanilla ice cream and sorbet.

- Serve fresh melon wedges with slices of lime.

- This instant cannoli filling comes from friend Deborah Krasner: Place 16 ounces ricotta cheese in a food processor or blender. Add ⅓ cup sugar and ⅓ cup cocoa powder and whirl. Serve in tiny bowls with fresh fruit, and cookies, or spread in a cannoli shell (available at Italian bakeries or specialty food shops). You can also add various flavors, like vanilla, rum, or the zest of an orange or lemon, or add chopped pistachios.

- Instead of offering sweets, serve a cheese course. Find a reputable cheese shop or a grocery store or specialty food shop that stocks a good variety of fresh cheese. Ask for samples and buy three to five varieties, depending on how many people you're serving and how big the rest of the meal is. For four to six people, choose 3 to 4 cheeses. For 10 to 20 people, choose about 6 to 8 cheeses. Look for a combination of soft cheeses and hard cheeses and always check out locally made cheese. A few favorites: Gorgonzola, Roquefort, Stilton, or another pungent blue cheese; Gouda; a sharp cheddar; Parmigiano-Reggiano; Gruyère; a hard sheep's milk cheese from Spain like Manchego or Idiazabal; a soft, fresh chèvre (goat cheese) or a hard aged goat cheese; and a rich, soft, creamy cheese like Explorateur, Camembert, or Brie. Serve the cheeses with an assortment of breadsticks and crackers, apples and pears, walnuts and almonds, fresh or dried figs, and biscotti for a sweet touch. To drink, try a good Port or red wine. A small bowl of sun-dried cranberries, cherries, or raisins offers a tart flavor that can cut the richness of the cheese.

Mocha Cake ☕☕

Old family recipes can be tricky. As they pass from generation to generation, small details can be dropped and ingredients inadvertently changed. But when I received this recipe from my husband's great aunt Dot, the instructions were very specific. "Use Swan's Down brand cake flour; it's very important! Beat the yolks and sugar until light and let stand twenty minutes." Aunt Dot is no longer here to ask, so I followed the recipe precisely and the results were superb. These coffee-flavored sponge cakes are layered with a sweetened mocha-flavor whipped cream filling and decorated with chopped walnuts.

6 eggs, separated
1 cup sugar
3 to 4 tablespoons instant espresso or coffee
1 cup cake flour (Swan's Down brand, if possible)
1 teaspoon baking powder
1 pint heavy cream
3 to 4 tablespoons confectioners' sugar
¾ cup walnuts, finely chopped

Grease two 9-inch cake pans and line with wax paper.

In a large mixing bowl, beat the egg yolks for about 2 minutes. Gradually add the sugar and beat another 2 minutes. Let stand for 20 minutes.

In a separate bowl, beat the egg whites until stiff peaks appear.

Add 1 tablespoon of the coffee to the sugar/yolk mixture and beat well. Sift the flour and baking powder into the mixture and fold in. Gently fold in the egg whites until incorporated. Divide the batter between the two pans and bake on the middle shelf for 30 minutes.

Remove from the oven and let cool. Gently release the cakes from the pan and gently peel off the wax paper.

In a mixing bowl, beat the cream until almost stiff. Add the confectioners' sugar and 2 tablespoons of the coffee and beat until just stiff. Taste the icing; if you want a stronger coffee flavor, add another tablespoon of coffee.

When cool, place one layer of the cake on a serving plate. Spoon almost half of the whipped coffee cream on top and spread evenly. Top with the second layer and cover the top and sides with the remaining icing. Sprinkle the top of the cake with the walnuts and chill before serving. The cake should be served within 6 hours of baking and icing.

Makes 8 servings

Ultimate Ice Cream Sandwich

This may strike you as "kid food," but if that's the case I never want to grow up. This dessert is only as good as the ingredients you use to make it: store-bought, bakery-bought, or homemade cookies are sandwiched with your favorite ice cream, sorbet, or frozen yogurt. Half the sandwich is then dipped into melted chocolate for a quick glaze.

The recipe can be made a day ahead of time; wrap in wax paper or foil and keep in the freezer.

½ cup semisweet chocolate chips, or a 4-ounce semisweet chocolate bar,
    cut into chunks
½ to ¾ cup ice cream, frozen yogurt, or sorbet (anything from vanilla
    to raspberry sorbet), slightly softened
8 large cookies (oatmeal raisin, chocolate chip, whatever is your favorite)

Heat the chocolate in a small saucepan set over *very low* heat until melted, about 5 minutes. Stir to create a smooth sauce.

Meanwhile, place about 2 heaping tablespoons of ice cream on one cookie; stack another cookie on top to create a sandwich. (You may need more or less ice cream depending on the size of the cookie.) Use a spoon to coat half the cookie sandwich with the melted chocolate. Repeat with the remaining cookies, ice cream, and chocolate sauce. Place sandwiches on a small cookie sheet in the freezer until the chocolate has hardened—about 10 minutes.

Makes 4 servings

8
Menus

Creating a menu is a personal choice. The following menus are meant to be suggestions, ways to combine recipes from this book into full and festive meals. You can create easy, simple menus by preparing one or two recipes from the book and supplementing them with store-bought soup, salads, breads, meats, or dessert. Or you can put together an elaborate, multicourse menu for a special occasion. Recipes are indicated by a page cross-reference.

TWO MENUS FOR SPRING

Menu One:

The snow is gone and the grass is turning green. There is a feeling of hope and freshness in the air and you feel like having a dinner party. These two menus celebrate the fresh flavors of spring—taking full advantage of fresh baby spring spinach, new peas, asparagus, strawberries, and rhubarb.

- Grilled Shrimp, Mango, and Spinach Salad (page 92)
- Leek, Mushroom, and Asparagus Risotto (page 106)
- Roasted Spring Asparagus Salad with Dill Vinaigrette and Crumbled Feta (page 174)
- Country Italian bread
- Shortcakes with Strawberry-Rhubarb Sauce (page 228)

Menu Two:

- Spring Pea Soup (page 79)
- Cheese and Pepper Twists (page 52)
- Roast Salmon on Garlic Spinach with Cherry Tomatoes and Mushrooms (page 206)
- Prosciutto-Wrapped Asparagus Bundles with Garlic Butter (page 179)
- Orzo
- Rhubarb Crumble (page 226)

EAST MEETS WEST

You want to serve something different and exciting. You crave new tastes that will get people talking. With very little effort, you can pull off this Asian-flavored menu (culling flavors from China, Vietnam, and Thailand).

- Spiced Nuts (page 42)
- Ice-cold Thai beer
- Vietnamese-Style Spring Rolls with Shrimp (page 54)
- Green Curry Chicken with Peas and Basil (page 120)
- Steamed basmati rice
- Fresh mango slices
- Panna Cotta (page 244)

FATHER'S DAY FEAST

Do it for Dad, Grandpa, or a special man in your life, or simply do it for yourself. This meal lends itself to eating outdoors: under a tree, on a patio, or on the lawn.

- Tomato, Avocado, and Red Onion Salad with Roquefort Dressing (page 88)
- Grilled Steaks with Provençal Herbs (page 136) or,
  Steak Sandwiches on Garlic Baguettes with Arugula and Tomatoes (page 98)
- Warm Potato Salad with Lovage (page 90) or,
  Mediterranean Couscous Salad with Roasted Vegetables (page 176)
- Crusty bread and rolls
- Three-Layer Mint Brownies (page 252)
- Fresh Watermelon or Melon Wedges

BACKYARD BARBECUE

The sun feels hotter than ever. Your brother calls to say he and the kids are driving by on their way home from the beach. How about a barbecue? As long as you don't have to be cooped up inside a hot kitchen, you're game. Try serving some, or all, of the following cool-down recipes.

- Assorted Raw Vegetables and Corn Chips
- Mango Salsa (page 65)
- Grilled Chicken Done Two Ways (page 126) or,
  Grilled Flank Steak with Fresh Corn-Tomato-Basil Sauté (page 128)
- Warm Potato Salad with Lovage (page 90)
- Grilled Zucchini with Lemon (page 147)
- Seven-Layer Bars (page 246)
- Ultimate Ice Cream Sandwich (page 258)
- Lemonade or limeade
- Ice-cold beer

WHEN THE DOORBELL RINGS AND THERE'S "NOTHING" IN THE HOUSE

You're thinking of heating up a can of soup and making a few slices of toast, watching that video you rented two days ago, and calling it a night. You put on sweats and a T-shirt when the buzzer rings. It's your old friends from the book club. They were in the neighborhood, wanted to say hi, hope they're not interrupting, and all that. You figure you can watch a video any night. "Come on," they say. "We'll take you out to dinner." But no, you already have on sweats and don't feel like moving. Let's do dinner at home instead.

This meal evolves from canned beans, pasta, frozen peas, walnuts and store-bought sorbet or ice cream. Maybe you can all watch the video together.

- White Bean Dip (page 61)
- Assorted crackers
- Rigatoni in Creamy Walnut-Pea Sauce (page 108)
- Green Salad with Sun-Dried Tomato Croûtes (page 85)
- Sorbet with fresh fruit slices (page 254)

VEGETARIAN MENUS

You don't need to be a vegetarian to find these menus appealing.

Menu One:

- Mango Salsa (page 65) and chips
- Cuban-Style Black Bean Soup (page 170)
- Assorted crusty breads
- Roasted Spring Asparagus Salad with Dill Vinaigrette and Crumbled Feta (page 174)
- Lemon Poppy Seed Cake (page 236)

Menu Two:

- Roasted Pear and Mixed Green Salad (page 86)
- Glenn's Tuscan Focaccia (page 172)
- Rigatoni in Creamy Walnut-Pea Sauce (page 108)
- Roasted Winter Root Vegetables (page 152)
- Three-Layer Mint Brownies (page 252)

Menu Three:

- Orange-Marinated Olives (page 43)
- Vidalia Onion Tart (page 182)
- Stuffed Tomatoes Provençal (page 214)

- Roasted Summer Beans with Sesame-Soy Glaze (page 151)
- Poached Pears with Caramelized Raspberry Sauce (page 224)

Menu Four:

- Roasted Beet and Fennel Salad (page 178)
- Leek, Mushroom, and Asparagus Risotto, made with vegetable broth (page 106)
- Sautéed Baby Spinach with Garlic (page 150)
- Crusty rolls
- Eve's Lemon Cheesecake (page 238)

BRUNCH

Don't ask people to arrive too early or this will feel too much like work. Serve a variety of juices, good, strong coffee, cocoa for the kids, and a few bottles of white wine or champagne with fresh-squeezed orange or grapefruit juice (cranberry is also nice) for those who have been up for a while.

- Potato and Cheese Pancakes (page 104) or,
  Spanish Potato and Pepper Tortilla (page 102)
- Spanish Chopped Salad (page 71)
- Maple-Glazed Ham Steaks (page 142)
- Rolls, biscuits, or muffins, and an assortment of breads
- Sweet butter and assorted jams, jellies, and marmalade
- Fresh fruit salad or fruit kabobs
- Plain and vanilla yogurt served with bowls of honey, chopped nuts, and dried fruit (to mix into the yogurt)
- Panna Cotta (page 244)

BIRTHDAY BASH

Next Saturday my husband will turn forty-five. It's not one of those huge birthdays that require special gifts and cards and a party to end all parties, but it feels significant. He says the scales are tipping and it's not in his favor. Our youngest daughter thinks this means he's getting fat. "No," he tells her. "Worse than that."

It's going to be a busy week. There are deadlines to meet and endless activities for the kids. There won't be much down time for planning a celebration. But with some basic organization, I can pull together one of his favorite meals with very little effort.

(continued on page 266)

New Year's Day Bash

In life certain rules of etiquette apply. When you have a baby, you send out a birth announcement. When you graduate from college, you have a graduation party. When you finish renovating your home you invite everyone you know to a house-warming bash so they can see how it all turned out.

"Let's have a huge open house on New Year's Day," my husband proposed in late June when our renovation was finally complete. "We'll invite everyone." The word *everyone* caused my heart to skip a beat. I imagined every soul we knew parading through my new kitchen, examining the faucets and knobs, peering into the new refrigerator and pantry, and checking out the potency of the new cook top. Even worse, I pictured all those close friends and casual acquaintances judging my culinary abilities as I produced platters of finger food and desserts prepared in my new kitchen. I imagined them whispering to one another, "Yes, she may have an impressive kitchen, and she may write cookbooks, but we knew she wasn't really a great cook!"

I spent a good part of the summer and, this is hard to admit, the fall mulling over the various scenarios of how this open house might play out. Thanksgiving came and went, and as we cleaned the turkey platter and the huge roasting pans, I looked at my husband and asked, "Still interested in a New Year's Day open house?" He didn't look nearly as enthusiastic as he had in June. By the beginning of December, as the usual holiday hoopla began to build to a frenzy, I sat him down late one night (always get them when they're tired is my theory) and asked him again if he *really* wanted the open house. He looked exhausted and defeated. "It's going to be a lot of work," he finally said. "Why don't we wait till next summer when everyone can be outdoors and we can grill?" I practically danced. I saw my holiday season opening up into a period of light, uncommitted bliss.

So we sailed through Hanukkah and Christmas, and then, somewhat mysteriously, on the morning of December 29, this man whom I've been married to for almost two decades woke up, looked me deep in the eyes, and said, "You know, we should have the party."

"You're nuts!" I screamed. "Are you trying to ruin New Year's or just make me crazy? No way. Absolutely not!" No less than two hours later, I was on the phone calling friends.

I spent the next two days cooking and cleaning and shaking my head in amazement at the number of guests that we had invited— seventy-two! On New Year's Day, I popped two turkeys in the oven (two 12-pounders, which roast much faster than one huge turkey), peeled potatoes, poached pears, and sautéed baby spinach with garlic. At four that afternoon the first guest rang our new doorbell, which continued to ring all day and night until the house was filled. The good news was that everyone brought a bottle or a dish and, much to my utter amazement, all the food was delicious. The house was together (as much as it was ever going to be) and the party was fun, festive, and a surprise to all—most particularly the host and hostess who couldn't believe they had pulled it together within forty-eight hours!

The moral of the story? Having only two days to pull the open house together forced my husband and me to focus on what truly mattered: a few favorite crowd-pleasing dishes, good champagne, good friends, and a feeling of wanting to celebrate without all the excessive planning and worrying. I had a great New Year's Day. It may just be an annual event (but we probably won't decide on that until next December 29!).

This dinner party serves eight, but can easily be doubled. It requires preparing one or two dishes before the day of the party, but the rest can be put together in less than a few hours. Because my husband is aware that he's getting older, I decide not to buy or bake a traditional birthday cake, but instead to make two of his favorite desserts: poached pears with a caramelized raspberry sauce and crunchy meringues with chocolate. Who could want anything more?

- Red Caviar Dip (page 62)
- Pita toasts (page 63)
- Marinated Grilled Butterfly of Lamb (page 202)
- Yogurt "Cheese" with Mint, Scallions, and Cucumber (page 64)
- Couscous
- Grilled Zucchini with Lemon (page 147)
- Green salad with herb vinaigrette
- Poached Pears with Caramelized Raspberry Sauce (page 224)
- Birthday Meringues with Chocolate Sauce (page 248)
- Champagne

THEME DINNERS

Here are a few dinner menus that focus on the foods of a particular country. Try to serve a regional wine to match.

Italian Feast:

You met them at a Fellini movie. Or traveling through Tuscany. Or you all took an Italian language course together and share the dream of moving to Italy. Sharing this meal could be just as good as getting on a plane. Well, maybe.

- Roasted Red Bell Peppers (page 46) or,
  Spinach, Prosciutto, and Red Bell Pepper Crostini (page 48)
- Sue's Meatballs and Spaghetti (page 190) or,
  Double-Dipped Chicken Parmesan (page 188)
- Glenn's Tuscan Focaccia (page 172)
- Robust Chianti
- Panna Cotta (page 244)
- Fresh fruit platter

Turkish Feast:

This is the meal to serve when you want flavors that will wake up all of your senses—a menu that is truly memorable.

- Turkish-Style Stuffed Grape Leaves (page 58) or,
  Stuffed Turkish Peppers (page 192), served at room temperature
- Turkish Lamb Kabobs (page 134)
- Turkish Shepherd's Salad (page 74)
- Yogurt "Cheese" with Mint, Scallions, and Cucumber (page 64)
- Rice Pilaf (page 155)
- Sautéed Baby Spinach with Garlic (page 150)
- Fresh fruit
- Almond Crisps with Amaretto-Glazed Almonds (page 222)

Summer Party with an Asian Twist:

This menu has a decidedly Asian flavor and is ideal for an outdoor party, picnic, or summer luncheon. All the dishes can be made several hours ahead of time and packed in plastic containers if you're traveling to the beach or a picnic spot.

- Chinese-Flavored Fried Chicken with Ginger Dipping Sauce (page 124)
- Asian Slaw with Peanuts (page 91)
- Almond Crisps with Amaretto-Glazed Almonds (page 222)
- Ripe summer peaches or watermelon wedges
- Iced ginger tea
- Ice-cold Asian beer

Mediterranean Dinner:

You love olive oil, garlic, tomatoes, and basil. You dream of Provence, Tuscany, and the Riviera. Put your dreams together in a dinner for some special friends.

- Tomato, Basil, and Garlic Soup with Rouille (page 162)
- Vidalia Onion Tart (page 182) or Spinach Tart (page 184)
- Green Salad with Sun-Dried Tomato Croûtes (page 85)
- Grilled Steak with Provençal Herbs (page 136)
- Mediterranean Couscous Salad with Roasted Vegetables (page 176)

(continued on page 270)

Leftovers: A State of Mind

Leftovers may be thought of as the glass half empty or the glass half full. When you open your refrigerator and see a piece of grilled chicken, a zucchini, some cheese, three eggs, and a hunk of dry, leftover bread you may say: a) "There's nothing to eat, let's go out," or b) "I'll make a spinach, chicken, and cheese frittata. You open the wine."

Here's what happened today: I looked in my refrigerator and found a container filled with basmati rice cooked two nights ago, a piece of roast chicken from last night, a half bag of spinach, and a few peanuts. I saw a meal—not just a little of this and a little of that. I took out a skillet and added a dash of olive oil. I sautéed a clove of chopped garlic and a shallot I found at the bottom of my onion bin and let them cook slowly. I cut the chicken off the bone and cut it into bite-sized pieces and threw it into the skillet along with the spinach. Once the spinach was tender, about a minute later, I added the rice and a splash of soy sauce. I looked back in the fridge and found some canned chicken broth. I added the broth and a dash of hot sauce and let the rice and chicken and vegetables simmer for a few minutes. Then I poured my new concoction into a bowl and sprinkled the peanuts on top. I had a delicious, Asian-style rice dish. This is not a dish I would normally have thought up. I let the leftovers dictate.

One of the great things about entertaining and inviting guests to a meal is that you almost always end up with leftovers. Start thinking about leftovers as possibilities waiting to happen rather than second-class food. If you've grilled salmon and have lots left over and know you won't get to it in the next few days, freeze it. It will seem a lot more appealing to you a month down the line. Thanksgiving turkey or holiday ham is a great example. Who wants to eat tons of leftovers after the big feast? But if you freeze the turkey off the bone (or slice up the ham and freeze it) and take it out a few weeks later, you'll be hungry for that food again.

Whenever you roast a chicken, lamb, or beef be sure to keep the bone and any scraps of meat for making soup. Even a leftover chicken carcass (with little or no meat) can make a fine broth. Take the bone and place in a large pot. Cover with cold water. Add a few peeled, quartered onions, some chopped carrots and celery, a handful of parsley, a peppercorn or two, and a generous dash of salt and bring to a boil. Lower the heat and let simmer until flavorful and reduced, one to two hours. You can then add leftover meat, beans, pasta, other vegetables, or a dash of hot sauce, pesto, or olive puree for added flavor.

Soup is only one idea for leftovers. Consider using leftovers as fillings for tacos, burritos, and tortillas (and add fresh avocado, tomato, and cilantro), omelettes, frittatas, pizza toppings, stir-fries, cold salads, and sandwiches. After a big party we usually have leftover night: I get a good loaf of bread, place all the leftovers on the table, make a salad, and let everyone make his or her own sandwich, salad, or leftover plate. Let the party go on!

- Plum and Nectarine Tartlets (page 230)
- Espresso with slivers of lemon rind

Spanish Luncheon:

You want something light, but special. You'll have to make most of it ahead, because time is tight. The flavors of Spain make you feel good. Why not share the feeling?

- Assorted sherries
- Gazpacho (page 81)
- Spanish Potato and Pepper Tortilla (page 102)
- Spanish Chopped Salad (page 71)
- Roasted Potato Wedges (page 153)
- Country bread
- Lemon Tart (page 234)

THE COCKTAIL PARTY

Talk to someone you trust at your local wine shop and choose a good selection of reds and whites. Supplement your wine with good bottles of rum, vodka, gin, and a well-aged Scotch. What about a martini party? Cut up lots of lime, lemons, and orange wedges, a collection of interesting Italian sodas and mineral water, and invite a group of people as mixed as your drinks!

   This menu borrows from locales as diverse as Italy, Turkey, and Vietnam. But at a cocktail party, unlike a dinner where each dish wants to complement the next, the more flavors, the better. And best of all, almost all these dishes can be prepared ahead of time (some require a last-minute pop in the oven), freeing you up to be with your guests.

Menu One:

- Spiced Nuts (page 42)
- Orange-Marinated Olives (page 43)
- Red Caviar Dip (page 62)
- Pita toasts and a selection of good breads and interesting crackers
- Gingered Crab Cakes (page 60)
- Spinach, Prosciutto, and Red Bell Pepper Crostini (page 48)

- Vietnamese-Style Spring Rolls with Shrimp (page 54)
- Selection of cheeses sprinkled with walnuts, sun-dried cranberries, and golden raisins

Menu Two:

- Clams and oysters on the half-shell with lemon wedges
- Shrimp and Pork Dumplings with Soy-Sesame Dipping Sauce (page 56)
- Beef Satay with Coconut-Ginger Dipping Sauce (page 50)
- Turkish-Style Stuffed Grape Leaves (page 58)
- Turkish Shepherd's Salad (page 74)
- Mango Salsa (page 65)
- Ultimate Guacamole (page 66)
- Pita toasts and chips

DESSERT PARTY

This is the party to give *after* an event—a play, graduation, an evening activity—when you want to have friends over, but don't feel like producing an entire meal. Dessert parties allow everyone to eat lightly at home and then celebrate later. You can pick and choose from this menu or make all of these sweet treats.

- Bowl of fresh seasonal fruit salad, or platter of fresh fruit
- Cheese platter with walnuts and pear and apple slices
- Spiced Nuts (page 42)
- *Kipferln* (page 221)
- Shortcakes with Strawberry-Rhubarb Sauce (page 228), or seasonal fruit
- Birthday Meringues with Chocolate Sauce (page 248)
- Three-Layer Mint Brownies (page 252)
- Sorbet and ice cream sampling
- Champagne
- Coffee and a selection of tea
- After-dinner drinks

Setting the Table: Creative Solutions Without Spending a Small Fortune

My good friend Valerie Jorgensen (one of the owners of R. Jorgensen Antiques in Wells, Maine) has an amazing ability to transform any room into a warm, inviting environment for entertaining and any table into a work of art. Val's secret is that she does this without spending a small fortune. Here are some of her ideas for organizing, or reorganizing, your house or apartment to make the most of the space you have and create a dynamic, inspired setting for you and your guests.

- *Assess your space:* When you look at the place where you'll be entertaining, you want to focus on the whole room, not just the table. Ambience comes from the space as a whole. It's all about creating mood.
- *Does the size of the room fit the size of the party?* If the room is large, but you're having a small party, consider setting the table in a different room of the house—a corner of the living room or the den, for instance.

To create a cozy, less formal feeling at the table, borrow chairs from other rooms in the house and combine upholstered chairs with dining chairs. Dim the lighting in the room to place the focus on the people around the table, rather than on the whole room. When your guests arrive, turn off large overhead lights. Light the room with table lamps, accent lamps, or picture lights (highlighting individual artwork or sculpture). This creates an inviting mood. The table lighting and candles can be lit just before seating your guests, which allows the table to be a bit of a surprise.

- *Gather or buy tall branches (flowering or not) or tall grasses in pots to fill voids in the room.* If you have very tall ceilings you can set tall branches in a vase on the table top as a support for hanging ornaments (old holiday ornaments, pinecones, glass icicles, or even costume jewelry hung from transparent fishing line). Make sure that the bulky part of the branches (with leaves or flowers) is above a seated person's eye level.

- *If the room is small, but the number of guests is large,* here are a several things you can do to make the space feel more comfortable. Remove any unnecessary furniture, lamps, books, or excess "stuff" from the room. Save a special bouquet of flowers for a sideboard or the entrance to the room rather than cluttering your small table. Decorate overhead and leave the table free for food. If you have a chandelier or any type of hanging light, you can decorate it with light vines, such as bittersweet or curly willow, and wrap it in and around the fixture. If you want flowers on the table, use multiple small common garden flower bouquets in "humble" containers (like jelly jars, juice glasses, votive candle holders, tall clear vinegar jars) rather than a large, overscaled flower arrangement, which can add to a feeling of being crowded.

- *In general, forget expensive flower arrangements and consider some of these alternatives:* Place several bowls filled with a different color vegetable on the table as a centerpiece, making sure that everything is kept under a seated person's eye level. Mound red cherry tomatoes, yellow lemons, maroon cranberries, or orange tangerines. Pick up on a color in your dishware and play off it. If you have blue dishes, any strong color fruit or vegetable will look great. If you have muted earth tones, artichokes or eggplant are excellent choices. Tight clusters of broccoli or asparagus can be wrapped with ribbon or raffia and stood up in little wooden produce crates (ask for the little crates at your local produce shop).

- *Line a couple of baking sheets with sheet moss or sheets of florist's green grass (available from a florist or craft supply shop).* This becomes a backdrop for a natural centerpiece of found objects from your garden (pinecones, acorns, leaves, rocks) or a collection of candles of varying heights. Use your imagination.

- *Buy an inexpensive live twig wreath at a craft supply shop to use as a border for a fresh plant/candle centerpiece.* Place a large plastic saucer or tray under the wreath. Cluster small pots of live plants in the middle (ivy, six packs of summer annuals like pansies or Johnny jump-ups, or small clumps of red and green grapes, flowers or vegetables) and fill in with a tall, chunky candle. Use leaves from ornamental kale or cabbage to hide the pots. The plastic saucer or tray underneath allows you to water the flowers to keep them fresh and not worry about damaging your table.

- *Assemble groups of clear glass bottles and vases of varying heights or shapes.* Fill each of them with one type of object (acorns, pebbles, small black-and-white rocks, small fruit or vegetables). Stand crisp leaves of kale or chard in wide-mouth containers and line them down the center of your table.

- *Showcase some of your hidden treasures.* Bring out sentimental bowls (Grandma's china) for a special event. Float a few flowers in these bowls or fill with small, live plants or mounds of moss (available in bags at craft supply shops).

- *Look around the house for items to decorate the table with.* Consider bringing out small sculptures, artwork, garden ornaments, ribbons, camp memorabilia, ceramic tea pots, little holiday angels, toy trains or soldiers, dolls from other countries, folk art birdhouses, or a collection of Santa Clauses.

- *For a children's party, have the kids build a centerpiece out of Tinkertoys or Legos.* At holiday time you can create a centerpiece from small wrapped boxes sitting atop raffia or tinsel creating a festive backdrop. You could also place a small Lego kit at each child's place to give him something to do while he waits to eat.

• *For family gatherings:* Find a collection of old family photos (going back as far as you can) and place small framed pictures on the table. This will encourage family storytelling. You can take the old photos to a copy center or scan them on your computer. Roll the copies into a scroll and tie with beautiful ribbon or raffia. Place one scroll at each setting as party favors.

• *Tablecloths and place mats:* If you love your table, don't cover it with a tablecloth. Show it off. If you don't love your table surface, or simply want to protect it, there are several approaches you can take. If you have a cluttered space, think about using a solid-colored tablecloth. To add sparkle, you can also use inexpensive sheer fabric to layer over a solid-color tablecloth. Lay it out as a banner or runner; it doesn't need to completely cover the table.

• *Contradict yourself.* If your china, glassware, and table are formal, try using rattan, straw, or sisal for place mats. If you have a country table, set the table using your special china and glassware.

• *Layer place mats over a tablecloth.* Experiment with positioning. Layer different-colored or patterned place mats along the table. Run one pattern or color horizontally, the other vertically.

• *Instead of a tablecloth, use a patterned sheet.* Then put solid-color place mats or solid-color plates on top. Consider using attractive tea towels as mats.

9
Potluck Parties

POTLUCK WEDDING: NO TABBOULEH, PLEASE

Back in the early '80s, around the time I first moved to Maine, I was invited to a potluck wedding in the woods. We barely knew the couple, but we were new in town and thrilled to be included in their special day. Dozens of people gathered among majestic pine trees. The women all wore long, flowing dresses and the men had on Indian shirts and Birkenstock sandals. Both the bride and groom were barefoot with flowers wrapped into their long braids.

All the guests had been asked to bring a dish to

the event. Knowing the couple's preference for vegetarian fare, I chose to make a large bowl of tabbouleh, flecked with fresh mint, cherry tomatoes from my garden, and bits of zesty scallions. I went to put my salad on the serving table that they had placed in a large, sunflower-filled field. There lined up on that long wooden table was bowl, after bowl, after bowl, of tabbouleh. I kid you not—there must have been close to twenty bowls of the bulgur-based salad. I laughed so hard I thought I wouldn't make it through the oh-so-groovy ceremony. And then we feasted: on tabbouleh, bread, cheese, and wedding cake. The bridge and groom seemed oblivious to this culinary comedy. No one went home hungry, but it was a grain-filled day I have never forgotten.

I tell this story because just last year a very close friend announced she was getting married. She called to ask if I would help her orchestrate the food, because she planned on having a potluck wedding. Laughing, I told her the story of the '80s wedding. We both agreed the first rule for her celebration would be: no tabbouleh!

Inviting 140 guests to a potluck wedding is risky business, but my friend's wedding was an elegant, beautiful, and thoroughly delicious event. A stranger arriving at her gorgeous New Hampshire lakeside home would have thought she had hired one of the region's best caterers. Although she spent a good deal of time and effort planning the meal, it was her friends and family that really made it happen. My friend felt a little squeamish about holding a potluck wedding, but she felt that financially she couldn't swing a caterer for that large number of people. So rather than reduce her wedding and leave out many key people, she figured she'd invite everyone and have them all help create her day.

Many people cringe at the thought of asking guests to bring food to their party, but potlucks have always been popular because we all live crazy, stress-filled lives, and cooking for a crowd doesn't always figure into the equation. If you host the party and provide the plates and silverware and a comfortable room to sit and eat in, why not ask friends to contribute?

Listed below are many of the tips I shared with my friend to help her create her wedding. These ideas can be used to plan any type of potluck event—whether it's a simple neighborhood get-together, a book club meeting, camp barbecue, family reunion, or your own wedding. Some of the most successful parties with the best food I've ever attended were potluck. The beauty of a potluck event is that guests only have to worry about preparing one dish, so they can really give it their best effort.

- *On the invitation, or when calling, make it clear that you are having a potluck event.* Ask guests to RSVP by sending you a note or calling and letting you know if they can help. Make it clear for those traveling long distances, or anyone who feels burdened by the request, that it is perfectly acceptable to arrive without a dish. And for those who claim they can't cook, or simply don't have the time, ask them to bring a bottle of wine, a box of chocolates, bread, pie, or a cake from a good bakery.

- *Plan your menu as if you were hiring a caterer.* You should try to have a menu as close to your vision as possible. Write out a list of first courses and hors d'oeuvres you'd like to serve. Think about the main course. Do you want to have a centerpiece-type main dish? Or would you rather have lots of salads and side dishes? Plan the dessert. Even if you will be hiring a professional to bake a cake, you might want to serve a fruit salad, bowls of ripe seasonal fruit, chocolate-dipped fruit, homemade chocolates, or cookies with dessert. Write down everything.

- *When friends call to RSVP ask them what they like to cook.* Some people will feel most comfortable putting together a simple salad. Others might want to make something more substantial. When someone says, "I'll make a side dish," you can read her the list of possible side dishes from your "dream menu" and see if any of them sound interesting. Ask your guests if they have a favorite recipe. Ask them to commit to the dish you discussed, and mark it down on your menu: "Susie and Jonathan bringing some version of potato salad." "Joe and Frank bringing a meatless main course." "Jane and Tom will make a cold soup." Slowly your menu will come together. Late callers might say, "What do you still need?" Don't be shy. Tell them. "Well, we're all set with salads and dessert, but I could really use a first course. Do you have a favorite?"

- *How much to ask for?* If you're having a large party (say, for 100 people), ask people to cook for at least half the number of guests. At my friend's wedding, with 140 guests, she asked people to cook for forty. Because so many of her friends were happy to cook she had an incredible array of dishes and, although some disappeared sooner than others, there was more than enough food for everyone.

Just to give you an example of how one party evolved, here's what I advised my friend to ask for when people responded to her invitation. The meal, which was to be served around four o'clock on a hot August afternoon, would revolve around grilled salmon (this is what I offered to make) and a ten-pound poached salmon (another friend offered to make this). She asked other friends to contribute several dips and platters of raw vegetables; a dozen types of cheeses (two friends brought entire wheels of locally made cheese); several types of bread; a selection of marinated olives; herb-flavored oils to dip the bread into; at least a dozen different green salads; a half dozen kinds of potato salad; several vegetarian main course salads; a few noodle or pasta salads; bowls of ripe (and preferably local) fruit; sushi rolls (she has a few friends who love to make sushi); chocolate-dipped summer berries; and a huge nonalcoholic punch.

She hired a friend to make her wedding cake and she and the groom provided all the wine, beer, champagne, drinks, coffee, and tea. Out of 140 guests, about eighty-five brought a dish. Imagine a table with eighty-five plates and bowls of homemade food, filled with the colors of summer, and you'll get a sense of how beautiful this meal turned out to be.

- *Once you've figured out who is going to bring what, be sure to ask everyone to follow a few basic "rules" that can make the difference between potluck party hell and potluck party success:*
- Ask all guests to bring their food in the platter or bowl it will be served in.
- Ask everyone to bring serving spoons, forks, or knives to serve his or her dish with. Be sure to have a few extra serving spoons and forks ready for those who forget.
- Make sure everyone marks his or her name on the bottom of his or her bowl so you won't need to spend the next three months figuring out who left the great-looking blue bowl at your house.
- If refrigeration is an issue, ask guests to bring their food in a cooler. That way you won't have to worry about where everyone's dish will be kept cool until it is served.
- Set aside a room or an area of your kitchen where guests, upon arrival, can drop off their coolers and finish off any last-minute preparation to their dishes.
- If you're having a large party you might want to hire someone to help organize the food. Guests drop off their food and cooler with the person in charge and can give him any last-minute directions for serving the dish. This way guests can go off and enjoy themselves and let someone else arrange their food.
- If you're having a smaller, simpler event you can simply ask guests to place their food on the table ready to serve, or place it in a low, preheated oven until it's time to eat.

POTLUCK: RECIPES THAT WORK

When you're traveling to someone else's house or apartment for a potluck party you want food that is portable and that can be prepared entirely (or almost entirely) ahead of time. If you're bringing a dish that will need to be heated or reheated, make sure to check with your host to see if there will be room in the oven or on the stove. Bring your finished dish in the serving bowl, plate, or casserole you'll be serving it in, and make sure to bring your own serving spoon, fork, or knife. This makes life a lot smoother for the host.

The following recipes are all ideal for a potluck party—whether you're hosting one or bringing the food to a friend's house. When traveling, be sure to wrap your food tightly, either in a plastic container, aluminum foil, a box, a picnic basket, and so on. Double wrap everything, particularly if you're traveling by car, to make sure the food and juices don't end up on the floor before you get to the party.

In general, make the dish at home and reheat at the party over low heat or in a 300 degree oven until hot.

Appetizers

- Spiced Nuts (page 42)
- Orange-Marinated Olives (page 43)
- Roasted Red Bell Peppers (page 46)
- White Bean Dip (page 61)
- Red Caviar Dip (page 62)
- Spinach Dip (page 63)
- Yogurt "Cheese" with Mint, Scallions, and Cucumbers (page 64)
- Endive Spears Stuffed with Herbed Goat Cheese (page 44)
- Mango Salsa (page 65)
- Ultimate Guacamole (page 66)
- Spinach, Prosciutto, and Red Bell Pepper Crostini (page 48)
- Cheese and Pepper Twists (page 52)
- Turkish-Style Stuffed Grape Leaves (page 58)
- Beef Satay with Coconut-Ginger Dipping Sauce (page 50); grill or broil the beef at the party
- Vietnamese-Style Spring Rolls with Shrimp (page 54)
- Spanish Chopped Salad (page 71)
- Turkish Shepherd's Salad (page 74)

Soups

- Spring Pea Soup (page 79)
- Gazpacho (page 81)
- Quick Thai-Style Coconut Soup (page 80)
- Vichyssoise (page 164)
- Tomato, Basil, and Garlic Soup with Rouille (page 162)
- Cuban-Style Black Bean Soup (page 170)
- Turkish Lentil and Vegetable Soup (page 168)

Salads, Breads, and Tarts

- Double Corn Muffins with Chives and Cheddar (page 82)
- Glenn's Tuscan Focaccia (page 172)
- Garlic Bread (page 84); wrap in foil and heat at the party
- Roasted Pear and Mixed Green Salad (page 86)
- Tomato, Avocado, and Red Onion Salad with Roquefort Dressing (page 88)
- Asian Slaw with Peanuts (page 91)
- Grated Carrot and Sun-Dried Cranberry Salad (page 87)

- Asian Chicken Salad with Mandarin Oranges and Soy-Glazed Pecans (page 94)
- Roasted Spring Asparagus Salad with Dill Vinaigrette and Crumbled Feta (page 174)
- Mediterranean Couscous Salad with Roasted Vegetables (page 176)
- Roasted Beet and Fennel Salad (page 178)
- Vidalia Onion Tart (page 182)
- Spinach Tart (page 184)

Main Courses

- Tan Tan Noodles (page 112); cook the noodles at the party just before serving
- Salmon Cakes (page 116) with Tartar Sauce (page 67); make the cakes at home and cook at the party
- Green Curry Chicken with Peas and Basil (page 120)
- African Chicken, Spinach, and Peanut Stew (page 122)
- Chinese-Flavored Fried Chicken with Ginger Dipping Sauce (page 124)
- Quick Sausage and White Bean Stew (page 138)
- Roasted Winter Root Vegetables (page 152)
- Summer Vegetable Hero with Green Yogurt Dressing (page 100)
- Roast Garlic Mashed Potatoes (page 154)
- White Beans Provençal (page 144)

- Double-Dipped Chicken Parmesan (page 188)
- Stuffed Turkish Peppers (page 192)
- Braised Oriental-Style Short Ribs (page 130)
- Veal Stew with Leeks and Olives (page 196)
- Lamb Stew with Ginger (page 198)
- Braised Lamb Shanks with Five Onions (page 200)
- Layered Sweet and White Potatoes with Maple-Sage Cream (page 209)
- Sweet Onions with Roasted Chile and Feta Stuffing (page 210)
- Stuffed Tomatoes Provençal (page 214)

Desserts

- Almond Crisps with Amaretto-Glazed Almonds (page 222)
- *Kipferln* (page 221)
- Chocolate Rugalach (page 250)
- Seven-Layer Bars (page 246)
- Poached Pears with Caramelized Raspberry Sauce (page 224)
- Pineapple Upside-Down Cake (page 232)
- Rhubarb Crumble (page 226)
- Plum and Nectarine Tartlets (page 230)
- Mocha Cake (page 256)
- Lemon Tart (page 234)
- Lemon Poppy Seed Cake (page 236)
- Eve's Lemon Cheesecake (page 238)
- Pavlova (page 240)
- Three-Layer Mint Brownies (page 252)

TABLE OF EQUIVALENTS*

LIQUID AND DRY MEASURES

U.S.	METRIC
¹/₄ teaspoon	1.25 milliliters
¹/₂ teaspoon	2.5 milliliters
1 teaspoon	5 milliliters
1 tablespoon (3 teaspoons)	15 milliliters
1 fluid ounce (2 tablespoons)	30 milliliters
¹/₄ cup	65 milliliters
¹/₃ cup	80 milliliters
1 cup	235 milliliters
1 pint (2 cups)	480 milliliters
1 quart (4 cups, 32 ounces)	950 milliliters
1 gallon (4 quarts)	3.8 liters
1 ounce (by weight)	28 grams
1 pound	454 grams
2.2 pounds	1 kilogram

LENGTH MEASURES

U.S.	METRIC
¹/₈ inch	3 millimeters
¹/₄ inch	6 millimeters
¹/₂ inch	12 millimeters
1 inch	2.5 centimeters

OVEN TEMPERATURES

FAHRENHEIT	CELSIUS	GAS
250	120	¹/₂
275	140	1
300	150	2
325	160	3
350	180	4
375	190	5
400	200	6
425	220	7
450	230	8
475	240	9
500	260	10

*The exact equivalents in the above tables have been rounded off for convenience.

Index